Secrets of Crime
Fiction Classics

ALSO BY STEPHEN KNIGHT

*The Mysteries of the Cities:
Urban Crime Fiction in the Nineteenth Century*
(McFarland, 2012)

Secrets of Crime Fiction Classics

Detecting the Delights of 21 Enduring Stories

STEPHEN KNIGHT

McFarland & Company, Inc., Publishers
Jefferson, North Carolina

LIBRARY OF CONGRESS CATALOGUING-IN-PUBLICATION DATA

Knight, Stephen Thomas, author.
    Secrets of crime fiction classics : detecting the delights of 21 enduring stories / Stephen Knight.
        p.   cm.
    Includes bibliographical references and index.

    ISBN 978-0-7864-9398-2 (softcover : acid free paper) ∞
    ISBN 978-1-4766-1898-2 (ebook)

    1. Detective and mystery stories—History and criticism.   I. Title.
PN3448.D4K575 2014
809.3'872—dc23   2014037945

BRITISH LIBRARY CATALOGUING DATA ARE AVAILABLE

© 2015 Stephen Knight. All rights reserved

No part of this book may be reproduced or transmitted in any form or by any means, electronic or mechanical, including photocopying or recording, or by any information storage and retrieval system, without permission in writing from the publisher.

Cover: © 2015 iStock/Thinkstock

Printed in the United States of America

McFarland & Company, Inc., Publishers
  Box 611, Jefferson, North Carolina 28640
    www.mcfarlandpub.com

For Rosa

Table of Contents

Preface   1

Introduction   3

Part I: Beginnings

1. *Caleb Williams*, William Godwin   13
2. *Edgar Huntly*, Charles Brockden Brown   23
3. The Dupin Stories, Edgar Allan Poe   33
4. *The Moonstone*, Wilkie Collins   44
5. *Monsieur Lecoq*, Émile Gaboriau   55
6. *The Leavenworth Case*, Anna Katharine Green   65
7. *The Mystery of a Hansom Cab*, Fergus Hume   76

Part II: Mainstream

8. *The Adventures of Sherlock Holmes*, Arthur Conan Doyle   87
9. *The Murder of Roger Ackroyd*, Agatha Christie   97
10. *Strong Poison*, Dorothy Sayers   107
11. *The Yellow Dog*, Georges Simenon   117
12. *The Big Sleep*, Raymond Chandler   127
13. *The Talented Mr. Ripley*, Patricia Highsmith   137

Part III: Diversity

14. *Cotton Comes to Harlem,* Chester Himes	149
15. *Indemnity Only,* Sara Paretsky	159
16. *The Name of the Rose,* Umberto Eco	169
17. *Southern Seas,* Manuel Vázquez Montalbán	180
18. *The Naming of the Dead,* Ian Rankin	190
19. *Postmortem,* Patricia Cornwell	200
20. *The Girl with the Dragon Tattoo,* Stieg Larsson	210
21. *Sacred Games,* Vikram Chandra	220
Index	229

Preface

This book combines two aspects of my lengthy career as a commentator on crime fiction. The focus on specific, separate books is the inheritance of a reviewer, always with something new to describe, something to speak to but also to hear speak. I stress that because my other career, as a scholar and critic of the genre, a cultural historian of criminography, has tended to set aside the voices of the separate books and authors for a more distanced narrative about patterns and shapes emerging over time. However, as I argue in the introduction, now that crime fiction is beginning to be taken seriously in higher education and academic publishing—there are many courses and a range of new critical books, especially essay collections by young scholars—it is appropriate for the older and more tried of the traditional literary critical moves to be finally brought home to the genre, that is, to listen to the texts themselves. As D. H. Lawrence famously remarked, we should trust the tale, not the teller—and what a psychothriller writer he would have made.

As a hybrid of the instant access of reviewing and the lengthy pondering of critical scholarship, this study owes much to generous help. I have had specific support as a prodigal returnee at the University of Melbourne, where Vice-Chancellor Glyn Davis has provided a fellowship; in the same city I have gained much from students at the Free University of Melbourne, who first heard and helped refine many of the thoughts presented here—we met in tough-guy tradition at Dexter's Bar. Much of this work could not have been managed without the excellent systems and dedicated skills of the librarians who have helped me assemble materials, notably at the University of Melbourne but also in the grand State Library of Victoria (a replica of the former British Library itself have now lost to tourism) and in the University of Sydney's world-ranking crime fiction collection.

I also, like any writer, especially in such a popular field, have had support, information, advice, veiled threats about omissions and proffered therapy about opinions, from well-read and mostly polite people. Specific thanks, of an accomplice kind, go to Maurizio Ascari, Anna Kay, Stewart King, Becky Munford, and Lucy Sussex. As in many mysteries, the relatives have been involved; many thanks should go to the two Margaret Knights, sister and wife; equally familiar has been recurrent input from daughter Elizabeth, even when she has been rather busy, and it seems right to dedicate this chronicle of exciting drama to her new and so far guilt-free daughter Rosa.

Introduction

Crime fiction operates as a major fact of literature, in large part through its massive sales—it is said a third of all fiction currently sold belongs to the genre—and it dominates film and television as well. In the last generation, crime fiction has taken a credible, if not yet matchingly dominant, position in the education industry. Courses on the subject have multiplied across the globe, and a flow of new analysis has appeared, often in specialized essay collections, which frequently note how the form has recently responded to the concerns of oppressed groups—non-whites, women, lesbians, the formerly colonized—and how crime fiction has in the last decades provided a socially analytic instrument in many languages and regions, notably Central and South America, South Africa and India.

For its first two centuries crime fiction remained more or less excluded from critical taste and high-canon respect and had to accept being reviewed at the very end of the book sections. Wilkie Collins and Edgar Allan Poe suffered the stigma of being popular and were not taken seriously in their national literary assessments; Arthur Conan Doyle internalized the prejudice by hoping to wake up as Walter Scott. Now, that situation is changing as students are writing essays and theses on the genre and there is a real secondary literature to be consulted. But there is still a noticeable absence, a body of work that is not yet lying in the library of crime fiction criticism.

Books and essays on the genre are almost all surveys, either generic, historic or about an author's general contribution—often thematically subtle but usually broadly based, making connections, but primarily operating in a mode distinctly distanced from the texts themselves.

What has not been undertaken is simply to look in detail at crime fiction texts to identify what is precisely going on in them, how they work, what they say or do not say—that is, to pay attention to the voices of the texts themselves.

To hear such voices is the normal mode of literary criticism: the routine professional essay will be a detailed study of *Hamlet,* or *Emma,* or *The Waste Land*—but not *The Moonstone* or *Sacred Games*. This book, however, does pay close attention to a selected series of major crime fiction texts, from the very beginning to the absolute present. If the genre is of serious value it should stand up to this scrutiny, and if we are serious as critics we should be able to do it this way round. The traditional crime fiction study has a few lines on each text—perhaps a paragraph for a major one—then on we go, inherently dominating the form and asserting its simplicity by never allowing it to speak up for itself. The only apparent contradiction to this rule lies in the infrequent introductions that have been written, usually for major and older texts, usually in university press series. But are they in fact a contradiction? T. S. Eliot's often-cited example on *The Moonstone* relates almost entirely to Dickens. Later introductions read for this study often struggle to find material other than biography and description to fill the space demarcated by those quaint little Roman numerals.

As a criminographical critic, to give a crime fiction text room to speak you need to understand the form itself—it was not invented by Edgar Allan Poe, for example, and there actually were American clue-puzzle writers of some importance ("S.S. Van Dine," Rex Stout, and "Ellery Queen"). There also exist important non-English early versions of the genre from Eugène François Vidocq to Gaboriau and beyond, all capable of influence. Attention should be paid both to the way a narrative develops in terms of the overall patterns of crime fiction and also to what variations are made from those patterns in each text in terms of innovations of form and theme, and also what connections are thereby constructed with the contemporary context.

To make the text speak it is first necessary to give an account of it. The synopsis is regularly used in these chapters and has many advantages. Work I have published and am continuing on the very long books in the 1840s-born Mysteries genre, from Paris with Eugène Sue, London with George Reynolds, Philadelphia and New York with George Lippard and E. Z. C. Judson (aka "Ned Buntline"), depends on making synopses. Through this can be avoided the embarrassing errors of fact or sequence that are remarkably common in less plodding (and less veridical) scholars, but discoveries also emerge—the very process of synopsizing reveals the way the texts move across social and thematic levels, vary their tones and treatments, redouble their themes, interweave their elements. The process of making a synopsis is a challenging and sometimes puzzling one itself, being both central to and simultaneously based on a critical understanding of the text. Much is left out, so what is left in will have real weight: at times a brief description or statement will seem crucially recordable—in Simenon it may be a mood-indicating gesture, in Eco a subtle political reference, past or present.

If the work is in this way permitted to speak for itself, both groundbreaking and contextually significant issues will be heard, like American settler landtaking in Brockden Brown or religious extremism in Chandra; or, potentially as important, such issues may be deliberately sidelined, such as real London crimes in Conan Doyle and social politics in Christie.

While respecting the texts, some extra-textual voices are also worth hearing. Young though crime fiction criticism may be, there are now commentators to consult on what the texts might want to say, and in these chapters reference is regularly made to the most useful opinions. Those selected are writers who are reasonably accessible to modern readers in libraries or on the Web, and the references given at the end of each chapter are to the most readily available versions of their work.

Thinking through an approach in these ways is only a start for a book like this. The crucial process is deciding just whom you will include. Key factors are the concepts of being popular and influential: both have been required here, and operating in full form. A very high-selling writer with no real influence, like Edgar Wallace, has not been considered, nor has someone of considerable influence but limited success, like Anthony Berkeley Cox, initiator of the psychothriller. In scanning the field, Poe, Conan Doyle and Christie seemed the only unmissables: all three have been massively popular (though in Poe's magazine-based case, sales are hardly an issue), and also operating as major influences in both form and theme.

If you insist, as any historically and generically aware person must, that Poe was a major developer, not a creator, of crime fiction, then there must be evidence for that from an earlier period, and so Godwin and Brockden Brown offer themselves. Both shape in complex and vigorous form the first real signs of individual detection, starting a whole chain of followers, and also appropriately indicate that the genre is both English and American in origin. Though it might seem surprising that the opening texts of a genre are complex and elusive, that is in fact the usual pattern: *Hamlet* has been followed by many far simpler visions of a self-doubting intellectual; romance fiction has never matched in terms of interrogative subtlety its source in Jane Austen. The elusive uncertainties about class in Godwin and race in Brockden Brown, and identity in both, have a remarkable modernity about them.

Other early forces were both popular in their own right and clearly formative in their influence. Anna Katharine Green, though not producing the first American crime novel by a woman, was far better known and had much more impact than "Seeley Regester" (Metta Victor Fuller) with *The Dead Letter*

(1867); Émile Gaboriau was for many around the world the first voice of serious and series-based police detection, and Fergus Hume's remarkable success showed what crime fiction could do in the market, as well as, by its Melbourne setting, indicating this was indeed a world genre.

The seven authors Poe, Godwin, Brockden Brown, Collins, Green, Gaboriau, and Hume comprise the part of this book called "Beginnings," while Conan Doyle represents the first of the "Mainstream" authors who developed a now-recognized genre operating in full confident form—in his case with the city-based rational specialist, in Christie's with the classic clue-puzzle mode, and Sayers providing the archetypal English amateur with title and monocle—the latter at least functional as a magnifying glass. Others in the "Mainstream" section realize other forms—Simenon as the French detective version stressing paternalistic, even priestly, policing; Chandler with the best-known, most-imitated American private eye; and Highsmith offering the subtlest and most widely acclaimed culmination of the crime novel focused on how and why, rather than who.

It was tempting to add a seventh to the "Mainstream" part of this book, to balance up numbers. The book was long planned as having twenty-one selected titles—based on the length judged necessary for each chapter and also, in less earnest mode, as a number that signified the adult status of crime fiction criticism and also suggested that might be a gamble. But three neat and lucky sevens would not work. When I focused on the final part of this book, representing forms of "diversity," it became clear that while another author might be justifiable as "Mainstream" there were too many demanding candidates for "Diversity" to let that happen.

Starting chronologically as it does with Chester Himes (never a mainstream man), that third part of this book demanded eight texts to show the range across which modern authors have determinedly diversified the only recently established tradition of the genre. After Himes spoke with vivid vigor for his race and Paretsky was leader of the feminists, Eco offered ultra-modernity in both historical and postmodern crime fiction (as well as an allegory of the disrupted present) and Vázquez Montalbán starts the Hispanic surge in crime fiction, in post–Franco Spain, where it has been a major genre of self-analysis, as also in the transatlantic regions. Ian Rankin is taken as the strongest of the recent British devolutionary crime writers, also at the subtlest heights of the police procedural, while Chandra takes the postcolonial possibilities of crime fiction further, into both the Indian mega-city and international religio-terrorism. Technical modernity is presented by Cornwell in her mix of forensic detection and serial-killer crime, and Larsson's novel trilogy speaks to an even higher-tech world where the honest journalist and the woman super-nerd grapple with the legacies of espionage and international business corruption, as well as personal vengeances.

In addition to selecting writers, it was necessary to choose actual books. In some cases there was only one—thanks for that go to Godwin, Hume, Eco, Larsson, Chandra—but this process has often been as challenging as selecting authors. Among multiple choices I have made decisions on the basis of which made the most substantial contribution. In a few cases, especially where influence is immediately powerful, especially in terms of the tone and technique of detection, I have chosen a first book, as with Green, Chandler, Paretsky, Cornwell. With Poe I have dealt with all the Dupin stories, but in other cases I have chosen and tried to justify that choice a title that seems to reveal most fully the nature of the writer's contribution—these are Brockden Brown, Collins, Gaboriau, Christie, Sayers, Simenon, Highsmith, Himes, Rankin, Vázquez Montalbán, and this process was why the first set of Conan Doyle short stories was selected, not the earlier novellas.

Many other writers have been considered and regretfully rejected. One category was those who, while popular and fascinating, did not have any real influence on the genre—J. B. Williams and the 1860s "New York Detective" series; G. K. Chesterton with his Father Brown stories; R. Austin Freeman of the dedicated medical mystery; the American clue-puzzlers "Van Dine," Stout and "Queen"; and in reverse Peter Cheyney, the English tough-guy writer who sold as well as Christie in wartime and was much admired in France. There were also some who had considerable impact, but it was dominantly transmitted by another writer: Hammett's brilliance is realized largely through Chandler; Sjöwall and Wahlöö are displaced as radical Swedes by Larsson; the powerful Mexican Taibo is, and felt, close to Vázquez Montalbán; James M. Cain, seen from the present, is less important than his more assertive successor Jim Thompson and both yield to the subtler, more widely acknowledged international crime novel by Highsmith. Then there were fine writers who basically followed someone more striking, like Mignon Eberhart modernizing Green's American woman-oriented mystery, or P. D. James condensing Christie and Sayers in the classic English tradition; Peter Corris, whose enduring Sydney PI Cliff Hardy is essentially transpacific from Marlowe's Los Angeles; Janet Evanovich with her vigorous downmarket version of Paretsky; Tony Hillerman developing the critique of white dominance that Chester Himes had forcefully begun; Peter Temple extending to Australia Rankin's concept of the politically aware anxieties of ultra-modern policing.

There were others it seemed especially hard to omit, as their material and approach was not really represented by the selected authors—Margaret Millar's woman-based psychothrillers like *The Iron Gates,* the "Barbara Vine" novels by Ruth Rendell starting with *A Dark-Adapted Eye,* the searching political thrillers of the French Didier Daeninckx and the Italian Leonardo Sciascia, the South African writers Margie Orford and Dialwe Tlholwe, the new Aboriginal Australian voice of Nicole Watson. Space and the dominant importance of the selected texts left no room for all of them. We may need another collection of those authors and books that have been too original to be fully influential: maybe there will even be room for a "cozy," perhaps with a dog detective.

That "Diversity" insisted on being the largest category is testimony to the vigor of the crime fiction form, and a structural reason why in sales and bookshop presence it is increasingly dominant. But it goes further. The ever-widening extent of topics and methods of detection is matched by the striking fact that the most recent titles discussed tend also to be the most politically serious and wide-ranging, both nationally and internationally. With Vázquez Montalbán, Rankin, Larsson, and Chandra, crime fiction is dealing centrally and weightily with major aspects of international crime, whether based in terrorism or forms of business, and linking those dire forces to national social and political manipulations of people in the present.

There are other issues that emerge from listening to the texts and their authors. It is common for these writers to have grown up without a father—ten at least: is the detective a form of paternal substitute? A parallel distance effect may lie behind the power with which writers strange to a city when young have created it memorably in their fiction. Then it is strikingly, even ridiculously, common for these authors and their texts to have been rejected, often frequently, by publishers. Most interesting, and even gratifying, of all, the detail of synopsizing and contextualizing the authors and the chosen texts has provided evidence for the complexity and originality of the material and the genre itself. That is, this closely text-based study of classics of crime fiction has generated detailed material to explain why these books have been phenomenally successful in terms of sales and readers and deserve a place among the classics of literary history.

Texts Used

1. William Godwin, *Caleb Williams.* Ed., with Introduction, David McCracken. World's Classics Edition. Oxford: Oxford University Press, 1982.

2. Charles Brockden Brown, *Edgar Huntly, or, Memoirs of a Sleepwalker.* Ed., with Introduction, Norman Gabo. New York: Viking, 1988.

3. Edgar Allan Poe, Dupin stories. *Tales of Mystery and Imagination.* Everyman's Library. London: Dent, 1975.

4. Wilkie Collins, *The Moonstone.* With Introduction by Sandra Kemp. Penguin Classics. London: Penguin, 1998.

5. Émile Gaboriau, *Monsieur Lecoq.* Vol. 1. only. Ed., with brief conclusion and Introduction, E. F. Bleiler. New York: Dover, 1975. For complete two-volume edition, see Project Gutenberg version, translator not given.

6. Anna Katharine Green, *The Leavenworth Case: A Lawyer's Story.* Introduction by Michele Slung. New York: Dover, 1981.

7. Fergus Hume, *The Mystery of a Hansom Cab.* Introduction by Simon Caterson. Text Classics. Melbourne: Text, 1999.

8. Arthur Conan Doyle, *The Adventures of Sherlock Holmes,* in *Sherlock Holmes: The Complete Facsimile Edition.* Ware, Herts: Wordsworth, 1996.

9. Agatha Christie, *The Murder of Roger Ackroyd.* London: HarperCollins, 2002, 1953.

10. Dorothy Sayers, *Strong Poison.* With Introduction by Elizabeth George. New English Library. London: Hodder and Stoughton, 2003.

11. Georges Simenon, *The Yellow Dog.* Trans. Linda Asher. London: Penguin, 2003.

12. Raymond Chandler, *The Big Sleep.* London: Penguin, 1948.

13. Patricia Highsmith, *The Talented Mr. Ripley.* New York: Vintage, 1999.

14 Chester Himes, *Cotton Comes to Harlem.* Vintage Crime. New York: Vintage, 1988.

15. Sara Paretsky, *Indemnity Only.* Introduction by Sara Paretsky. New York: Dell, 1990.

16. Umberto Eco, *The Name of the Rose.* Trans. William Weaver. London: Picador, 1984.

17. Manuel Vázquez Montalbán, *Southern Seas.* Trans. Patrick Camiller. New York: Melville House, 2012.

18. Ian Rankin, *The Naming of the Dead.* London: Orion, 2007.

19. Patricia Cornwell, *Postmortem.* New York: Pocket, 2003.

20. Stieg Larsson, *The Girl with the Dragon Tattoo.* Trans. Reg Keeland. London: MacLehose, 2008.

21. Vikram Chandra, *Sacred Games.* London: Faber, 2006.

Part I
Beginnings

1
Caleb Williams, William Godwin

Caleb Williams was originally published in 1794 as *Things as They Are, or The Adventures of Caleb Williams,* and it also has two endings. Four days after writing a grim conclusion, Godwin changed his mind and provided a more positive, though still demanding, final sequence. The novel has other complexities. It does focus on a hidden murder and detection occurs throughout, but we know about the crime quite early and the main issues are the social and personal consequences that are caused by knowledge of the crime, especially on Caleb, its discoverer. The novel where, as the notable historian of crime fiction, Julian Symons, said, "[t]he characteristic note of crime literature is first struck" (33) is also one of the most testing and least comforting examples of the form.

It can, as Symons continues, be described as a very early psychological novel and could be seen as what will become the psychothriller. But it has also been taken as a fictional and individualized counterpart to Godwin's major critique of the current social system, *Political Justice* (1793)—he thought the novel up in the week that book was being published. *Things as They Are,* in conception and original title, belongs to the period of revolutions in America and France and it offered a deep critique of the national situation in Britain, shown in the novel as the dominance of upper-class wealth, supported by the legal system. Godwin's preface ended by saying, "Terror was the order of the day and it was feared that even the humble novelist might be shown to be constructively a traitor" (2). That preface was withdrawn in the first edition "in compliance with the alarms of booksellers" (1).

The crime is personal as well as political. The title *Caleb Williams* was widely used from the start, and in 1825 William Hazlitt remembered how it spoke directly to the reader as if "the events and feelings had been personal"

(McCracken, vii). The novel recounts a privately based unveiling of crime and corruption—the word "detection" is used of Caleb's activities. He is by no means a confident or settled detective and the law is itself suspect, but many elements of what will become the readily identifiable patterns of crime fiction can be found in the novel. *Caleb Williams* looks forward to the most politically challenging and most psychologically unsettling of the classics of crime fiction, and a study of the form that starts with Godwin will have a wider and more socially connected understanding of the origin and meaning of the genre than one that wrongly states, as is commonly repeated, that it was entirely invented by Edgar Allan Poe.

At the start Caleb announces dramatically he will tell about "a theatre of calamity" (3) connected to his relationship with Ferdinando Falkland, a landowner in the north of England who employs him, a poor but well-educated young man, as secretary/librarian. The first volume tells the story of Falkland's previous life: he was small in stature but graceful, learned and considerate. He spent time in Italy, where he was much admired and also resolved a potential crisis. A lady appeared to be favoring him over an impulsive nobleman, Count Malvesi, who challenged him to a duel, but Falkland managed to avoid it and reunite the couple, showing his nobility and, importantly, retaining his reputation for courage—fame will always be crucial with him.

Falkland returns to "the residence of his ancestors" (16), and soon enough more trouble emerges. Another local squire, Tyrrel, is hot tempered, and when a yeoman farmer, Hawkins, refuses to let his son become his hunting servant (he wants the boy to grow up a free man) Tyrrel destroys him through his wealth and misuse of the law and has the son jailed. Tyrrel goes on to harass his own cousin Emily Melville, a poor woman who dies in misery. Falkland behaves as an excellent social leader, nobly active in directing a fire rescue and sympathetic to Tyrrel's victims, but when he leads the local people in excluding Tyrrel from the local assembly Tyrrel suddenly returns and knocks Falkland down.

Later that night Tyrrel is found stabbed to death: Hawkins and his son are accused, and their guilt established though "accumulated evidence" (104)—bloodstained clothes and a knife broken in the body—and they are executed. Falkland feels shame, because Tyrrel's death means no honorific compensation is possible for his being knocked down and publicly humiliated. There is even a rumor that Falkland was involved in the murder, but he proclaims his honor and reputation to a public inquiry and is cleared. But he only enjoys "the empty remains of honour and fame" (102), is very unhappy, and becomes little more than a recluse.

At the start of volume 2 Caleb, now Falkland's employee, suspects him of murder. Caleb will be "a spy on Mr. Falkland," which like most later detectives he finds "a strange sort of pleasure" (107). The Tyrrel case is symbolically recalled: Falkland and Caleb debate the history of Alexander, a great man who murdered a friend, and in another parallel a local peasant is goaded into killing another man. At times Falkland shows himself in a rage, at others he weeps "tears of anguish" and Caleb, convinced "this is the murderer!" is himself in "a kind of rapture" (129).

When a fire breaks out at the house, Caleb goes to an attic to save valuables. He sees a large trunk and recalls that very early in his employment he heard Falkland "hastily" shut and lock the trunk, then very angrily call Caleb a "spy" (8). Caleb seizes some tools, breaks the lock and is raising the lid when Falkland appears and puts a pistol to his head. Shortly after, Falkland confesses the murder of Tyrrel to Caleb. Falkland's reason for confessing is "the love of fame" (130): he fears Caleb's exposing him but believes that as Caleb knows the truth, his "faith" in Falkland will protect his honor.

At first Caleb feels "lulled in a certain degree to security upon the verge of the precipice" and is even worried about "the unjustifiable means by which I had extorted from him a confession" (138), but Falkland becomes steadily less trusting and more tyrannical. Falkland's half brother Mr. Forester and Caleb become friendly, and when Falkland finds them together he assumes Caleb is betraying him and is very aggressive. Caleb runs away: a letter from Forester brings him back to the house, but now Falkland "shuddered at the very possibility of detection" (160) and is increasingly nervous. Before long Caleb is accused of theft; some jewels and a watch are found in his trunk. He tells Forester that Falkland is his enemy but is not believed, as Falkland is his master, and he is sent to the prison where Hawkins and his son were held.

The prison scenes show England has its own versions of the Bastille and that a simple noble person like Brightwel, a learned soldier, can die through oppression. Caleb escapes but hurts his leg in the process and is easily recaptured. Then one of Falkland's servants visits, is shocked at Caleb's treatment, and brings him some tools: he escapes again, breaking through the wall with great difficulty.

Volume 3 begins with Caleb being pursued from jail but enjoying "the sweets of liberty" (210). He is attacked and robbed by thieves, including a thug named Gines. Then Caleb meets a generous man who turns out to be Captain Raymond, leader of the gang of thieves, effectively outlaws. Raymond is, like Robin Hood, against "tyranny and perfidiousness" (220) and the gang expels Gines for misbehavior and agrees to protect Caleb, not taking the large reward on offer for his arrest. Caleb tries to talk Raymond and the gang out of criminal activities but fails and leaves, in disguise for the first time: he hears people speaking of "Kit Williams the notorious housebreaker"—his story has become public and garbled.

He buys a ticket on a boat to Ireland, but with an Irish accent as part of his disguise, he is arrested as an Irish mail robber. His guards take most of his money and free him, and he finds his way to London, disguises himself as a Jew, lives secretly in the East End, and through a friendly woman intermediary sells articles to the press, many on famous criminals. Gines reappears, now employed by Falkland as a thief-taker to find Caleb, but at the woman's warning he escapes, to set up as a watchmaker's assistant. By now his "appearance was wasted to a shadow" (266), and he hears a hawker selling the adventures of Caleb Williams, a newssheet Gines has created, which helps him find Caleb and take him before a magistrate. Caleb tries to indict Falkland for murder, making this charge public for the first time, but the magistrate will not accept the accusation, as Caleb is Falkland's servant—he would only accept it if Caleb were an accomplice to the crime: Caleb comments that "six thousand a year shall protect a man from accusation" (277).

With Caleb back in the prison he first escaped from, no one appears against him in court and he is freed. Gines takes him to see Falkland. He has been watching Caleb and did not want him in jail, unlike Forester. Had Caleb been genial, Falkland would have been kind, he says. Now he demands Caleb sign a rebuttal of the charges, but he refuses and insists it was all through "your mad and misguided love for fame" (283). Falkland leaves, making threats, but his servant brings Caleb £20.

He settles in an "obscure market-town in Wales" (289) where he works as a watchmaker, a math teacher, and then an etymologist. He meets a family led by Laura, part–Italian: they have mutual intellectual interests and he thinks of marrying her daughter. But people turn steadily against Caleb, including finally Laura, on the basis of the story Gines has publicized. Caleb leaves again, now not bothering with disguise. He meets Collins, Falkland's old steward, who cannot believe ill of Falkland and feels Caleb has become "a machine" (310), with automatic responses. Caleb tries to go to Holland but is stopped by Gines: Falkland will not let him leave the country. Caleb decides he will leave his papers about Falkland to Collins and thinks about the trunk—but we never find out what was in it.

Finally, in Falkland's county town, before a magistrate (who is reluctant to accept the charge) Caleb accuses Falkland of murder. They meet with the magistrate: in the revised ending Falkland is in a terrible state and Caleb feels pity. He thinks Falkland did show him "forbearance" and he in turn should have "opened his heart" (322) to him. He sees Falkland as an essentially noble spirit destroyed in "the corrupt wickedness of human society" (325). Presumably this revised ending is changing Caleb from being "a machine" to a human, and in a parallel way Falkland confesses his fault, saying, "Williams you have conquered" and "I have spent a life of the basest cruelty to cover one act of momentary vice" (324).

Falkland dies three days later and Caleb endures "the penalty of my crime," guilt for making miserable and finally destroying such a noble spirit—though finally he feels that Falkland did "imbibe the poison of chivalry with thy earliest youth" and lived for "the phantom of departed honour" (326). It is a partly positive ending: despite the damage done to him, Caleb has in a way triumphed—a position that is, Gary Kelly notes, much more positive than *Political Justice,* though having its own "degree of sentimentalism" (186).

In the original ending, however, quoted in David McCracken's edition, Caleb was once more rejected: Falkland answered his charge in terms of his life having been "uniformly benevolent and honourable" and the magistrate accepted this, dismissing Caleb's case as "so bare faced and impudent a forgery" (330). Two pages of manuscript are missing, but then Caleb is in prison, evidently part-mad. Finally he scrawls a note to Collins: he cannot recall who Falkland was, has strange dreams, is immobile, and thinks of his own gravestone saying, "Here lies what was once a man" (334).

Godwin wrote that stark conclusion a day after visiting in jail his friend Joseph Gerrald, about to be transported for fourteen years for sedition—or in fact planning a new "British Convention" of fairer laws. But Godwin reverted to a more idealistic, if also difficult, resolution—though, as Philip Shaw argues (366), also one that asserts Caleb's semi-sublime fascination with Falkland rather than a simple desire to punish a crime. The reworked ending was not the only positive change. For the 1796 second edition, as well as a good deal of sharper verbal detail and the previously canceled preface, Godwin elaborated the story by adding the lengthy sequence in Wales about Laura and her family, changing the peasant who was goaded to murder from a violent beast to a saintly man and making Caleb in London more suicidal: he also less purposefully changed some of the names—Gines was originally Jones, for example—and also, without evident reason, altered Falkland's mysterious "chest" to a "trunk."

When the novel first appeared, some responses were less than serious: one reviewer felt it lacked a love interest, another found the politics dull and worth cutting out, and by early 1796 there was a play in London called *The Iron Chest,* which changed the names, introduced female partners for all, as well as songs, and made the secretary's outraged innocence the only real issue (the chest contained a bloodstained knife). Others did notice the politics: the government-supporting *British Critic* felt this was an attack on "religion, virtue, government, laws" (Marshall, 150), seeing the links with *Political Justice,* but some reviewers applauded the novel's intense, serious tone.

The original ending had been consistent with the dark critique of *Political Justice,* which was itself rewritten in later editions to dilute its aggression to state politics. In *Political Justice* Godwin addressed "the moral concerns of mankind" (I. 316) and argued that all social mechanisms were corrupt—like Falkland's obsession with fame and the power of the wealthy over the law; he also asserted that a truly enlightened order could be established only by individuals speaking to one another in rational terms. As McCracken puts it and as the revised ending argues, "he had vast faith in the individual's ability to develop his reason and natural benevolence so that he could live peaceably and usefully with other men" (viii). It is, as Kelly notes, "tempting to interpret the entire novel in terms of the arguments of the philosophical treatise," in that where *Political Justice* was "designed to revolutionize the political views of the public, *Things as They Are* was just as clearly designed to revolutionize the sentiments of the individual" (182–83).

The young Falkland was a model of this, bringing reason and justice to bear on the awkward encounter with Count Malvesi—where he admitted to his own thoughtlessness—and his genuine benevolence in the face of Tyrrel's brutish exercise of the power of wealth and position, especially in seeking "a right understanding with him" (28). Caleb, too, tries to be an individual bringer of peace and truth and at the end, in the revised ending, feels he has failed to speak in a peacefully truth-telling way to Falkland.

The idealistic notions of "philosophical anarchism"—Godwin is the first to develop this position—are behind some of the unusual features of the book: that Falkland sends Caleb £20 to sustain himself on the run, that he does not want him jailed unlike the harder Forester, that he confesses both at first and at the ending, and also that Caleb retains an underlying affection and respect for Falkland, whatever tyranny he has been persuaded to enact by the delusions of honor.

Falkland is finally described as having drunk "the poison of chivalry" (326), and he is throughout obsessed with his public standing: the fact that he cannot arrange any public humiliation of Tyrrel once he is dead to compensate for having been himself humiliated in public is more distressing to him than any personal guilt at having murdered Tyrrel. Godwin connects this public system of honor with the self-preservation of the landed wealthy, supported strongly by the legal system run by magistrates who are themselves men of that class: this is what he calls things as they are.

In the light of that strong social and evaluative theme, the novel might well be seen as the first political novel rather than the first psychological novel.

Both Falkland and Forester have names that imply ownership of land, and Falkland, on the one hand, was also "undoubtedly modelled" (Marshall, 150) on Lucius Cary, Viscount Falkland, a leading Royalist in the seventeenth-century Civil War—Kelly notes that the English Revolution was being much discussed in the 1790s (202–4)—Tyrrel, on the other hand, is a name redolent with crime, the surname of the man who on behalf of the future Richard III murdered the princes in the tower and also of the man who, probably not accidentally, shot to death King William II in the New Forest in 1099. The hero's name also has positive and anti-authoritarian implications: Marilyn Butler suggests (71) it may be no accident that Williams was the alternative surname used by Oliver Cromwell, and Godwin surely would have known that Caleb was the name of one of the agents Moses sent into the Promised Land, as he was trained to be a Dissenting minister like his father.

That context of radical Protestantism and an insistence on personal responsibility is evident through the novel: Paula Clemit comments that the "atmosphere of terror owes much to the narratives of religious persecution" that Godwin knew (v), and Shaw reports his stress on them in his introduction to the 1832 edition of *Fleetwood* (362). His education in Dissenting academies was well away from the establishment paths of a major school and Oxford or Cambridge; he was very familiar with Rousseau's socially critical philosophy and had met Tom Paine, author of the very influential radical book *The Rights of Man*.

If a dissenting politics seeking a place and way for individuals to live more rationally is the essential theme of *Caleb Williams*, part of its context is also the Gothic and the sublime, as is stressed by Maurice Hindle in general and also in terms of sources by Shaw (362). But the novel also offers many features common in crime fiction: a secret murder, a prestigious criminal, a lower-class inquirer, the framing and hounding of the inquirer, collateral impact on others of good character, the inquirer's recourse to disguise, deception, mobility, urban marginalization, opposition to inquiry from the legal authorities, the use of wealth and power to conceal crime, a resolution outside the legal system, a substantial price paid by the inquirer for revealing the crime.

There is even a striking structural link to later crime fiction in the fact that, as Godwin explained in the *Fleetwood* introduction, he imagined the story backwards. As he was publishing *Political Justice* he conceived the conclusion of his story (with the grim first ending) and worked out the pattern of volume 2 and volume 1 in that order—he then slowly drafted his manuscript from the beginning. This is very similar to the way in which some clue-puzzle writers, including Christie, worked out their solutions before they drafted the plots.

A deeper link to crime fiction lies in the social and political positioning of the novel and the form. Early crime stories like those found in *The Newgate Calendar* stories normally produced their resolutions by someone observing the murderer and reporting it to the local magistrates (see Knight, chap. 1). As Shaw notes (362), Godwin read many of these and other crime narratives before writing his novel, but he goes further than this simple system of crime solving. Both Caleb's inquiries and those made in volume 3 by Gines are different from the social security system of the *Calendar* pattern. They are not yet formal detectives: Gines is a specialist, but he is a decidedly negative figure, and Caleb is never conceived as a regular, systematic inquirer. He does not have another case to take up after this novel, and he is not in any real way what a Foucauldian approach (see Worthington, chap. 2) would call a disciplinary detective, using rational and scientific skills to solve the problem. Yet it is striking that the roles Caleb takes on to support his inquirer's position are all those of a skilled worker with considerable cerebral powers: first appointed as secretary/librarian, when on the run he becomes a writer, a watchmaker, a math teacher and, most strikingly intellectual of all, an etymologist, a man detecting the origin of words.

If Caleb is in this way the shadow of a future disciplinary detective, he is also at the meeting point of detection and what the late eighteenth-century commentator Edmund Burke had called the sublime. His arguments were well-known to Godwin though not admired by him, and Butler argues (69–70) that Burke was a physical model for Falkland. As Maurizio Ascari has shown, early crime fiction has much contact with the Gothic tradition, which celebrates both the anxiety and the excitement that Burke found central to the sublime, and Caleb's mixing of high-flown noble rhetoric with recurrent self-abasing terror makes him in many ways a figure of the early criminal sublime. Hindle argues that Caleb's feeling and language work in this way ("Theatres of Calamity," 22) and Elizabeth Inchbald, playwright and friend of Godwin, gave him contemporary Gothic status, saying in a letter that she found his second volume "sublimely horrible—captivatingly frightful" (Clemit, vi).

As a politically driven inquiry into concealed crime committed by the powerful, where the inquirer suffers heavily and the legal authorities, high and low, are turned against him, *Caleb Williams* has a structure and an impact much like that of later crime fiction. What is surprising is what sort of crime fiction Godwin powerfully previsions. The characteristics listed above as being common between *Caleb Williams* and later crime fiction do not belong to the tradition of the intellectual detective, from Auguste Dupin through Sherlock Holmes to the forensic modern specialists, nor yet to the carefully controlled, and controlling, police from the 1840s magazines through Crofts' 1920s

Inspector French to the modern worldwide procedurals in print and film. They fit rather with the heroic detective, either amateur as in sensational fiction or, and more strongly, the private-eye hero (and more recently heroine) of the American tradition, who suffer for their inquiries, face great pressures to reveal the truth, and are rarely aligned with the legal system. This connection is in fact an existing though mostly unnoticed tradition. American crime writing only briefly picked up the European model of the all-knowing detective, with Anna Katharine Green leading on to "S. S. Van Dine," Rex Stout and "Ellery Queen": Poe's highly cerebral stories are set in Paris. The dominant American pattern of Hammett and Chandler goes back through the dime novels to "Jem Brampton the New York detective" of the 1860s, and that can be seen as continuing the earlier concept of contested detection in the face of negative social forces that Godwin is the first to imagine and Brockden Brown developed in America.

Godwin did not pursue further any of the forms of crime writing. His later novels were more idea based—*Fleetwood* (1805) attacked Rousseau's idea of "natural" education and *St Leon* (1799) and *Mandeville* (1817) both dealt with seventeenth-century settings of problems in politics and philosophy. *Cloudesley* (1830) is about a man who redeems himself from a criminal life, but the social politics of both crime and inquiry were not by then of central interest to Godwin—he had accepted the change of title to *Caleb Williams* in the new edition of 1831 and now held more widely idealistic Romantic views. He even might not unfairly be in part honored for the work of his daughter Mary Wollstonecraft Shelley: it is possible to see some links between her great novel *Frankenstein* (1818) and Godwin's attempts to outline in *Caleb Williams* the possibility of establishing a new kind of man—and the huge difficulties involved.

In the long repression of the Napoleonic Wars Godwin became widely seen as undesirably disruptive: Percy Shelley was astonished in 1812 to find Godwin was still alive and writing. But he was deeply respected in his time as a thinker and a serious radical, read by the major Romantics and many others; Mary Shelley said in her notes for his long-planned but never-written life, that his major novel spoke to the oppressed but also to the uncertain and somewhat anxious holders of power (Clemit, vii). Godwin is still well-known, especially in Continental Europe, for the innovative power of *Political Justice* and is honored by those who, following Peter Kropotkin and Pierre-Joseph Proudhon, find intellectual anarchism a powerful concept and even a guiding star in the puzzling present. But Godwin's major gift to succeeding readers has been his bold, exciting and extraordinarily imaginative novel *Caleb Williams,* at once the fictionalization of contemporary radical thought and, in a real and serious way, the first move in the direction of the genre of crime fiction.

References

Ascari, Maurizio. *A Counter-History of Crime Fiction, Supernatural Gothic, Sensational.* London: Palgrave Macmillan, 2007.

Butler, Marilyn. *Jane Austen and the War of Ideas.* Clarendon: Oxford, 1975.

Clemit, Paula. "Introductory Note," in William Godwin, *Caleb Williams, The Complete Works of Godwin*, Vol. 3. London: Pickering and Chatto, 1992.

Hindle, Maurice. "Introduction," in William Godwin, *Caleb Williams.* London: Penguin, 1988.

———. "Theatres of Calamity: Godwin, Burke and the Language of Gothic," in *Crime and the Sublime.* Ed. Maurizio Ascari and Stephen Knight. Special issue of *La Questione Romantica* 2 (2010): 15–25; reprinted in *From the Sublime to Crime.* Ed. Maurizio Ascari and Stephen Knight. Monaco: Libero, 2014, 21-62; E-publication.

Kelly, Gary. *The English Jacobin Novel 1780–1805.* Oxford: Oxford University Press, 1976.

Knight, Stephen. *Form and Ideology in Crime Fiction.* Bloomington: University of Indiana Press, 1980.

Marshall, Peter H. *William Godwin.* New Haven: Yale University Press, 1984.

McCracken, David. "Introduction," in William Godwin, *Caleb Williams.* Ed. David McCracken. World's Classics Edition. Oxford: Oxford University Press, 1982.

Shaw, Philip. "William Godwin (1756–1836)," in *A Companion to Crime Fiction.* Ed. Charles J. Rzepka and Lee Horsley. New York: Wiley-Blackwell, 2010, 361–68.

Symons, Julian. *Bloody Murder: From the Detective Story to the Crime Novel: A History.* Revised second edition. London: Pan, 1992.

Worthington, Heather. *The Rise of the Detective in Early Nineteenth-Century Popular Fiction.* London: Palgrave Macmillan, 2005.

2

Edgar Huntly, Charles Brockden Brown

Larry Landrum, Jr., calls *Edgar Huntly* (1799) "America's first detective novel" (1). Charles Brockden Brown was a great admirer of Godwin and an active member of a literary and intellectual circle operating in both Philadelphia and New York. Most of the novels Brockden Brown produced in a remarkable burst of creativity deal with interpersonal dramas—including some psychic conflicts within a single personality. But in *Edgar Huntly* he took Godwin's use of criminal inquiry as a way of speaking critically about the state of the nation and Americanized it, combining the uncertainties of immigration with the confrontation between landtakers and Native Americans, without losing contact with the intensity of the drama about the emergent individual that was a marked feature of Godwin's work and his own.

From the shooting of a young teacher at night to the final apparent suicide of another young man on a mission of damaging folly, the novel is a dramatic story of action and disorder in newly independent America, caught between European practices, including malpractices, and the American situation—the very wild frontier country, the resistant activities of Native Americans, and the difficult formation of the newly independent country and its consciousness, from old inhabitants with set attitudes and volatile newcomers from Europe. Events are observed, studied and often clumsily instigated by Edgar himself, young and naïve as well as brave and baffled. As an inquirer he shares both the zest and the negative impact of Caleb Williams, while the country of the upper Delaware north of Philadelphia provides a region more grandly and threateningly sublime than any British writer could imagine. Brockden Brown also outstrips Godwin in his dramatic, and sometimes melodramatic, use of the theme of the double, both between people and also within an individual, a psychic uncertainty that is especially realized through the major theme of sleepwalking—the novel's subtitle is *Memoirs of a Sleepwalker,* and about this time Brockden Brown worked on a story that seems parallel to the first part of *Edgar Huntly,* which he published in 1805 as *Somnambulism: A Fragment.*

Born in 1771 to a long-established Quaker merchant family now living in Philadelphia, Brockden Brown trained as a lawyer, but in 1793, in contact with a New York literary circle, he adopted full-time writing, mostly producing essays and editing periodicals. But in four busy years, 1798–1801, he wrote seven novels—and an eighth was apparently lost. Three of the best-known are city based and focus on potentially violent dramas of the self, notably the impact of ventriloquism and the false projection of a second identity in *Wieland* (1798) and the unfinished *Carwin the Biloquist* (1803–5)—but there is also a good deal of social drama like the impact of the 1793 plague in *Arthur Mervyn Part 1* (1800) and *Ormond* (1799). These novels also give a large role to women, and in addition Brockden Brown wrote a dialogue-based book, *Alcuin* (1797), which draws heavily on the groundbreaking feminism of Mary Wollstonecraft, Godwin's wife: two other novels from this period, *Clara Howard* (1801) and *Jane Talbot* (1801), written in the form of letters, deal extensively with woman-centered issues.

Edgar Huntly is unusual in Brockden Brown's work for being almost entirely set outside the city and having mostly offstage roles for women—though they remain important as foci for male feelings and intentions. A central theme of the novel is realizing the uncertain individuality, values and success of a young American person of his time, aware like Caleb Williams of both the grandeur and the anxiety of the Burkean sublime. But Edgar also seems a figure for the emergent American nation: Brockden Brown deliberately set the novel in mid-1787, in the very months when the American Constitution was, with substantial publicity, being written in Philadelphia, and this strange, confused activity on the wild frontier northeast of the city may well be meant to parallel the possibilities and difficulties of a new American social world, just as the drama of *Caleb Williams* had cast a searching and also doubting light on the possibility of a new social order to transcend the class-ridden and deeply conservative condition of England.

Edgar Huntly, like *Caleb Williams,* tells a story that mixes lengthy speeches and confessions with sudden and baffling action, and it both outlines and also makes continuously puzzling the position, attitudes and impact of the central figure. Brockden Brown starts his preface by both recognizing and displacing the genre of Gothic excitement. While "the sympathy of the reader" has by "preceding authors" been invoked by "Puerile superstitions and exploded manners; Gothic castles and chimeras," this writer as "a native of America" finds "incidents of Indian hostility, and the perils of the western wilderness are far more suitable" (3). "These, therefore, are, in part, the ingredients of this tale" (4).

Effective as publicity for a new book, especially in an American market, this is only a partial description of a novel that operates in several areas. The wilderness will emerge as both setting and theme, and the second half will involve Indian attacks. The meaning of events will be revealed through sleepwalking, which Brockden Brown presumably does not mention in his preface because that theme continues from his earlier work. Brockden Brown's narrator is more evidently unreliable than Caleb Williams; his only overt mission is to explain events and even himself to his beloved, to whom the whole novel is a letter (their relationship remains, at best, on hold). The mystery remains integral to the novel's system of delivery as well as its events. *Edgar Huntly* operates as both an anxious symbolic story of the very new republic and a compelling prediction of the psychothriller: it can credibly be seen as *Caleb Williams* rerealized, and in many ways both emphasized and sophisticated, in the new transatlantic world of the sublime.

Edgar has no evident occupation; he lives with his uncle on a farm northwest of Philadelphia, close to wild country and not long vacated by the Delaware Indians, the Lenape people. His friend Waldegrave, brother of the girl he loves and a teacher in a charity school for African Americans in Philadelphia, has been found shot at night, and Edgar has walked to the farm out of curiosity—like Caleb, this is his strongest and most lasting characteristic. He arrives at night, detours past the huge elm where Waldegrave was shot, and sees a man there, digging a hole. Edgar follows him back to Inglefield's farm, where Waldegrave lived, and finds the next day he is Clithero Edny (the novel, unlike critics, rarely uses his surname—its tone is intensely intimate).

Edgar watches Clithero and finds he is a good worker, who talks in his sleep and sometimes disappears at night. Edgar can get no more out of him but then follows him at night on a long and dangerous walk. He sees Clithero disappear into a cave and not emerge. But he returns home the next evening, and Edgar follows him again—they meet, and Clithero explains himself.

He grew up in Ireland in humble circumstances and as an orphan was fostered by a very generous lady, Mrs. Lorimer. Her twin brother Arthur Wiatte was troublesome: he opposed her marriage to a man she loved, named Sarsefield. After she married someone he thought more respectable (who has now died), Wiatte became a highwayman and was transported, but he was apparently drowned when the ship sank. Clithero becomes Mrs. Lorimer's steward and loves her niece, Wiatte's daughter Clarice. He feels this is wrong and gives notice, but Mrs. Lorimer knows his feelings and that Clarice shares them: she approves and keeps him on. Suddenly Sarsefield returns: he has traveled the world as a soldier, even with "banditti" in Italy, and is now keen to see Mrs. Lorimer again, and she him. But all of a sudden her wicked brother also reappears—Clithero and Sarsefield keep him away, but one night he tries to rob Clithero in the town and in a struggle is shot dead. Clithero knows Mrs. Lorimer loves her twin in spite of everything, and feels she will die without him, so with strange logic he feels it will be better to kill her rather than submit her to such pain. In her bedroom, as he is about to plunge a knife into a sleeping form, Mrs. Lorimer catches him by the arm: it is Clarice in the bed. He struggles free, sees Mrs. Lorimer fall, assumes she has died, and takes off into the night—and away to America. There, as Edgar has seen, he is gripped with guilt most of the time and goes into the wilderness for a form of lonely grief-stricken relief in the caves.

Edgar responds with more investigation. He follows Clithero into the wild but loses him, then back at Inglefield's house he investigates Clithero's box: this is made with high skill learnt from Sarsefield (in Ireland). But Sarsefield was also Edgar's own mentor (in America before he returned to Ireland) and he manages to open the box, finding a secret spring—but Clithero has built it so that it cannot be shut again. In the box are only tools, yet the next day when Clithero returns he smashes it to pieces, knowing it has been opened. Edgar continues his detection, digging up the hole under the elm where he saw Clithero digging, and finding a small box, which has in it Mrs. Lorimer's own account of her optimistic treatment of her brother. Edgar then misses his letters from Waldegrave. Edgar had promised to copy these for Waldegrave's sister but has recently decided to edit them, so as not to upset her—some expressed serious religious doubts. His uncle says that he heard someone upstairs the night before, where the letters were.

A man suddenly arrives to see Edgar, a friend of Waldegrave's named Weymouth. He invested a small amount of money as a merchant and through his efforts and many wanderings made a good deal of money through his "enterprise." He sent $7,500 back to Waldegrave for safekeeping. Edgar knows Waldegrave received this amount, but has seen in his papers no statement of where it came from. It was a puzzle to his sister, who inherits all he has. Edgar is sympathetic to Weymouth, feels he may find evidence, but thinks he deserves the money in any case. Weymouth leaves and is not heard of again.

There is a drastic change of tone and location and the start of a long series of wild adventures. Suddenly Edgar wakes up in the dark, poorly dressed, and in some sort of pit. He manages to climb out and is menaced by a cougar. He kills it with a tomahawk he finds and is so hungry and thirsty he eats its meat and drinks its blood—and feels very ill. He sees Indians sleeping at a cave and one on guard: he kills the guard and rescues a bound girl. With great difficulty they reach a rough hut. The other Indians arrive: they go in and he hears the girl scream as they break her ribs; when they come out he shoots two of them and then a third. He sees white men come and carry out the girl, but he cannot speak and faints against an Indian; the visitors take him for dead and leave. Finally, when he is walking back over the mountains, he sees a man watching him at a distance. He shoots and misses him, and the man and his party shoot at Edgar as he jumps into the river from a height. Being a very good swimmer, he eventually manages to save himself, though the bank is very steep. On the way back he hears of an Indian raid on a house and assumes that Huntly's has been attacked and his sisters and uncle killed. This is what happened to his parents and a sibling long ago, when he and his sisters were away from home.

He staggers into a house. Sarsefield is there and even Waldegrave's missing letters. Sarsefield, recently back in America, saw Edgar sleepwalking into the wild, led a search for the letters, and then sought him after the men at the hut said they saw him dead. It was Sarsefield and his men who shot at him in the river, thinking he was one of the last of the Indians they were trying to round up, and Edgar shot a hole in Sarsefield's sleeve. Two Indian captives are brought to the house, and one escapes through Edgar's bedroom window. Edgar learns his uncle is dead, but he is the only one and he was killed leading an attack on the Indians. His sisters (who never appear in the novel) are safe.

Clithero reappears. He has in the wilderness found Mrs. Lorimer's manuscript—evidently Edgar dropped it when wandering asleep before he fell in the pit. Clithero did not realize she was alive until Edgar tells him now. Since then he has gone into the wilderness and is living at the old hut where Edgar took the wounded girl. This originally belonged to a Scottish settler who disappeared, and it has for some time been lived in by Old Deb, whom Edgar, who can speak her language and gets on with her, calls Queen Mab. She is the last of the local Delawares and feels she owns the land. It comes out that she was behind the recent invasion as a payback for settler hostility and—most surprisingly—that Waldegrave had been killed by an Indian on a single mission of vengeance.

Sarsefield goes back to his wife, the former Mrs. Lorimer, who has joined him in America. Clithero is determined to go and see her—he doubts she is alive, and if she is he may plan to kill her: he seems quite deranged. Edgar writes to Sarsefield about this, but his wife reads the letter, becomes very anxious, and miscarries their baby as a result. Sarsefield manages to intercept Clithero and has him certified. He is on a ship taking Clithero to an asylum in Philadelphia when he jumps off: as rescuers arrived he "forced himself beneath the surface" (285). Sarsefield writes angrily to Edgar about the part he has played and criticizes his "rashness." Sarsefield's letter and the novel end with the word "Farewell."

Edgar's complex story is built from three interwoven elements. The frame story is the murder of Waldegrave with Edgar's detective-like "curiosity" in solving this, both for his own interest as a friend and also because of his love for Waldegrave's sister Mary, the "thou" to whom the whole story is addressed. There was a man famous for teaching African Americans in Philadelphia, like Waldegrave, Antony Benezet, a leading Quaker reformer, who died—not murdered—in 1784. This murder story was evidently part of the early fiction piece called *Sky-Walk*, now mostly lost, which Brockden Brown wrote by early 1798 and focuses on what became the Clithero–Mrs. Lorimer story, and the Benezet connection is apparently meant to suggest how serious social losses can be caused by dangerously erratic behavior. For most of *Edgar Huntly* we are led to think that Waldegrave's murder was somehow linked to Clithero, and this was probably the outcome in *Sky-Walk*—its central figure, looking forward to Edgar, is referred to as the "Man unknown to Himself" (Krause, 317). In *Edgar Huntly*, however, this crime is finally, and almost casually, absorbed into the others caused by the resistance of the Native Americans.

The presence and threat of the Delaware people, in the text called "Indians" or often "savages," is a major part of the novel that was not apparently a presence in *Sky-Walk*. Though that name refers to a wild region, which is much traversed by the hero, it does not include hostile indigenes as in *Edgar Huntly*—their only substantial presence in any of Brockden Brown's work. Edgar starts off with some respect for these people—he can, we later hear, speak Delaware and has been friendly with "Old Deb," the eccentric matriarch who still lives on their original lands. But all the natives come to seem more threatening, and he is increasingly hostile to them, killing one with a tomahawk and others with a rifle—his own rifle, which he has regained from them. He is mistaken for an "Indian" by a rescue party and shot at, and his last contact with them is when one escapes through Edgar's own bedroom window.

This is a strange long sequence, heavily emphasized in the novel. As Peter Kafer argues (177–80), the Philadelphia Quakers, both Brockden Brown's family and many of his friends, were firmly liberal towards the indigenous people, and it seems improbable—especially because the topic is not raised in any of the other fiction or other writing—that Brockden Brown would have been personally hostile towards Native Americans, even though attacks like those in the novel were occurring in the 1780s. Rather, he appears to represent these commonly held anxieties as part of the mix of emergent American feelings. Kafer suggests (180–83) that the violence of and towards the "Indians" in the novel is simply a displacement of the hostile feelings of the Philadelphia Quakers towards the aggressive "Revolutionary" Americans of the period, who were frequently new emigrants, often from Ireland, and could be seen as another kind of "savages." This highly strained argument, while relieving modern anxiety about Brockden Brown's apparently anti–Native American stance, has no detailed support from the text. There are, through the novel, some other traces of an anti-immigrant feeling—Clithero, with his self-melodramatizing and his tendency towards violence, is from Ireland, and so is the enigmatic and essentially negative Sarsefield; Brockden Brown was very likely aware that this is the surname of a Protestant military hero from the late seventeenth century.

The political force of the novel is not directly involved in the third major strand of story, which starts early, as soon as Edgar sees Clithero digging under the elm where Waldegrave died, and only ends in the grim events of the last pages as Edgar's clumsy intervention leads Clithero to suicide and his former patroness Mrs. Lorimer, as Mrs. Sarsefield, to lose her child. Clithero the clumsy dreamer from Ireland and Edgar the almost as clumsy and almost as dream-racked young American often overlap: in Grabo's discussion of "doubles, twins, look-alikes, and second selves" (xi) they are the most striking pair—including both being mentored by Sarsefield as well as entering the wild country in parallel. But there are elements of the double about Sarsefield and Wiatte, Mrs. Lorimer and Clarice, and Waldegrave and Edgar. Grabo comments that on this basis of doubleness the novel's action and meaning "originates in the psychology of somnambulism" (xi), where people act when asleep to express their desires without the standard constraints of the superego. Brockden Brown was well aware of the research published by the major British scholar Erasmus Darwin in this field, including his view that when asleep man was "a much less perfect animal" (see Krause, 336).

The major pair of doubles operates through their parallel somnambulism, just as Clithero digs to hide Mrs. Lorimer's statement, and Edgar will hide the letters from Waldegrave that both challenge his stability of mind and threaten his relations with Mary. Yet both the doubled characters feel strongly, if improbably, positive: Clithero thinks he will save Mrs. Lorimer from a wretched life by killing her; Edgar, as Krause notes (345–46), is always positive in his expectations, in this like an Enlightenment optimist. His plan to use sympathy as therapy can be seen as an application of the current theory of "homeopathy"— though in fact almost all the violence actually performed in the book is by Edgar himself and both men have disastrous impacts on those about them.

Just as Clithero's bungling good-heartedness led him to plan to kill Mrs. Lorimer and nearly murder his beloved Clarice, so Edgar, having imitated Clithero's desperate walking, becomes not so much a fierce enemy of the "Indians" but himself actually like their negative stereotype, killing the cougar and stalking and shooting them with skill and malice. He is first reduced to the same location and state as Clithero and then linked in blood and what seems like death with another Indian—and he stabs another to death in a Clithero-like muddled version of mercy. After the drastic events at Old Deb's hut Edgar felt he had "imbibed from the unparalleled events which had lately happened a spirit vengeful, unrelenting, and ferocious" (184)—in a word, become like them, "savage." By staying in Old Deb's hut (a sequence Brockden Brown amplified in revision; see Krause, 300) Edgar seems to share her identity—and Grabo notes how often "the occupation of another's place" suggests a sharing of identity in the novel (xv).

With Waldegrave dead, Edgar, the uncertain American, has had only untrustworthy models of behavior such as Clithero and Sarsefield. The older generation is brave enough—Huntly gives his life leading an attack on the Indians—but the Indians are there because he took their land in the first place, and Edgar's parents and a sibling have already paid for it with their lives. With the tainted inheritance of Europeans like Clithero and the confident and at times cruel Sarsefield and the stark history of land-taking, there is no room for a moral and calm approach to American modernity. Even the determined walking of Clithero and Edgar, while a trait that Brockden Brown shared, has negative implications. As they walk the land, with Edgar insisting several times that nobody at all, white or not, has been there before, they are the image of landtakers: no one at the time could miss the connection with the notorious "Walking Purchase" of 1753, when the natives agreed to cede as much land as a man could walk in a day—and the would-be settlers hired professional walkers who took for them far more than the former owners had imagined possible.

At the end, the always innocent, if also always foolishly positive, Edgar is left without resolution—just like Caleb Williams. Finding the answer to the mystery has merely instigated a whole range of other troubles, and just as Godwin left the exposed problems of class, power and law to be pondered and slowly tinkered with, so Brockden Brown laid out for Americans the disturbing bases of their society, torn between brutal land-taking, inadequate inheritances from Europe, and the uncertain procedures being invented in the new country. Central among them was the Constitution that was being produced as Edgar and Clithero ranged erratically across the former country of the indigenous Delaware people.

Without using, even without seeking, the confident closure of most crime fiction, both Godwin and Brockden Brown deployed the idea of inquiry into crime as a way of opening up in a startlingly new way the socio-political structures of their countries that most preferred to ignore, and both novels have only grown in stature as more has been understood about the contexts to which they related and the powerful uses to which these transatlantic originators of crime fiction put the possibilities of this new genre.

Brockden Brown was read widely: Percy Shelley and other late Romantics admired him very much, and Cooper, while never willing to praise his work, "borrowed shamelessly from Brown" (Fiedler, 145) and paid him the tribute of reusing the idea of white Americans encountering Indians in the much less disturbing form of Natty Bumppo, the white but quasi-native "Deerstalker." Poe considerably admired Brockden Brown's intense quality and obviously used *Edgar Huntly* for the first half of his fantasy story "The Tale of the Ragged Mountains" and reworked the idea of doubles like Edgar and Clithero suggestively in "The Purloined Letter" and more deeply in "William Wilson." Hawthorne also owed a major debt to Brockden Brown, putting him in his "Hall of Fame" with Homer, Shakespeare, and Scott.

Brockden Brown's anti-realist mix of mystery and uncertainty, well described by Calanchi, was less appealing to later mainstream American authors and critics, committed as they were to humanist realism, and he had no place in F. O. Matthiessen's very influential book about the "American Renaissance" in fiction. He began to be of interest again fairly recently in terms of psychiatric readings, as in David Brion Davis's chapter "The Disordered Mind," which explores Clithero's "homicidal insanity" (98) and sees his killing of Arthur Wiatte as Oedipal. This reading was made central to Leslie Fiedler's major statement in *Love and Death in the American Novel* (1960) where he calls *Edgar Huntly* a book "not so much written as dreamt" (396). Fiedler saw Cooper as redeeming the frontier threat simplistically in terms of Rousseau's noble savage but feels Brockden Brown was confronting the complexity of the American experience, offering, as Sydney J. Krause puts it, a national foundation myth about "the American Adam's return from the Garden of his origins" (400). Since Fiedler's long, searching chapter about *Edgar Huntly,* many writers and researchers have seen much of importance in Brockden Brown's complex explorations in the personal, social and national uncertainty of the early American male citizen, though it is notable that the emphasis tends to fall on the psychological rather than the political elements of Brockden Brown's analysis: Steven Watts in a well-received study emphasizes what he calls Brockden Brown's exploration of the "hidden, dangerous dimension of rational individualism" (123) and does not deal with the "Indian" issue at all.

Charles Brockden Brown's other novels show he had the power to write testingly about the relationship between people in the developing American cities—including their relationship with their sense of an inner self, or even a fictitious, ventriloqual self. In *Edgar Huntly* he allied that power with a complex view of the country itself and its former owners. By adding to the early

Sky-Walk the whole "Indian" issue, he created a dense and complex study in social and personal politics. The effect is strikingly like the way in which Raymond Chandler would much later condense two stories with quite different themes into one complex "cannibalized" novel, and it is possible to see the American thriller tradition as having kept alive some of the rich uncertainties of the complex power of *Edgar Huntly*. Just as *Caleb Williams* seems to link most strongly with the personal-political mix of the Hammett tradition, *Edgar Huntly* is the first of many novels to explain American values through crime fiction.

References

Calanchi, Alessandra. "Tender Is the Wild: Subliminal Soundscapes and the Aural Sublime in Charles Brockden Brown's Proto-Crime Fiction," in *From the Sublime to City Crime*. Ed. Maurizio Ascari and Stephen Knight. Monaco: Livero, 2014, 70-106; E-publication.

Davis, David Brion. *Homicide in American Fiction, 1798–1860: A Study in Social Value.* Ithaca: Cornell University Press, 1957.

Fiedler, Leslie. *Love and Death in the American Novel.* New York: Dell, 1960.

Grabo, Norman S. "Introduction," in Charles Brockden Brown, *Edgar Huntly, or, Memoirs of a Sleepwalker.* Ed. Norman S. Grabo. New York: Viking, 1988.

Kafer, Peter. *Charles Brockden Brown's Revolution and the Birth of American Gothic.* Philadelphia: University of Pennsylvania Press, 2004.

Krause, Sydney J. "Historical Essay," in Charles Brockden Brown, *Edgar Huntley, or, Memoirs of a Sleepwalker.* Ed. S. J. Krause and S.W. Reid. Bicentennial Edition. Kent, OH: Kent State University Press, 1984, 295–400.

Landrum, Larry, Jr. *American Mystery and Detective Novels: A Reference Guide.* Westport, CT: Greenwood, 1999.

Steven Watts, *The Romance of Real Life: Charles Brockden Brown and the Origins of American Culture.* Baltimore: Johns Hopkins University Press, 1994.

3

The Dupin Stories, Edgar Allan Poe

For many commentators Poe was the originator of crime fiction. That idea is contradicted by the presence of novelists like Godwin and Brockden Brown who created inquiries into hidden crime, the uncertain self and the deep structures of their society, and also by the flow of less ambitious fictional explorations of malpractice in the early nineteenth century, usually involving a lawyer or doctor as an agent of inquiry. But Poe was the first to imagine what have become basic techniques of the genre: a clever person looks at the puzzling facts, sees connections invisible to others and reveals the culprit in the dramatic conclusion of the story. That structure of intelligent mystery solving is buttressed by the fact that Dupin is not an official policeman or even a paid private detective (though he is consulted by the police and money does come his way) and is given a bravura appeal by the range of learned reference, subtle comment and melodramatic flourish with which he delivers his amazing analytic explanations.

Early inquirers like the real French police detective Vidocq, whose *Mémoires* appeared in 1828–29, Samuel Warren's doctor stories and the "Philadelphia Lawyer" series (see Knight, chap. 1) depended on information, confession and coincidence for explanations. Poe's Dupin generates the solutions from his own remarkable brain, and so a fantasy of intellectually driven security is created, which was extremely successful with committed readers. Poe himself did not make much of these stories: there were only three, spread over four years, and in that period he also wrote a story essentially mocking what he was doing in them ("Thou Art the Man"). His fame rested first on his poetry—"The Raven" was his big breakthrough in January 1845—and then on learned and quasi-scientific inquiries like his cryptography-solving exercises and his long late essay "Eureka." The French and many later readers admired especially the sheer horror of stories like "The Pit and the Pendulum" and "William Wilson," which, while they go back to Brockden Brown for inspiration, depend on Poe's exploration of the disturbed mind and the concepts of doubleness, not on his interests in crime and detection. All those roles that Poe fulfilled with brilliance were of interest to the strongly growing audiences of the miscellany magazines of the period, in Britain and the United States, and his impact was more original and extensive than just being a mythical inventor of crime fiction: it was he who first gave the form imaginative and intellectual power.

His short and often-troubled life began in Boston in 1809, the second son of actors of Irish and English origins. By the time he was two his father had left home and his mother had died of tuberculosis: he was fostered by John Allan, a rich merchant from Virginia, whose name he adopted. This elevated southern upbringing would mix oddly with Poe's northern bohemian elements, both in his writing and in his activities. After several years abroad—including some schooling in London—Poe studied languages for a year at the University of Virginia but left with money problems, probably through gambling. He drifted away from the Allan family, enlisted as a soldier under the name Edgar Perry, and upgraded to officer school but left in a year, having published poetry in a modest way. He reconnected with his family through his aunt, but this new life was also less than orderly: his brother died of alcoholism in 1831 and Poe married his thirteen-year-old cousin in 1835, by which time he had found his role in life by beginning work as a literary editor and writer.

His novel *The Narrative of Arthur Gordon Pym of Nantucket* appeared in 1838 and made less mark than it deserves. In 1839 his first story collection was named *Tales of the Grotesque and Arabesque:* the title proclaims both his area of interest and his intellectual command of it. The terms go back to the German Romantics, especially Friedrich Schlegel and E. T. A. Hoffman, and "grotesque" means a tale of horror delivered with full sensationalism, while "arabesque," implying "elaborate" rather than "Moorish," refers to a subjective disturbance that is recounted in a calm and intelligent way. Hoffman is the model, but it might also be seen as a version of Charles Brockden Brown's inner excitements. Stories from the early 1840s like "The Pit and the Pendulum" and "A Tale of the Ragged Mountains" clearly depend on Brockden Brown for their basic ideas, and the early and powerful "William Wilson" projects the idea of a double personality into the areas of elaborated horror. The notion of "arabesque," implying intelligent explanation, was taken further in the early 1840s in what Poe called his three "tales of ratiocination." Here intellectual analysis became a method of explaining mysterious events and creating stories of detection in a much more formal way that had been imagined

3. The Dupin Stories

by Godwin or Brockden Brown or the minor doctor and lawyer inquirers Poe would certainly have known from the magazines. He mentioned Warren in his work, and he knew well the "Philadelphia Lawyer" stories started in the American *Gentleman's Magazine* by 1838, as he became editor of it for a year in 1839.

"The Murders in the Rue Morgue" appeared in March 1841. The title sounds designed for one of Poe's flamboyant parodies, but the tone is serious, holding to the arabesque, not the grotesque. Like the Philadelphia Lawyer story "The Murderess," it starts with a quotation, here in English from Sir Thomas Browne—foreign languages will soon gather. Then comes, again as in the lawyer model, a lengthy and high-toned statement: where the Lawyer speaks about the criminal capacities of women, the Poe narrator discourses on methods of analysis. Though the language is lofty, there is real engagement with ordinary life: he argues that chess, being only abstruse, is not nearly as complex as draughts, where success depends on comprehending the identity and intention of your opponent. Throughout these stories will run what can be called this subtle-simple paradox, the notion that what might well seem a simple approach is in fact more complex than one at first seeming more elaborate.

Then, also as in the Lawyer stories, the narration begins as an example of the opening discourse—but Poe first has to introduce his detective. The narrator, who is merely "residing" (381) in Paris and so might be an American, met him in a library. They are both dedicated to books, read all day, and adventure out at night, a lifestyle matched by the "time-eaten and grotesque mansion" in the Faubourg St Germain—they live in a "retired and desolate" (382) part of this traditionally noble quarter. Dupin is both energetic and reflective, and when thinking deeply he seems physically distant: there is "a double Dupin—the creative and the resolvent" (383)—to remind us of Brockden Brown's doubles. The example given of Dupin's thought process is a much-imitated sequence. He observes his friend, reads his thoughts, and breaks into them with a comment—and then explains in detail how he managed this. It is both a set piece of genius at work and also a readily followable exposition of science as understandable. Ronald Thomas has seen Poe as linking crime fiction and science, calling Dupin a "triumph of modern science" (112), but in fact the passage substitutes empirical data for scientific method, as Conan Doyle will in the Sherlock Holmes myth. Poe sweeps on with more facts, creating quotations from newspapers (also used in the Philadelphia Lawyer stories) about a horrific murder. Dupin and his friend discuss this, and Dupin says the police lack any real method—they are looking too closely at things: another subtle-simple paradox lies in their "undue profundity" (392).

So Dupin and his friend visit the Rue Morgue house, where Dupin "scrutinised everything" (393)—including the bodies—but there is no grisly detail or analysis: Dupin just goes home and thinks in silence. The model is that of disciplinary specialism, with an expert statement to come. The subtle-simple paradox is mentioned—he says the police have "fallen into the gross but common error of confusing the unusual with the abstruse" (394). He, however, understands all and is just waiting for a visitor to explain it all, and though he is a man of the mind, he produces a pair of pistols—there is some action, or at least the promise of it, in Poe's stories.

The famous outcome is that there is not in fact a murderer, merely an orangutan run amok. Though the savage violence against women and the terrifying entry to a locked upper apartment seem like a contemporary urban nightmare—and Dupin and the narrator also live alone in just the same sort of building—it is in fact just a freak event. Dupin knew the source of the violence from the hair, the superhuman agility needed to get in and out, and the language (when no human can identify it, it must be inhuman). Thomas sees this as all science based (40–56), but most of it is logical observation. The mix of logic and science (though some have challenged the hair identification as then impossible) is compelling, and there is no problem in the outcome. The pistols are put away unused and the Prefect of Police is informed without taking too much offense—though Dupin reminds us that he is "somewhat too cunning to be profound" (409)—and we end with a lighthearted quotation from Rousseau to round off this exercise in finding functional security through a cleverness that is also fully imaginative.

A review by Margaret Fuller in 1845 recalls the story made "a great impression" (see Carlson, 17), and Poe was evidently happy with the approach, because in the following year he took a bolder step, deciding to apply the same method to a real New York murder. Mary Rogers, famous as "the beautiful cigar girl," was found dead in July 1841, attacked physically, perhaps sexually, before being thrown in the Hudson River. The police made little headway, and Poe went to work. He made her name French and set the murder in Paris as another case for Dupin. "The Mystery of Marie Roget" appeared in three installments, in November and December 1842 and February 1843.

Marie worked in a perfumery for a year, then disappeared for a week, saying she had been in the country. Five months later she disappeared again and her battered body was found in the Seine. A reward was offered; the police chief visited Dupin with "a liberal proposition" (414), and he begins to investigate. The newspapers have discussed the case in detail, being particularly interested in how long it takes a body to rise in water. Then some boys find signs of a fight and some of Marie's clothes scattered in a wood near an inn kept by Madame Deluc, who says she saw a girl with a "man with a dark complexion" and following them "a gang of miscreants" (421). But then Marie's fiancé, St Eustache, suddenly kills himself with laudanum: it is suggested there has been press talk against him, but the actual cause seems the very similar real suicide, apparently through grief, of Mary Rogers' fiancé, Daniel Payn. Press "insinuations" (432) are made against Marie's employer, including that he has wrongly identified her body. Dupin discusses all this in detail—this story is longer than the first. He theorizes in scientific mode about bodies in water, debates whether the clothes were ripped or deliberately torn, and doubts the presence of a gang: he suggests the clothes were dumped as a distraction—what will later be called a red herring. He favors as murderer an unknown sailor lover of Marie who has been away a lot, could handle a boat (to dump the body), and might well have a dark complexion. The sailor's discovery seems to be where the story is heading: it ends by predicting that "corroboration will rise upon corroboration, and the murderer will be traced" (452). The editor comments merely that "the desired result was brought to pass" (452) and the story concludes with, for Poe, a fairly restrained discourse about "the Calculus of Probabilities."

What happened in late 1842 showed why Poe was unwise to take on a real crime. Mary Rogers was last seen on Greenwich Street, New York, a notorious site of brothels and abortion parlors. Late in 1842 a Mrs. Loss confessed on her deathbed (she had been accidentally shot by her son) to being involved in an abortion that went wrong, after which Mary's body was attacked to make her death look like a result of rape-murder and thrown in the river. As John Walsh has argued, Poe appears to have deferred publication for a month, missing January 1843, which enabled him to insert reference to a possible "accident at Mme Deluc's" (445), and, without withdrawing the mystery sailor as favored villain, added two paragraphs trying to separate Marie from Mary. At least Dupin had been right about the clothes and the absent gang and the apparent violence as covering up a different death, but the real cause of Mary Rogers' death was undoubtedly part of the well-known scandal of abortion in the city—and that probably is why she was away previously for a week and returned "in good health but with a somewhat saddened air" (412). The version in the 1845 collection, as Walsh shows in detail, made further minor changes backing away from the single killer theory but also removing Madame Deluc's name.

The uncertain outcome inevitably makes the story rather ineffective, but it is in any case much wordier and less focused than "The Murders in the Rue Morgue." While the commitment to quasi-scientific writing seem to function well for Poe, this step towards True Crime just did not work. The failure apparently made him in the last Dupin story withdraw into something entirely more controllable, an imaginary story effectively without crime at all but also one where in a much shorter compass he produced one of his finest and most stimulating works—not only a model for crime fiction writers in its elegant realization of the mystery of the obvious but also remarkable in the modern period for stimulating major theorists into their own versions of its possible meanings.

"The Purloined Letter" was published in September 1844 (though the anthology it appeared in is dated 1845) when, although his wife was very ill and he was drinking more, Poe remained highly productive—"The Balloon Hoax" was widely enjoyed and "The Facts in the Case of M. Valdemar" is a brilliantly condensed piece of horror. The new Dupin story only reaches some eight thousand words, little more than half "The Murders in the Rue Morgue," and quite lacks the detailed reportage and discussion of the other two. Poe starts with Seneca saying, in Latin, "Nothing is more hateful to wisdom than too much guilefulness" (454)—the last word in Latin is *acumen* and Poe means it, as Seneca does, as over-fussy analysis focusing, not the sweep of imaginative insight that he and Dupin are demonstrating: it is the subtle-simple paradox given some distinction.

As before, Poe recalls "The Murders in the Rue Morgue" and now "Marie Roget" as well. Here there is no opening method discussion: the Prefect of Police arrives at once and sketches out the problem. The Minister D—— has stolen a letter that is very embarrassing to the Queen and has been using it "for political purposes, to a very dangerous extent" (457). The Queen needs it back: she saw him take it but could not speak because someone else was there—the King, evidently. The Prefect thinks Dupin will be interested because the puzzle, though simple, is also "so excessively odd" (455). Knowing the Minister needs the letter at hand, they have for three months been looking for it in his house and those of his neighbors: they have even taken up the carpets and searched under the wallpaper.

A month later the Prefect returns. They have not found the letter. Dupin asks what was the reward? Fifty thousand francs the Prefect replies. Dupin teases him a little, asks for a check, and hands over the letter. The Prefect "appeared absolutely thunderstricken" (462), writes a check, and rushes from the room, all in silence. Action and surprises are emphasized in this story, partly by the more limited discussion, partly by being just more dramatic. Dupin begins to explain to the narrator, picking up the simple-subtle paradox in reference to the guessing game "even and odd": you can win by making your face look like your opponent's—but the police have not tried to think like Minister D——. Dupin knows him, as both a mathematician and a poet: he argues the latter skill is further reaching and has brought the power of simplicity. If you want to hide a name on a map, Dupin says, you make it as large as the map. He decided the letter was in fact not concealed, so visited the Minister and at once saw in a cheap letter rack a badly torn letter addressed to D—— himself. That was the opposite of what was being sought, so Dupin assumes it is the purloined letter, goes home and makes a copy. He visits the next day for his allegedly forgotten snuffbox and, while he is there, by pre-arrangement a man fires a musket in the street. As D—— looks out, Dupin exchanges the letters.

The letter was hidden in plain sight. Dupin makes a lot of money—at the time fifty thousand francs was about four professional annual salaries, so at least half a million dollars in modern terms. On the blank letter he wrote, knowing D——— would recognize his handwriting, a quotation from Crebillon's classical tragedy *Atrée*, linking D—— to Thyeste, who is punished for betraying his brother—by way of ending, Dupin and Poe play on the detective/criminal double.

Well-controlled, better-paced and more dramatic than the other stories, this and "The Murders in the Rue Morgue" have been the classic originary instances of the all-knowing detective. It seems deeply sad that Poe wrote no more in this mode, but then he had only four more years to live, with many disruptions in them, and in any case did not seem to value highly what he saw as "ingenious" stories (Carlson, 92). Poe's November 1844 story "Thou Art the Man" was basically parodic detection—Sayers in her 1928 introduction said it has "a certain repulsive facetiousness" (72–73). A man disappears, and his close friend (though of only six months) Charley Goodfellow is very upset, acts as detective and finds clues to accuse a local. The narrator, a local resident, describes the arrival of a large box of wine that the dead man had promised Charley. When it is opened the man's rotting body sits up and looking at Charley appears to say, "Thou art the man." Charley collapses, confesses his guilt, and then dies. The narrator, who found the body, has investigated the matter and observed Charley's dubious behavior. He arranged the wine delivery, pushed a strip of corset whalebone down the body's throat and doubled it over so that when the lid was raised it also rose—and to make the accusation he uses his ventriloqual skills (clearly referencing Brockden Brown). At once spectacular, parodic and predicting the shock revelation of the classic mystery, this story may show Poe enjoying his burlesque skills, but it also suggests he did not share the high value that succeeding generations have placed on the Dupin stories—the manuscripts of them are apparently less well finished than other stories, though that could also mean they are closer to Poe's productive unconscious.

Some commentators enlist "The Gold Bug" as a crime story because its solution comes from a complicated cryptogram, but it was Conan Doyle, in "The Adventures of the Dancing Men," who brought this device into the crime fiction mainstream, and it seems proper to see it as just part of Poe's extraordinary range, just as "The Man of the Crowd," a puzzling examination of the urban public, is often seen as a major text in the development of urban alienated consciousness.

Poe's inheritance and reputation have been both rich and complex. He would have been very pleased that his stories appeared in French from 1846 on. The Goncourt brothers saw a connection between Dupin and Voltaire's mythic detective Zadig (see Carlson, 87) and Baudelaire thought Poe a kindred spirit: the first of his very influential translations appeared in 1848. For Baudelaire, Poe's great quality lay in the bold imaginative excess of the stories, both the horrific grotesque and also the intellectually refined arabesque: Baudelaire felt he had himself had thoughts like those of Dupin on the subtle-simple paradox in "The Purloined Letter." But other writers read the Dupin stories as part of the intellectual detective tradition, admiring their emphasis on both empirical detail and imaginative analysis. Gaboriau's first detective, the elderly amateur Tabaret, owes a good deal to Dupin; Conan Doyle referred to Poe favorably in his first Holmes story, *A Study in Scarlet*, and named him as his own inspiration in a 1909 speech celebrating Poe's centenary. American scholars and reviewers in the early twentieth century consistently returned to Poe as the originator of the form, notably in an essay of 1907 in *Scribner's Magazine* by Professor Brander Matthews (see Carlson).

But those who were constructing the canon of American literature were not so open to recognizing Poe's importance. He had himself been a serious opponent of the highly valued school of "transcendental poets"—he belittlingly named them "Frogpondians" and found little to respect in the much-admired Longfellow. While poems like "The Raven" have always been enormously popular with the public, Poe's standing as a national poet has never been among the highest. His prose, not being in the dominant humanist-realist novel tradition, was seen, like that of Mark Twain, as merely popular, so below serious national notice—though in France, England and Russia it was always acknowledged as of high importance. Like Brockden Brown, Poe had to wait for a wider range of interests and a much stronger valuing of the psychically and mythically dynamic to be rated more highly in modern times: Jeffrey Meyer said Poe was the first to deal with "the disintegration of personality" (282).

While scholars and critics of crime fiction have seen him as the originator of the classic mystery story, major theorists have also found important themes and attitudes embedded in his narratives. A recent Web site has set out ways of reading "The Purloined Letter" in terms of modern critical theory (www.eng.fju.edu.tw), arguing that it responds to the semantic analysis of A. J.

Greimas and can also be read in terms of the disciplinary surveillance that Foucault has discussed and is often taken as a basis for detective fiction. Major theorists have written directly about this fertile story, as reported by John P. Muller and William J. Richardson in *The Purloined Poe* and as discussed in an essay by John T. Irwin. Marie Bonaparte, a between-wars Freudian psychoanalyst, felt the letter over the fireplace is a symbol of the clitoris, and so maternal sexuality, and that Dupin here represents Poe himself negotiating psychically between the King, as his long-lost father, and the Minister D—— as the foster father, John Allan. At a different level Lacan argued in a widely influential essay (discussed by Irwin) that the letter is a "pure signifier" that symbolizes desire in two versions of the primal scene, where D—— and then Dupin steal the letter. Finally, Jacques Derrida and his interpreter Barbara Johnson both, as Irwin also explains, reinterpret the letter as a symbol of ultimate—and very postmodern—undecidability.

Against this welter of analysis, the meaning of "The Murders in the Rue Morgue" seems fairly modest: the Bonaparte interpretation is rich with symbolic anxiety, focusing on Poe's obsession with controlling his mother's sexuality. The daughter stuffed up the chimney has been symbolically returned to the womb to deny his father's part in her creation—or perhaps his own—and the beheaded mother has suffered symbolic castration. Against this psychic melodrama, Bonaparte merely offers "The Mystery of Marie Roget" as expressing Poe's sado-necrophiliac feelings for his wife.

In these Freudian readings the orangutan merely represents feared paternal violence—murder used as a figure for sexual power—and it has been noted that many of Poe's stories, including all the Dupin mysteries, involve murder or at least threats against women. But Elise Lemire has suggested the animal raises racial issues. She cites the commonness then of "monkeys as parodies of black barbers" (184), the babble-type speech of the animal and "the spectre of interracial sex" (195) as features linking the murderous threat to African Americans. Poe's Philadelphia was the scene of much racial debate; but as the violator is finally revealed as a mere beast, the threat is finally silenced. There has been a substantial debate over whether Poe was indeed a racist or whether he just tuned his editing and writing and editing to the white and often racist readership of magazines. It is true he often symbolizes threats and evil by forms of blackness but also that his close friend George Lippard was a dedicated antislavery spokesman: the debate may reveal more about modern American concerns than the socio-political depths of Poe's work. If there is a conscious politics in Poe's stories it is anti-modern and anti-urban, taking refuge in the rich world of his imagination and his remarkable range of reference. Scholars have occasionally found errors in his no doubt often speedy writing—he confuses

La Bougive and La Bruyère as French writers in "The Purloined Letter"—but in general the learning as well as the acute analysis shown in Poe's work is very impressive, was seen in that way by his often-learned French admirers, and itself offers a world of reliable values in learning alone.

However, not everybody in his period admired him, and his obituary in the *New York Tribune* said that "few would be grieved" by Poe's death. This was by Rufus Griswold, a rival editor who managed to become Poe's executor and set out to destroy his reputation. To the collected works of 1850 Griswold added a "Memoir of the Author," which denounced Poe as addicted to drinks and drugs and included, as evidence of his unacceptable behavior, letters, some of which were forged. Poe's friends attacked Griswold, but his widely disseminated libel long held power, seeming somehow matched to Poe's apparently wayward and anti-mainstream personality and writing. He did drink a lot but never took drugs, and he could certainly be difficult, mostly to his employers—but his life was also disrupted to the point of tragedy. After losing both parents and his wife, he died after being found in crisis in the street after he had been campaigning for a liberal candidate in the Baltimore elections. Poe had been drinking hard for the last years up to his wife's death in 1847, but he had also kept on working, with "Eureka" a major success from that period.

Poe's reputation, like his life, has been both brilliant and troubled, and he remains for many critics outside the pantheon of American great writers—but his work also remains vividly alive and in print, and in the areas of science fiction and crime fiction he is revered as massively influential. He was not the actual originator of crime fiction, but he did something more difficult—he imagined a shape and a central theme for the fiction of the detective. In 2011 Warner Brothers and ABC made a pilot for a series with Poe himself as an 1840s Boston detective, but it did not catch on. That seems right: he is not just a mythic personality; he is a great and very influential creative artist. A major part of his impact is the few brilliant detective stories, including the misconceived "Marie Roget," which define the necessary imaginative limits of crime fiction. His finest memorial is the way in which writers have for close to two hundred years shaped their stories, novels and scripts in both the spirit and also the specific technical mode that Poe invented for the first great detective, the Chevalier Auguste Dupin.

References

Carlson, Eric W. *The Reputation of Edgar Allan Poe: Selected Criticism Since 1829.* Ann Arbor: University of Michigan Press, 1960.
Irwin, John T. "Detective Fiction as High Art: Lacan, Derrida, and Johnson on 'The

Purloined Letter,'" in *The Selected Writings of Edgar Allan Poe*. Ed. G. R. Thompson. Norton Critical Texts. New York: Norton, 2004, 941–52.

Knight, Stephen. *Crime Fiction Since 1800: Detection, Death, Diversity*. Second revised edition. London: Palgrave Macmillan, 2010.

Lemire, Elise. "'The Murders in the Rue Morgue': Amalgamation Discourses and the Race Riots of 1838 in Poe's Philadelphia," in *Romancing the Shadow: Poe and Race*. Ed. J. Gerald Kennedy and Liliane Weissberg. New York: Oxford University Press, 2001, 177–204.

Meyer, Jeffrey. *Edgar Allan Poe: His Life and Legacy*. New York: Scribner, 1992.

Muller, John P., and William J. Richardson, eds. *The Purloined Poe*. Baltimore: Johns Hopkins University Press, 1988.

Sayers, Dorothy L. "Introduction," in *The Omnibus of Crime*. London: Gollancz, 1928, reprinted in *The Art of the Mystery Story*. Ed. Howard Haycraft. Second edition. New York: Carrol and Graf, 1992, 71–109.

Thomas, Ronald R. *Detective Fiction and the Rise of Forensic Science*. Cambridge: Cambridge University Press, 1999.

Thompson, G. R., ed. *The Selected Writings of Edgar Allan Poe*. Norton Critical Texts. New York: Norton, 2004.

Walsh, John. *Poe the Detective*. New Brunswick: Rutgers University Press, 1968.

www.eng.fju.edu.tw/Literary Criticism/Structuralism/purloin.

4

The Moonstone, Wilkie Collins

From when it first appeared in 1868 in Dickens' weekly periodical, *All the Year Round, The Moonstone* has always been a substantial presence in English fiction. Crowds of people queued to buy each new episode and people would bet on when, where and how the enormously valuable missing diamond would reappear. With *The Woman in White* (1858–59) Collins had established the sensational novel as a major form. He followed with the more challenging and less successful *No Name* (1862) and *Armadale* (1866) but then with *The Moonstone* condensed his power to create memorable characters with a puzzlingly complex plot and, most demanding of all, raised issues generating a good deal of social tension at the time

The Moonstone is not technically the first detective novel—the English *The Notting Hill Mystery* (1862–63) and the American *The Dead Letter* (1867) both precede it—but it introduces substantial complexity to the form. The evidence that is assembled is hard to find and just as hard to decipher; everybody has a special interest and a special range of errors; nobody comes close to guessing the actual final explanation. The novel is also very wide in its conceptual range: it looks back to Brockden Brown in the importance of somnambulism and the unconscious mind and looks forward generations in its skeptical treatment of the authoritarian practices that the period deployed without question in the areas of race, imperialism, gender and class. *The Moonstone* is, like the diamond itself, both brilliant and a puzzle—is the range and subtlety readers find in it Collins' conscious work? Or was it just the outcome of his powers as a sheer storyteller and creator of mysteries, who was himself, like his best detective, Ezra Jennings, under the influence of opium through the production of the novel—a feature that Collins stressed, and probably exaggerated, in his preface to the 1871 edition.

4. The Moonstone

Collins was born in 1824 in London, son of a successful artist, William Collins. They shared first names, but Collins chose to use his middle name Wilkie, from his godfather, the Scottish painter David Wilkie. Though Wilkie Collins could paint, he rejected his father's profession, worked for a tea merchant and then trained as a lawyer. But writing was his calling: he first wrote a biography of his father, then turned to novels—a Tahiti-based melodrama was never published, but after he met Dickens in 1851 Collins moved towards English-set social novels, with elements of crime and mystery. *Hide and Seek* (1854) has an amateur detective and *The Dead Secret* (1857) another; then *The Woman in White* uses both a painter and a woman to expose the crimes of aristocrats who are either weak, fake or foreign, all exploiting women who are brave and sometimes strong like the investigating Marion Halcombe.

Collins wrote *The Woman in White* consciously as a set of witness accounts, all converging on the complex truth of the matter. In 1856 he had visited a court proceeding and was impressed by "the succession of testimonies so varied in form and nevertheless so strictly unified by their march towards the same goal" (see Kemp, xxiii). In this multi-narrative method there is a conflicted social jury at work, not the simplicity of a single detective. In *The Moonstone* he developed this quasi-realistic approach, so the sense of a True Crime narrative takes on the complexities of a whodunit. His preface to *The Moonstone* starts by saying that where before he had traced "the influence of circumstance upon character" (xv), here he reverses the order, telling what the people are like in order to suggest what happened.

Basically the story of *The Moonstone* is quite simple, though it has several stages, and the climax is very well concealed. The great diamond itself was stolen from a sacred Hindu statue in 1799 by Captain Herncastle as the English took an Indian fortress. Back in England, knowing three Brahmins were seeking it round the world, he kept the stone in a bank, then left it to his niece Rachel Verinder to avenge himself on the family who had cut him off for his crime, by diverting the danger onto them. As the Verinder family steward Gabriel Betteredge, faithful but limited, explains in his long opening "narration," Rachel's cousin Franklin Blake, who has for some years been in Europe, brings the diamond for her eighteenth birthday party, avoiding the three Indians with a mix of caution and luck. At the house party is Rachel's other cousin, Godfrey Ablewhite, son of the diamond banker, and a barrister and major charity figure. He proposes to her but is courteously rejected: she prefers Franklin, and they paint her bedroom door together. He gives up cigars for her and sleeps badly as a result. She wears the diamond the night of her party, when Franklin mocks doctors for not helping his sleeplessness. She puts the Moonstone away in a bedroom drawer, and in the morning it has disappeared.

Investigations begin: even the unimaginative Betteredge is gripped by "detective-fever." Rachel will not speak to Franklin and shuts herself away as he leads the search for the stone. He suspects the Indians were in the house. The local Inspector Seegrave thinks the Indians acted with the servants, especially Betteredge's daughter Penelope, but is at Franklin's instigation replaced by Sergeant Cuff from London. Cuff finds the fresh paint on Rachel's bedroom door is smeared, but Rachel refuses him permission to hunt the servants' baggage for a paint-stained nightgown. He suspects she has taken the diamond to cover her own debts, helped by Rosanna Spearman, a servant who is plain and slightly deformed: Cuff knows her, as she has been in jail for theft, but Lady Verinder has helped her reinstate herself. Rosanna, obsessed with Franklin, attempts to speak to him, but he avoids her and she disappears: they trace her footprints in the sand and find she has killed herself in "The Shivering Sands."

Rachel denies to her mother any involvement in the theft, merely saying she will in time reveal why she has been silent. So Lady Verinder calls off the inquiry, Cuff leaves with a generous payment, and the long sequence called "The Losing of the Diamond" ends, with Franklin leaving Britain again and Rachel going to London. Lady Verinder says of Cuff "the circumstances, in this case, have fatally misled him" (183), but he does predict three things that all come true: they will hear more about Rosanna through a letter, the Indians will reappear, and Septimus Luker the moneylender will emerge as important.

"The Discovery of the Truth" is the rest of the long novel, in eight "Narratives," starting with Miss Clack, Rachel's gossiping ultra–Christian aunt, describing events in London. Through charities she knows Godfrey Ablewhite: there has been a rumor that he was involved in bringing the diamond to London, but this is dismissed by him and Rachel. Mr. Bruff, the family lawyer, who dislikes Godfrey and feels "appearances are dead against him" (225), accepts Rachel's statement of innocence and takes up the narration: he is sure the stone is with the moneylender Septimus Luker.

Bruff is followed by Franklin, who has now inherited his father's wealth and is back in Britain "to take up the inquiry again" (299). Rosanna left him a letter, and he and Betteredge find hidden in the sands a box containing Franklin's own nightgown stained with paint and a long letter expressing Rosanna's love and despair. Betteredge realizes with astonishment that Franklin was the thief. Then he meets Ezra Jennings, Dr. Candy's assistant, a man of colonial origin, who has been accused of some unstated crime, has a serious illness, and depends on opium. Candy has been very ill since the night the diamond was lost, but Jennings has reconstructed his rambling speech to suggest that, annoyed with Franklin for mocking doctors, he gave him laudanum so he would admit the next day that a doctor made him sleep well. Jennings, citing contemporary medical and psychological science, believes Franklin took the diamond under the influence of opium and that if they reenact the situation they may find out what he did with it. Franklin insists on seeing Rachel: she tells him she saw him take the diamond, and attends the reenactment, which Jennings narrates.

Franklin, sleepwalking in a drugged trance, takes a mock diamond but then drops it. He is exculpated, he and Rachel are happy together, but the mystery of the diamond remains. Sergeant Cuff, now retired, is stimulated by Franklin to take up both detection and the narration and now gets things right, though in a limited way. The year for which they believe the jewel has been pawned is nearly up, and Cuff, Franklin, two men and a boy watch at Luker's bank. He seems to give something to two different men, whom they pursue, with no outcome. The boy is missing: he has followed a tall, dark-skinned man to an inn. Cuff and the others break into his locked room: the man is dead. The dark skin is makeup: it is Godfrey Abelwhite, and by him is an empty box that contained the diamond. The Indians had got in through the roof; they escape on a ship to Bombay, and, realizing the police there will be waiting for them, take a small boat ashore somewhere in India.

Cuff has established that Godfrey led a double life with a very expensive mistress in a villa, had stolen trust funds, and was desperate for money: when it was clear Rachel's money would not be available soon enough, he agreed to break off that marriage and sought others. Then he inherited from an old lady enough to redeem the diamond and pay off his mistress. When he gave the stone to Luker, Godfrey had to explain how he got it: he told Luker he had watched Franklin, affected by the opium, come out of Rachel's bedroom with the diamond; Franklin asked him to take it back to the Ablewhite bank for safety. In the morning, when Franklin had no memory of this, Godfrey kept the stone.

Finally, the Indian expert Mr. Murthwaite reports that a huge ceremony has seen the diamond restored to the sacred statue, and the three Brahmins who have given up their lives and their high caste to recover the stone have separated.

The story has been slowly developed, with the minor characters of Betteredge, Clack and Bruff fully detailed as well as the major players, and then it comes to an end very quickly: from Franklin's exculpation to the end is less than a twelfth of the novel. This mix of paces is also the pattern of *The Woman in White* and another major sensational novel, *Lady Audley's Secret,* and presumably relates to the process of serial publication—hook the audience quickly, keep them reading steadily, and then manage a rapid climax. In fact, *The Moonstone* did so well that it was expanded when about halfway through from a twenty-six-week serial to a thirty-two-week one, probably explaining the slow movement of the Clack sequence. No one has ever seriously doubted Collins' technical skill in shaping a story, but there were contemporary objections: an 1868 review in the *Nation* said the characters "are nothing but more or less ingenious pieces of mechanism" (see Thoms, 156), and Dickens seemed equally annoyed, or conceivably jealous, saying in a letter, "The construction is wearisome beyond endurance" (see Peters, 311).

The novel has two major areas of operation. One is as a mystery, a complex puzzle with a range of possible solutions and hopeful interpreters, linking the Poe mastery of a final surprise explanation to the fuller Brockden Brown model that offers multiple uncertain ways of finding out the truth—and so Collins produces an experimental mystery novel without the simplifying closure of a major authoritative detective. The other way *The Moonstone* works powerfully is as a multilevel symbolic story raising and exploring a range of themes and issues, social and personal, areas of increasing interest in recent decades.

T. S. Eliot and Dorothy Sayers are among the many who have seen *The Moonstone* as the first real detective novel—and both thought it was the best. Many of the central elements of the classical detective novel are to be found consciously deployed here. It exhibits the limits of police detection; the powers of specialist detection; the country-house mystery; suspicion passing across characters, along with "red herrings"; the least likely person as culprit; the process of reconstruction and reenactment; the gathering of evidence; surprising links between characters; some elements of a "locked room" mystery; and a genuinely surprising final sequence of action and explanation.

Collins had adapted the idea of Poe's "The Purloined Letter" into brisk real detection by a lawyer in "The Stolen Letter" (anthologized in *After Dark* in 1856 but first appearing in *Household Words* as "The Fourth Poor Traveller," an 1854 Christmas story) and would have found about half the previously listed elements of crime fiction in Poe's work, some quite brief. He seemed convinced of the American sources of detection, having given his amateur detective Matt Marksman in *Hide and Seek* (1854) long experience there (including being scalped). Then in *The Woman in White* Walter Hartright, the rather weak artist hero, returns from a trip to South America a much more decisive and active man, and in the detection-rich story "The Diary of Anne Rodway" Anne's fiancé returns from America to complete her investigations.

The Moonstone is also critical of the emergent crime genre, offering a range of unsuccessful detectives: the local Inspector Seegrave merely blusters; Sergeant Cuff, the specialist, is brisker and smarter. He is apparently based on the real Sergeant Whicher, celebrated by Dickens in his *Household Words* police articles of 1850. As Andrew Mangham discusses (384–86), in the 1860 Road murder case (where a missing nightgown was also a key factor) he famously predicted an outcome that appeared wrong at the time but was justified five years later when the daughter confessed—but Cuff is here quite wrong to assume Rachel has taken the diamond. Franklin Blake attempts some inquiries as the amateur gentleman but basically gets nowhere, while Mr. Bruff the blunt lawyer does establish a few facts, some of them right. The closest the novel gets to a real detective is Ezra Jennings. His medical knowledge and understanding of somnambulism are linked by Collins to contemporary scientists (see Taylor, 187–88, and Pykett, 169–71), one of whom, Elliottson, the mesmerism specialist, was a friend of Collins, but the topic also goes back to *Edgar Huntly* and other novels by Brockden Brown. Yet Jennings solves only half the case, and the stone itself is traced by a final banal piece of street police work managed by Cuff and actually achieved by a small boy.

The Moonstone is also an anti-detective story. The formalist scholar Tzvetan Todorov famously showed that in classic mysteries the criminal hides the real events under a false narrative and only the detective can renarrate this lost story. The first part is certainly the case here, and the way Godfrey Ablewhite has misled everybody is a model for a mystery writer. But Collins' detectives only elucidate the non-crime of Franklin's taking the diamond: the Indians avenge the actual theft before it is comprehended. As Miller has argued, the detectives do not solve the crime—that is the result of communal interaction, and the community has been quite hostile to the detectives, especially Cuff (37–38). As a result, Miller comments, "a policing power is inscribed in the ordinary practices and institutions of the world from the start" (46). Although Collins employs detectives to explain minor details and tidy up (like finding Ablewhite's body), resolving crime is actually a social process, as it was in the 1840s urban Mysteries of Sue and Reynolds, which influenced Dickens in his great city novels *Bleak House* and *Our Mutual Friend*, and this process, as Miller shows (43), appears again in Dickens' unfinished *The Mystery of Edwin Drood*.

This pattern throws emphasis on social forces, and evidently Collins had more on his mind in *The Moonstone* than a mere detective-focused solution to a puzzle. The novel exposes to criticism a range of contemporary social and moral practices. The frame story and the noble behavior of the Indians is a serious challenge to mid-century English imperialism. The events of 1857 in what the English still call "The Indian Mutiny" (Indians see it as a justified rebellion) led many, including Dickens, to call for savage punishment of all who resisted British rule. Collins wrote an essay for an 1858 issue of *Household Words* that certainly condemned anti–English violence but also praised as worth following the values of the Hindu and Islamic religions. In *The Moonstone,* far from showing imperial confidence, he shows first the savage theft of the jewel and then the supreme dedication of the Indian men who seek to restore it to the temple. Lyn Pykett, in a section named "Race, Foreigners and Empire" (155–64), explores what she has already identified as Collins' interest in "the British burden of imperial guilt" (158), having also noted the effectively pro–Indian nature of some of Collins' earlier writing (161).

Related is the presentation of the half-white Ezra Jennings as both brilliant and suffering from unfair accusations in the past. He has loved and lost: he mentions the name Ella as he dies, and his combination of a mixed-race misfit and a capable scientist who alone makes headway against the mystery is a challenging presentation for the period. His reliance on opium and his odd appearance seem to make him an authorial double (Collins was very small, with a large head). Jennings speaks of "the ignorant distrust of opium (in England)" (386) in what sounds like Collins' voice. Peter Thoms sees a clear link between the two in terms of both their aspirations for human society and their deep sympathies for sufferers (165). Some critics have seen Jennings as a deliberate reminiscence of Keats, the ultra-sensitive but also radical romantic who (like Collins) suffered severe criticism from the conservative media (see Heller, 160–61): Keats' mother, Collins would surely have known, was named Jennings.

If a racial hybrid like Jennings can be admired, the novel finds much to condemn about English behavior. Godfrey Ablewhite is always a dubious character: Mr. Bruff turns out right to see Ablewhite as "a smooth-tongued impostor" (276). Collins planned him as a corrupt clergyman but backed off a little: his charity work is hypocrisy, he manipulates female sentiment for money, and he checked the terms of Lady Verinder's will before letting Rachel break their engagement. But the ultimate crime is his immorality and theft of trust funds and then the diamond: there is a potent irony in his black face being false and his crime being avenged by truly dark men of deeply faithful character. Other white men are unimpressive. Godfrey's banker father is a neurotic bully, who makes a major fuss when Rachel gives up Godfrey, and refuses to be her guardian: he feels both the loss of money and a sense of social slight. Dr. Candy is also represented as a weak bully in wanting to humiliate Franklin with drugs. Most commentators feel Gabriel Betteredge is represented as an honest servant, especially loyal to Lady Verinder and Rachel, but it is hard to avoid the sense that he is only self-interested, handled his wife brutally, is distant to his daughter, and is only a reliable narrator because of his lack of imagination. The meaning of his dependence on *Robinson Crusoe* invites consideration. Pykett sees this as "an ironic running commenary on imperialism" (160) and notes that Betteredge, though he does not mention the native servant, is in fact "more of a Friday than a Crusoe" (161). Collins may also be subtly thinking of Defoe's work as the original English novel, of a deeply empirical, unimaginative, self-confident kind—the sort of thing that his own work consciously questions.

That leaves Franklin Blake. He has resisted his unpleasant father (who had aristocratic fantasies); he is a man of some learning and racial tolerance, who feels real sympathy for Jennings and on parting calls him "our best and dearest friend" (432). Rachel loves Franklin dearly—indeed, he "was one of those men whom the women all like" (189)—but it seems he, too, is far from a model of ideal behavior, being self-indulgent and nervy and, as the plot shows, all too open to suggestion. Collins canceled a passage where Franklin reacts with some remorse to the suicide of Rosanna Spearman, deliberately leaving him overall fairly impassive and self-centered. It is curious that Franklin has real art skills, like Walter Hartright—and Collins' father, whose influence and profession Wilkie basically rejected—and they are as close as Collins gets to heroes.

Against these mostly unappealing and often oppressive men, the women have spirit but little real authority. Lady Verinder is wise and kind, but she fades away early in the story: remarkably, Collins' own strong mother died at about the same time—and he dedicated the book to her. Rachel is very strong willed and appears to be directing events, but in fact it is her devotion to Franklin, which survives the evidence of his crime, that is the major dynamic of her behavior and she plays an increasingly passive role in the novel as wife-to-be and soon enough mother: Tamar Heller reads Rachel's behavior towards Franklin as essentially hysterical (152–53). Rosanna Spearman also loves Franklin, but she is treated with some contempt by him and others. There is a class basis to that, which, with her plain appearance, makes her ineligible even for marital submission: her suicide is her acceptance of this fate, though Collins does preserve a dissenting pro-female voice in the angry response of her friend "Limping Lucy." These women succeed or fail in life through their relations with men, and it is noticeable that Miss Clack, whom commentators often find annoying, is herself stranded in obsessive Christianity by a failure to link with any man—she would obviously like it to be Godfrey. The secondary status of women is something this novel exposes but also accepts, though Collins had previously challenged it with Marian Halcombe and the potent criminal Lydia Gwilt in *Armadale*, as Mrs. Braddon also had through her murderess Lady Audley.

Substantial conservative assaults had been launched against sensationalism—the Archbishop of York attacked it publicly in 1864—and with the fuss that *Armadale* had caused, building on the controversial reception of *No Name*, featuring the bold and eventually happy illegitimate Magdalen Vanstone, Collins may have felt compelled to withdraw into a less pro-woman stance in *The Moonstone*. It is a challenge to relate his somewhat feminist sympathies with his own situation: he refused to marry his partner from 1858 on, Caroline Graves (even supporting her brief marriage to another man), and in the mid-1860s picked up with Martha Rudd, who was then effectively his secondary mistress—and later mother of his children.

Critics have seen deeper and more cross-cultural shapes in the meanings of *The Moonstone* than the contemporary politics of race and gender and the subtext of class. Recent commentators, led by Alfred Hutter, have read the whole drama in personal and psychiatric terms, quite stripping it of imperial and social implications. Charles Rycroft saw the key structure in Freudian terms between Rachel, the innocent upper-class woman expected to lead a life of sexual ignorance before marriage and silence after it, and Rosanna, a lower-class ex-criminal, daughter of a prostitute, whose passion for Franklin is symbolized by "The Shivering Sands" (see also Heller, 148, and Mangham, 386–89, for a discussion of this and other sexual symbolism)—she is eventually consumed by her overt desire. As Jenny Bourne Taylor notes, "the underlying tensions of the text concern not only the tacit definition of feminine sexuality but the problematic nature of masculinity" (177). Similar analysis sees Franklin's sexual claiming of Rachel symbolized by his theft of the diamond from its hidden place in her bedroom—and by the stain on his nightgown: he is much more symbolically involved than Godfrey, the sexually active hypocrite, who only seeks Rachel for her money and sees the diamond as just a source of money. Collins here, as elsewhere, appears to have been aware of sexual forces in his text: he originally called the diamond "The Eye of the Serpent" and that was an early title for the novel but was presumably blocked by Mary Braddon's *The Trail of the Serpent* (1860). He also gave Rosanna a name highly suggestive in Freudian terms, "Spearman."

Ranging from social satire to disturbing symbolism, *The Moonstone* combines a startling mix of the everyday and the amazing: Betteredge says they are returning "to meet the trouble and terror that were waiting for us at home" (166) and Dickens pointed to this special quality when he described the novel in a letter as "wild, and yet domestic" (Taylor, 176). Henry James elaborated on this when he said Collins produced "those most mysterious of mysteries, the mysteries which are at our own door" (Kemp, xiii). The impact of the book was not only in sales. Anthony Trollope borrowed its plot idea for his unusually lively *The Eustace Diamonds* (1871). Conan Doyle would reuse the concept of troublesome imperial theft in a more confident detective context for *The Sign of Four* in 1890. Most notably, it seems that Dickens himself in his last and unfinished novel of 1870, *The Mystery of Edwin Drood,* was constructing a plot with drugs and bafflement and a shock ending, looking, as its title suggests, to match his friend Wilkie at his potent art.

The lasting prestige of *The Moonstone* can be judged from the standing of some of the people who have written introductions over the years—Dorothy Sayers, T. S. Eliot, and Anthony Burgess were all intrigued by it—though Eliot's famous opening remark about it as the first and best detective novel does give way immediately to a long discussion of Dickens. Julian Symons was a serious admirer, calling it "a masterly performance" (60), and as a crime writer himself he was most impressed by the technique of "the shifting of suspicion from one character to another" (61).

Collins never again matched the detail and intensity of his great 1860s sensational novels. He grew increasingly ill, and his compensatory drug taking may have hindered him more, but after Dickens died in 1870 he became closer to the socially focused novelist Charles Reade, who coined the phrase "Fiction for a Purpose," and Collins' later work was focused on specific social problems rather than mystery and melodrama. When *The Moonstone* became a play in 1877, he omitted the Indians, the opium, Rosanna Spearman and Ezra Jennings and it ended not with the murder of Ablewhite but with him being pursued by the police: the play was less than successful, having lost most of the high symbolic drama of the novel.

Collins' role as a popular writer, a master of melodrama, for long kept him out of the sanctioned areas of high-canon serious literature. But the growing interest in recent decades in radical literature, and in novels about social and gender issues, has brought him back to the fore, and the sheer power of his deceptively simple writing, and his ability to construct plots not only full of twists and turns enough to please the most addicted reader of crime fiction but also rich with enticing symbolic suggestions, doubles, social questions and uncertain resolutions, has finally brought Collins a place among the finest writers. Where *The Woman in White* remains the first of the great sensational novels, *The Moonstone* is the richest and most complex of the books that shaped the form and suggested the possibilities of crime fiction.

References

Eliot, T. S. "Introduction," in Wilkie Collins, *The Moonstone.* World's Classics Edition. London: Oxford University Press, 1928.
Heller, Tamar. *Dead Secrets: Wilkie Collins and the Female Gothic.* New Haven: Yale University Press, 1992.

Hutter, Alfred. "Dreams, Transformation and Literature: The Implications of Detective Fiction." *Victorian Studies* 9 (1975): 181–209.
Kemp, Sandra. "Introduction," in Wilkie Collins, *The Moonstone*. Penguin Classics. London: Penguin, 1998.
Mangham, Andrew. "Wilkie Collins (1824–1889)," in *A Companion to Crime Fiction*. Ed. Charles J. Rzepka and Lee Horsley. New York: Wiley-Blackwell, 2010, 381–89.
Miller, D.A. *The Novel and the Police*. Berkeley: University of California Press, 1988.
Peters, Catherine K. *The King of Inventors: A Life of Wilkie Collins*. London: Secker and Warburg, 1991.
Pykett, Lyn. *Wilkie Collins*. Authors in Context Series. Oxford: Oxford University Press, 2005.
Rycroft, Charles. "The Analysis of a Detective Story," reprinted in *Imagination and Reality*. New York: International Universities Press, 1968.
Symons, Julian. *Bloody Murder: From the Detective Story to the Crime Novel: A History*. Revised second edition. London: Pan, 1992.
Taylor, Jenny Bourne. *In the Secret Theatre of Home: Wilkie Collins, Sensation Narrative and Nineteenth-Century Psychology*. London: Routledge, 1988.
Thoms, Peter. *The Windings of the Labyrinth: Quest and Structure in the Major Novels of Wilkie Collins*. Athens: Ohio University Press, 1992.
Todorov, Tzvetan. "The Typology of Detective Fiction," in *The Poetics of Prose*. Trans. R. Howard. Oxford: Blackwell, 1977, 42–52.

5

Monsieur Lecoq,
Émile Gaboriau

When Conan Doyle gave Sherlock Holmes a French grandmother, he was paying tribute to—and also claiming to surpass—the substantial French tradition in crime fiction, which was based on a longer experience of formal policing and specialist detection than that of either England or America. In 1828–89 the *Mémoires* of the criminal-turned-detective Eugène François Vidocq were best sellers in London as well as Paris, and the London stage celebrated his capacity to observe and infiltrate the criminal classes, with special emphasis on daring and disguise.

Balzac made recurrent use of Vidocq as Vautrin (also known as Collin), both major criminal and super-detective, in *Le Père Goriot* (1835), *Une Tenebreuse Affaire* (1841) and *Splendeurs et misères des courtisanes* (1847)—the second would inspire much of the second volume of Gaboriau's *Monsieur Lecoq*. Hugo split Vidocq, creating both Javert, the dedicated policeman of *Les Misérables* (1862), and his target, the former criminal Jean Valjean. The figure of the detective was absent in the massive "Mysteries of Paris" that Eugène Sue produced in 1843–44, followed up in G. W. M. Reynolds' *The Mysteries of London* (1845–46): in both, criminals operated at all social levels and were controlled in part by accident and in part by the representatives of social morality, not here narrowed down to a single detective.

There was a French version of *Les Mystères de Londres* before Reynolds, by Paul Féval (1843–44), but this was neither realistic urban crime nor anything like a detective story: it was a French revenge fantasy in which a pro–Napoléon Irishman leads an attack on the entire English establishment and just fails to launch his revolution successfully. But if Féval at first took crime fiction away from both realism and detection, he still had a crucial role to play. In his *Jean Diable* (1862) the hero is a multi-identity master criminal, but his opponent, himself capable of many disguises, is Gregory Temple, chief detective at Scotland Yard—generously, if unhistorically, placed back in 1816 (restoring Napoléon is part of the plot). Temple is a master of the detective art and has written a book titled *The Art of Discovering the Guilty*.

As Féval wrote this, he was employing as secretary a man named Émile Gaboriau, born in 1832 in the Charente region. He edited Féval's magazines, probably ghosted some of his work, picked up his techniques, and focused them better. Féval went on with a series called, after the first novel, *Les Habits noirs* (1863), about a central criminal dynasty: the worst villain in the first novel is called Lecoq; he is capable of many disguises and trickeries—but is finally killed by the hero, very strangely, beheaded with a safe door. Lecoq would be revived in Gaboriau's work and become the first major police detective in crime fiction, what Yves Olivier-Martin calls "the prototype" (50).

Gaboriau first wrote non-fiction commentaries and historical material and was strongly interested in the rich French genre of what E. F. Bleiler calls "factual crime" (vii). During 1864–65 Gaboriau wrote his first successful novel, *L'Affaire Lerouge*, which appeared early in 1866 as a weekly serial in *Le Petit Journal*. This full-length mystery starts with a grisly murder and develops through a wrongly suspected man. The police under Gévrol, called "the general," get everything wrong, and it is only when Tabaret, an elderly bookish amateur, is called in that the past of the characters is explored and finally, as is common in the period in France, a corrupt and vengeful aristocrat is found to be the basis of evil. Tabaret is an armchair detective not unlike Dupin, though somewhat more humble, and there is a small part for a young policeman named Lecoq, a reformed criminal, but all he really does is refer the case to Tabaret.

This must have changed round in Gaboriau's mind, because during this period he drafted a longer novel, *Monsieur Lecoq*. It appears likely that its weight and length seemed too much for cautious editors, and later in 1866 and 1867 Gaboriau published two other fairly short Lecoq novels. They both did well and set the scene for a major publicity blitz for his best-known novel in spring of 1868 in the magazine *Le Petit Journal* (see Bonniot, 148–50).

Both the intervening novels show Lecoq more senior and confident than the energetic self-proving youngster of *Monsieur Lecoq*, and they handle the historical explanations with less weight than the second volume of his major work. His first published Lecoq mystery was *Le Crime d'Orcival* (serialized 1866–67), which involved a sensational murder among the upper classes where Lecoq's power of detailed observation and the historical backstory combined to identify the villain; its successor *Le Dossier 113* (1867) is a big-city mercantile parallel, where the secure safe of a bank is robbed, a loyal employee is suspected, and eventually close observation and some history derived from Lecoq's rural enquiries bring forward a distinctly corrupt aristocratic criminal.

From the start *Monsieur Lecoq* (serialized in 1868, appearing as a novel in early 1869) is more detailed than its predecessors in its social and urban observations and its account of Lecoq's technique. It is quite searching in its account of national events of 1816 and their aftermath—very different from Féval's romantic patriotism about the period. The novel has two volumes: in English they have quite often appeared separately, with volume 1, *The Inquiry*, published as *Monsieur Lecoq* and volume 2 appearing under its subtitle as *The Honour of the Name*—and as the two were not always published at the same time, many English readers must have come to the end of what they thought was the novel to find only a suggestion of who the criminal might be, with Lecoq's promised investigation deferred till volume 2. In a way even more puzzling is the Dover reprint of 1975, which simply tacks the last few pages of volume 2 on to the end of volume 1, without any indication of this in the introduction by E. F. Bleiler, just a word on the cover that he has also "Edited" the book.

The story of *Monsieur Lecoq*, where he establishes himself as a major detective, begins in about 1830: a police patrol moves late on a winter night through a rough area by the Seine; Gévrol, still the "general," is in charge. They hear shots from a bar called La Poivrière (The Pepperpot) and break in. Two men are dead, and one soon dies after saying "Lacheneur" enticed him there. A fairly young man who has been wounded in the face and neck tries to escape but is caught by a young policeman, who is praised by Gévrol. The Widow Chupin, the bar owner, says the three took on the wounded man; Gévrol arrests her and the "murderer"; the young policeman expresses doubts, and Gévrol leaves him to investigate.

Lecoq is twenty-five or twenty-six, small and energetic. A Norman, he studied law, but his parents died and he became a law clerk, then an astronomer's assistant calculator. When Lecoq fantasized about some lucrative crimes, the astronomer said he should become a thief or a policeman. He found police work dull but feels this situation is his chance and with an elderly policeman, Father Absinthe, studies the evidence. As the police arrived, the "murderer" made a battle of Waterloo statement, "It is the Prussians who are coming" (8), and Lecoq believes he had let his accomplices escape. They find women's footprints in the snow outside, showing they met a man waiting there. Lecoq is like a bloodhound and even lies on the ground investigating; he asserts the waiting man was tall, middle-aged, in a cap and a brown wool coat, and wore a ring. They follow the women's footprints and find they took a carriage; Lecoq makes a plaster mold of the footprints and will trace the driver. Then they return to examine the bar. The women were not drinking with the young man and someone came back for something. The widow's apron pockets were turned inside out, and Lecoq finds a diamond earring on the floor: a map of the scene and the women's movements is provided in the text.

At the police station a man, apparently drunk, has turned up, been arrested and had access to the prisoners; Lecoq calls him the "accomplice." The third dead man was dressed as a soldier, but the clothes were condemned, so he was not in the army; the other two carried no papers. Judge d'Escorval praises Lecoq's report but is also rather distant. Lecoq thinks the "murderer" is a gentleman.

The judge visits the "murderer," who then tries to strangle himself. The initial judge is reported as having had an accident and is replaced by Judge Segmuller. The "murderer," now called "May" (in French, "Mai"), seems born again after meeting the new judge and gives some account of himself. He speaks three languages and says he is an itinerant fairground worker: when interrogated he weakens a few times but does not crack.

Lecoq finds May's trunk at a hotel—it come from Leipzig, fitting his story. Madame Milner, in charge there, says she does not know May or his name. Lecoq interviews at the bar the Widow Chupin's daughter-in-law; the "accomplice" looks in but gets away. She knows Lacheneur: her husband said he would make their fortune, but her husband denies this. Lecoq has found who bought the earring, but she sold it and there is no trace of its owner now. He hunts for Lacheneur, but time passes and the crime is nearly forgotten; most accept May's account of himself—only Lecoq and Segmuller disagree.

Lecoq starts to watch May from above his cell. After days, Lecoq sees bread thrown in and realizes May's singing is a signal; Lecoq obtains bread thrown out, with tissue paper in it bearing a coded message that he deciphers. But when he throws in a message, May gives it to the police, as if innocent. They all doubt Lecoq, and even the judge is giving up. At Lecoq's suggestion May is allowed to escape and followed. He gets money from Madame Milner, buys clothes, then takes a cab with a man and climbs a high wall into a big house belonging to the Duc de Sairmeuse. They seize the other man and search the house: there is no sign of May. The man is an escaped convict May met in a bar. Lecoq has the sudden idea that perhaps May is the duke.

Lecoq goes to consult Tabaret (whose career is summarized). He praises Lecoq but points out some errors. He also says the original judge was not in an accident and that May is the duke and has acted "to save his name and his honour intact." Lecoq will investigate: he says that if what Tabaret says is true, "I shall have my revenge" (366).

Volume 2, *The Honour of the Name*, begins in 1815 at Sairmeuse as the duke returns from exile: his house has been bought by Lacheneur, a former

5. Monsieur Lecoq

servant, with money the duke's aunt gave him to keep it in trust. Lacheneur's daughter Marie-Anne insists he return it now; the duke is not grateful but eventually gives Lacheneur some money. She is admired by Maurice, son of the Baron d'Escorval, a supporter of Napoléon, who is helped to keep his position by the Marquis de Sairmeuse, the duke's son—who also admires Marie-Anne. The duke wants him to marry Blanche, daughter of the very conservative Marquis de Courtornieu.

Lacheneur, with some support from Maurice, develops a plot against the duke, which turns into a peasant rising and an attack on the village of Montaignac, which is easily beaten back by soldiers led by the duke: there is a long trial where the duke is very bullying and after which twenty men, some innocent, are executed. Then d'Escorval is helped escape by the marquis, under pressure from Marie-Anne, but he is badly hurt in the escape. Lacheneur also escapes but is caught and executed.

Marie-Anne and Maurice are married in Piedmont. She returns to a house left her by an executed peasant of great strength, who loved her, and Maurice disappears in an Italian jail. The marquis has married Blanche de Courtornieu but has separated from her. She expects he still sees Marie-Anne, who has in fact had Maurice's child. Blanche employs the duke's agent Chupin to watch the marquis, who has ruined her father's standing with the king; her father has also been attacked by Lacheneur's son Jean in the forest and is now insane. The marquis has, due to his continuing feeling for Marie-Anne, agreed to save d'Escorval's reputation.

Through Chupin, Blanche finds Marie-Anne, goes to her house and poisons her (while Blanche's aunt waits outside); the dying Marie-Anne tells Blanche she is married to Maurice and has a child and asks her to look after it. As she leaves, Chupin is killed by Jean Lacheneur but survives long enough to tell his son about Blanche's guilt. Later the same night the marquis arrives with a letter of freedom for the Baron d'Escorval. The next night Maurice arrives at the house, back from Italy: he is stunned by Marie-Anne's death but then meets the marquis, who swears to avenge her.

After all this hectic action and reaction, Blanche and the marquis are reconciled, largely though her pretense of continued love. The duke dies, apparently in a fall from a horse but probably killed by Jean Lacheneur, who leaves for Paris, as does Chupin's son. Blanche is haunted by her murder of Marie-Anne and then her aunt threatens her with exposure; Blanche agrees to take her to Paris with them. In Paris with the new duke, Blanche hires a detective, Chelteux, to find Marie-Anne's son; he keeps at this for several years and later looks for Jean Lacheneur and is killed by him. Young Chupin is married, has a son, Polyte, but is then killed in prison. Blanche's aunt also dies.

The duke has been overseas for four years and now has gray hair. (It is about 1830, at the latest.) Chupin's son and widow know nothing, but Jean Lacheneur works out what Chupin knew and begins a plot against Blanche, using the Widow Chupin as an agent. Finally Blanche goes to the bar with her servant Camille and meets Lacheneur's three thugs, one of whom is to be presented as her son. Lacheneur is not there—he has fallen in a quarry and hurt himself. Blanche is disguised but has forgotten to take off her earrings. The duke, disguised as May, arrives; his faithful servant Otto has followed him. The thugs go for the earrings; the duke shoots two, pushes another over and kills him. As at the start of volume 1, the police arrive; the women run away and meet Otto. The duke tries to leave the back way, is trapped by the police and says, "It is the Prussians who are coming." Otto is the "accomplice" and his lady friend Madame Milner helps him with the "May as fairground worker" story. The repentant Blanche kills herself with poison.

In the epilogue, a mere ten pages, Maurice's son is returned to him by a repentant Lacheneur. In disguise, Lecoq visits the duke with a letter he has forged as coming from Judge d'Escorval asking for money in return for his secrecy. The duke writes his agreement, and Lecoq reveals himself. Soon afterwards the duke is found not guilty of murder and the story ends.

Gaboriau's novels brought a new structure and attitude to the developing genre of crime fiction. These were stories entirely focused on the puzzling nature of a single crime—not merely, like so many nineteenth-century novels, using a series of crimes or some past wrong as motives for human interaction. Where Collins spread the effect of a crime through many puzzled people, Gaboriau's newly focused structure was authorized through a single detective presence, and now false leads and puzzling confusions would amplify what had been in short stories a single-case structure into the ramified plot of a novel. Above all, the detective novel combined the capacity for perceptions, that Poe had perfected, with the street-level action that the English police detectives had brought into the form—William Russell's first story collection about Waters, published in London in 1856, appeared in French by 1858. This meshed with the long-held interest the French found in Cooper's stories—they coined the term "Cooperisme," and Dumas had relocated the concept as *Les Mohicans de Paris* (starting in 1854), where a Mysteries-style series of events is overseen by the detective-like Jackal, a dubious figure looking back to Vidocq as much as to Cooper's frontier hero; the young Gaboriau admired Cooper greatly (Bonniot, 161).

Most of these crime writers, in France and England, used the city for the basis of their innovative fictions, charting the multiple activities, mystifying differences and above all the sense of isolation, alienation and possible hostility of the new megalopolis. But Gaboriau was the first to link this rich, troubling context to the techniques and above all the explanatory focus of the detective novel—Régis Messac, an early and learned French commentator on the form, insists that Balzac is in many ways the father of Gaboriau's work, with his interweaving of social and locational tensions in the newly potent and newly volatile city.

Like Collins' works, selling both in cheap serial form and in relatively expensive complete novels, the new material appealed to a socially wide audience, but while Gaboriau certainly thrived on the streets he was also admired by the great—Disraeli, English novelist and prime minister, spoke highly of his work, and he was praised by somewhat different power-rich figures, the mighty late nineteenth-century German Chancellor Bismarck and Woodrow Wilson, who led America in the crucial post–1918 period.

Unlike most crime fiction before and after, Gaboriau locates true heroism, both physical and intellectual, in a serving policeman. The police procedural as a sub-genre will not be born until the 1960s work of "Ed McBain," and even then, and in its many TV versions and dilutions, the police heroes, increasingly of both genders, will need to show that they are also deeply, and even fallibly, human. None of those who accepted Gaboriau's shape of the crime-focused puzzle would have a hero policeman, especially Conan Doyle and including Anna Katharine Green and Fergus Hume, Gaboriau's most immediate transmitters into the Anglophone mass market.

What empowers the special, supersocial heroism of his detective is that as well as being a policeman, he is also a representative of that other new nineteenth-century force, outlined in general by Michel Foucault and linked to crime fiction by both D. A. Miller generally and Heather Worthington in the early period—the deployment of disciplinary expertise in the identification and control of social disturbances and aberrances. The fact that early detectives tend to be doctors and lawyers, or at least lawyers' clerks, is, as Worthington shows (chapter 2), a crucial deployment of disciplinary skills against criminal disruption. Both Dupin and Holmes are functional fantasies of such technical expertise, with, as Miller has outlined, much use of ideas of surveillance and intellectual prediction of behavior as modes of crime control. It is no accident that the verb "detect" derives from the Latin for "unroof": this idea of domestic surveillance was quite well-known in the period and is invoked consciously when Sherlock Holmes speculates in "A Case of Identity": "If we could fly out of that window hand in hand, hover over this great city, gently remove the roofs and peep in at the queer things that are going on" (147).

There is one other crucial feature of Gaboriau and Lecoq that is noticed by the astute French commentator Narcejac. The previous investigators, from

Vidocq to Dupin, all had wonderful successes in baffling contexts, but they never faced a criminal who was consciously their rival, who sought to twist and turn the evidence against detection, as does Clamaran in *Le Dossier 113*, for his own protection, or the Duc de Sairmeuse in *Monsieur Lecoq*, for the "honour of the name." Gaboriau seems the first to imagine the dual narrative that Todorov saw at the core of the classic mystery: Poe's orangutan or Collins' Geoffrey Ablewhite never consciously sought by inventing evidence to outwit the detective who was their only possible nemesis, but Gaboriau does for the first time imagine this elemental disciplinary battle of conflicting narratives at the heart of what can now be called legitimately a whodunit.

As well as these various deep-laid urban, disciplinary and narratological powers, Gaboriau gives Lecoq all the traditional detective skills. He can track a footprint as well as Cooper's hero; he can wait for days and surveil a prisoner like the concept behind the Foucauldian Panopticon; he can scour the city for evidence like Vidocq; and also like Vidocq he is theatrically formidable in disguise—at the end of *Le Dossier 113* he spectacularly reveals one of his identities as the abandoned lover of the wrongly suspected man's girlfriend.

This brave, active, polymorphous police disciplinarian was surely enough to catch readers' attention around the world. But in France there was an additional element: in the nineteenth century the national self-concept was consistently troubled by historically negative elements. The country's glorious past was compromised by being royal, aristocratic, and exploitative and the grandeur of the Napoleonic period had been defeated by its enemies and even traduced by its own excesses. It is not surprising that historical fictions and fantasy adventures gripped French audiences, from the Musketeers to Monte Cristo. Less easily distracted writers confronted the situation—Balzac by imagining an awkward new world of bourgeois values; Sue by inventing a non–French lord who supervised the Mysteries of modern Paris; Zola by ignoring the past and plunging into the conflicts of the socially mobile present. Gaboriau recurrently explains the problems of the present through its inheritance of the corrupt past, but after *Le Crime d'Orcival* he is not simply anti-aristocrat (and even there the lady is worse than the lord). In *Le Dossier 113* it is a fake aristocrat who causes the trouble. In *Monsieur Lecoq* the Duc de Sairmeuse as a young man acts with decency when his father rages back from exile and now, inheriting the threats, behaves with courage and skill in a world of brutish aristocrats and corrupt arrivistes to defend his family's name and eventually earn the statement "Not Guilty" for himself and, by implication at least, some of the aristocrats.

The underlying quietistic politics of *Monsieur Lecoq* are not dissimilar to those of other major crime writers, such as Conan Doyle, Christie and

Chandler. They all assert that good people can somehow live together and outwit the aberrant, and our superhero detective will enable that anxiously yearned-for outcome. But Gaboriau also established, for others to copy and develop, the familiar form of the mystery novel. It is clear that Anna Katharine Green before 1878 had been reading Gaboriau; Fergus Hume was specific about following him in seeking to establish himself in Melbourne in 1886; Conan Doyle makes Holmes early in *A Study in Scarlet* speak with revealing aggression to disavow any possible connection with Gaboriau: "Lecoq was a miserable bungler" (18), Sherlock says, and he goes on to say it took him six months to identify a criminal he, Sherlock, would have found in twenty-four hours. But in fact, apart from the police affiliation, as Bleiler comments, "much of Sherlock Holmes is based on this very Lecoq" (v), and Conan Doyle in his novellas uses Gaboriau's lengthy historical explanations. The posthumously published short narrative *The Little Old Man of Batignolles* (1876) may well, as Bleiler noted (xv), have influenced Conan Doyle more precisely: it has a medical student narrator, an austere detective (though rather more like Maigret than Holmes), and uses as evidence letters written in blood, a left-handed man and a dog that does not bark when it might have been expected to do so.

Gaboriau died tragically early in 1873 and was recognized in his time as a master of the form, with a special power of human realization. His contemporary Marius Topin saw Gaboriau as "a logician of the first order" (324), "a dialectician as rigorous and neat as Poe" (336), but who also added the novelist's gifts of "vivacity of writing, natural dialogue and the creation of vividly alive characters" (336). There was something mythic about the detective's name (his motto *semper vigilans,* "always vigilant," traditionally belongs to the Gallic cockerel), though it does also link to Vidocq, and Bonniot suggests also a reference to the Lecoq who was a major operative among the Paris police in the time of Louis XIV (191). French literary tradition has consistently seen Lecoq as generating Maigret and the modern heroes of the *romans policiers.*

Yet the strongest inheritance this gifted young writer left was that a mystery novel can be self-standing in generic terms as an intriguing and satisfying puzzle and can attract audiences that are both large and also extremely loyal. Gaboriau did much to construct the readership as well as the structure of classic crime fiction.

References

Bleiler, E. F. "Introduction," in Émile Gaboriau, *Monsieur Lecoq.* Ed. E. F. Bleiler. New York: Dover, 1975, v–xxiv.
Bonniot, Roger. *Emile Gaboriau ou la naissance du roman policier.* Paris: Vrin, 1985.
Miller, D. A. *The Novel and the Police.* Berkeley: University of California Press, 1988.

Narcejac, Thomas. *Une Machine a Lire: Le Roman Policier.* Paris: Denouel/Gonthier, 1975.
Olivier-Martin, Yves. *Histoire du roman populaire en France de 1840 à 1980.* Paris: Michel, 1980.
Stableford, Brian. "Introduction," in Paul Féval, *John Devil.* Encino, CA: Black Coat Press, 2005.
Topin, Marius. *Romanciers contemporains.* Paris: Charpentier, 1876.
Worthington, Heather. *The Rise of the Detective in Early Nineteenth-Century Popular Fiction.* London: Palgrave Macmillan, 2005.

6

The Leavenworth Case, Anna Katharine Green

There are several candidates for the title of the first major crime story by a woman writer. The earliest must be Catherine Crowe's *The Adventures of Susan Hopley* (1841), published in London as Poe's first detective story was appearing: the inquiries by Susan, a maidservant, are central to unveiling the crimes, but as the novel had no real influence it is best seen as a potent forerunner. *The Dead Letter* by Metta Fuller Victor, writing as "Seeley Regester," started appearing in 1865 and was published as a novel in 1866 and this does have a formal detective, Mr. Burton of the New York Police—but it did not sell very well or have any generic authority, and could only in a strained sense be called "major"; rather, it was archetypal of a period when the expanding world of publishing brought more women characters and authors into the genre, notably in series of short stories (and sometimes quite long ones) in London. Edward Ellis's Ruth Trail appeared in 1862–63 in *Ruth the Betrayer, or The Female Spy,* and Mrs. Gladden "The Female Detective" by "Andrew Forrester Jr." (now held to be J. S. Ware, who went on to be a prolific minor novelist) first appeared in 1862. She was imitated in Mrs. Pascal in *Revelations of a Lady Detective* (1864) by "Anonyma," probably the all-purpose male writer W. S. Hayward. The model traveled to America as in Harriet Prescott Spofford's two "Mr. Furbush" stories in 1865–56 and further when Ellen Davitt published in the *Australian Journal* in 1865 *Force and Fraud,* a novel focused on a murderous lawyer but without formal detection, and in the same magazine Mary Fortune started in 1866 her long-lasting "Mark Sinclair" series about a mounted policeman who often acted as a classic detective.

But the first widely read detective novel by a woman appeared in early 1878 when Anna Katharine Green published *The Leavenworth Case*; sales are reported to have reached 750,000 in fifteen years. This started her long career, reaching into the 1920s, and no doubt inspired many authors, especially women—Agatha Christie knew it when very young. It is the first novel that pays close attention to legal details and presents evidence of multiple possible guilt in a calm but also thoroughly puzzling way: as Murch comments, Green shaped "the pattern that became characteristic of most English detective novels written during the following fifty years" (159).

Born in 1846 with a New York trial lawyer for a father, from the city's striving middle class rather than its gilded upper-class set, Green was one of the first American women to have a university-level education. She started writing as a poet and with several slim volumes to her name wrote her first mystery novel; she apparently rewrote it very carefully, taking six years in all (DuBose, 6). Her father admired her work and she went to the publisher George Putnam, whom she knew through contacts in the city. The novel was very long and he required some cuts for it to fit in the new one-volume model (though she retained a division into books, two of the four are quite short). Putnam's was a respectable list well above the dime novel or western adventures and already contained serious women writers. The book did well in both sales and reputation–reportedly it was used at the law school at Yale University to remind students how misleading circumstantial evidence can be.

Green kept writing in the same mode, remaining loyal to her New York detective Mr. Ebenezer Gryce, reserved, secretive and a sufferer from rheumatism, far from the romantic intellectual figure Poe had imagined or the dynamic city activist J. B. Williams had in the mid–1860s created as Jem Brampton, "the New York detective," an early example of the brisk, manly figure who was appearing in simplified form as "Old Sleuth" and "Nick Carter" in dime novels as Green began to write. Régis Messac comments that Green's detectives from the start have great patience and proceed by making "a mass of small discoveries" (577), a pattern he sees as a more woman-oriented model, and later on she would deploy the idea of a female detective.

Green's innovative powers go along with an aura of respectable calmness. From the start *The Leavenworth Case* moves in a world that is quiet, elevated, urban, well mannered—and then starts to seethe with melodrama. It is subtitled *A Lawyer's Story* and Everett Raymond, a junior partner in a legal firm, is the narrator. When his seniors are away he learns that Horatio Leavenworth, an important client and friend of senior partner Veeley, has been found shot through the head in the library of his Fifth Avenue mansion. Leavenworth's secretary, Harwell, reports this and is seeking an adviser for the two nieces, who face an inquest in the house that day.

Raymond attends and meets the police detective Mr. Gryce, and the inquest begins. Leavenworth was found in the morning; there was no pistol present, and the maid Hannah is missing, but the butler says the house was locked up. Harwell left Leavenworth quite late at night in the library, when his niece Eleanore's door was open. He says he later heard a skirt rustling. When Leavenworth's body was discovered, Eleanore had it moved to his bedroom; and the cook says Eleanore left the library with a piece of paper. The fatal bullet came from Leavenworth's gun, found by his bed, now reloaded and incompletely cleaned.

Raymond and Gryce have heard one niece accuse the other of knowing about the crime: Mary, fair, delicate and beautiful, tells the coroner she knows nothing of the murder and did not see a paper in Eleanore's hand. The latter is dark and dramatic, and Raymond loves her at once. She says she always knew Mary would inherit; she saw the pistol the previous day in its drawer and denies cleaning it or putting it away. The previous night the butler brought the card of a gentleman caller, Mr. Le Roy Robbins. Later her door was open and she heard Harwell pass; a little later she heard the library door close but no pistol shot. She denies having any piece of paper and declines to answer further on that matter. She describes the library key, with a broken handle. When she hears her handkerchief was found in her uncle's room, with gun marks on it, she faints.

Mary tells Raymond and Gryce she and Eleanore are not good friends. Gryce's man finds Eleanore apparently hiding the library key. Mary, who argues a burglar has done all this, leaves the house with Raymond and posts a hurriedly written letter. He makes notes to counter the apparent suspicion against Eleanore. A reward is offered in search of Hannah. Eleanore is named by the papers as a suspect; to prove her innocence to Raymond she kisses the dead body. She and Mary argue in private; then Raymond tells Eleanore he will work to clear her. She will not explain the key and says the piece of paper no longer exists.

Gryce, who says he is not a gentleman, wants Raymond, as a gentleman, to befriend Henry Clavering, after whom book 2 is named. Raymond feels Eleanore has been used by someone. Gryce asks if he felt Harwell's evidence was reliable and says he knows nothing yet about Hannah the maid: his agent Q is looking for her. Eleanore has moved and is ill, but keeps in touch with Raymond. He visits Mary, who talks about the inheritance and about Eleanore, largely sympathetically; she wants him to help Harwell finish her uncle's book. He makes no progress with Clavering. When Mary meets him in the house one evening, he says Eleanore may be arrested—Mary insists that she is innocent but cannot explain the key. She is nervous, and Henry Clavering arrives at the house. Harwell asks Raymond to be spared discussing the murder but sees Clavering, asks who he is, and says he is the murderer. Mary leaves Raymond a note asking him not to come to the house again: Harwell will visit him to work on the book. The butler tells Raymond that Clavering visited the night of the murder under the name Le Roy Robbins.

The next day Clavering visits Raymond's office and tells him a story about "his friend," a wealthy Englishman, marrying an American girl in secret. Raymond assumes it is Clavering and Eleanore. Harwell is waiting in his office and relates a dream from the night before the murder, in which Clavering was the killer; Harwell also describes a lady's face from the dream. He saw a letter Clavering wrote to Leavenworth complaining about one of the nieces mistreating him. Raymond says Clavering is English and Harwell says Leavenworth hated the English.

Harwell has told Raymond that the Leavenworths went on holiday upstate to R—— (Patricia D. Maida suggests this is Saratoga Springs, 15), and Raymond assumes Eleanore met and married Clavering there. Raymond consults Gryce, who tells him the letter Mary sent was to Clavering: Gryce's man checked at the time. He has heard from London that Clavering, a wealthy man who returned there as if expecting a wife, has been writing to her care of Amy Belden upstate. Gryce has strips of a torn bloodstained letter, which Raymond puts together (as shown in the text): it is the complaint to Leavenworth from Clavering and was found with the key.

Mr. Veeley explains that Leavenworth had met in England an American woman who was brutalized by her English husband and left him, with her baby. After the husband's death they married and came to New York, but she and the child died. She was very like the woman Harwell described in his dream. Eleanore is at Veeley's and asks Raymond to abandon his efforts for her, but he refuses, when she asks to be told any news, he agrees and leaves sadly.

Raymond goes upstate to investigate, but Gryce's man Q is there and sends him home. In two days Q informs Raymond that the ladies did meet Clavering in R——. Raymond sees Gryce and tells him Eleanore married Clavering, but Clavering later complained to Leavenworth and visited on the night of murder as Le Roy Robbins. Raymond believes Clavering killed Leavenworth and Eleanore is protecting him. Gryce says he plans to disprove this and calls in the marriage witness Q has brought to New York: he identifies Mary as Clavering's wife. Gryce says he believes she is the murderer and Eleanore knows it. He is planning to arrest Eleanore to force Mary to give information. They argue about this; a note comes, saying Hannah has been found. She is with Amy Belden. Gryce wants Raymond to help Q investigate, as he is ill with rheumatism; he gives Raymond a cipher for telegraphs.

The fairly short book 3, titled "Hannah," tells how Raymond lodges at Mrs. Belden's house and finds "Mary Clavering" inscribed backwards on a window. Mrs. Belden says two ladies left a box of papers and one has asked her to destroy them. He advises against doing that on legal grounds and that night follows her to a barn where she hides the box. In finding it, he sets fire to the barn. The next morning Q (disguised as a woman tramp) wakes him up and says Hannah is in the house upstairs. Raymond and Q break in and find her dead; paper has been burnt in the grate. Q has through the window seen her taking a powder. It was Mary, Q has found, who wrote to seek the destruction of the papers in the box.

Mrs. Belden says she met Mary upstate. Her uncle objected to her marrying Clavering because he was English. They corresponded through Mrs. Belden, he using the name Le Roy Robbins. Eleanore discovered their correspondence and insisted on attending the wedding. Mrs. Belden says Mary said only her uncle's death would resolve the problem and she would wait for that, but Clavering was not satisfied with waiting. Hannah arrived very late the night of the murder and said Mary wanted her hidden. Mrs. Belden thinks Mary is innocent but suspects Clavering. Raymond tells Mrs. Belden he has the box of documents and then finds in Hannah's bed a hand-printed letter saying she was wicked and a man with a black mustache came out of the library the night of the murder.

In book 4, "The Problem Solved," Mr. Gryce calls the case "the deepest game of the season" (269). He thinks Hannah's "confession" is a fraud (they discover Mrs. Belden had recently taught her to write, not just print), and he finds Hannah was sent something quite bulky in a letter she received, apparently from Mary. The envelope was yellow; Gryce shows some of the ashes in Hannah's grate were of yellow paper and believes Hannah was sent both the "confession" and the poison. He and Raymond return to New York and Gryce traces the yellow paper for Hannah's "confession" in the Leavenworth flat, then examines the papers in Mrs. Belden's box. Pages from Eleanore's diary tell the story of Mary and Clavering, the marriage and the separation. Gryce tells Raymond he feels he has to arrest Mary for murder, calls him to his house, and makes a lengthy statement finally accusing Mary of being "the assassin of her uncle and benefactor" (301).

Suddenly Harwell rushes in, falls at Gryce's feet and shrieks that he is the murderer.

Gryce had arranged for both Clavering and Harwell to hear his accusation of Mary, to test them. Harwell did the murder for his obsessive love of Mary. She then arrives, apparently uncertain of Clavering. He in turn thinks she might be complicit. Harwell confesses his detailed cunning, including trying to inculpate Eleanore and pretending to love Hannah, who saw him leave the library. Mary rejects Harwell but also the wealth: she tears the diamonds from her ears and will rely only on "the husband she has so long and so basely wronged." Harwell says he did it all "for a shadow" (308).

Gryce is very pleased. He never believed a woman could have cleaned a pistol, and that was the false link in the case against Mary. Harwell's very full confession occupies a penultimate chapter: he acted all for Mary, did not really plot against Eleanore, and was desperate in his treatment of Hannah. Finally, Raymond says he and Eleanore are together in "a dream from which I have never waked" (331).

The Leavenworth Case is a confident and coherent piece of work: as Audrey Peterson comments, it gets straightaway into the plot and keeps it moving on (187); it looks forward fully to the clue-puzzle with everything hinging on the final explanation of confusing pieces of evidence, strands of suspicion and attempts at investigation. That combination had been found to some extent in Victor's *The Dead Letter*, which also stressed letters, including a reproduced one (Kate Watson, 123, notes that so did the English *The Notting Hill Mystery*, serialized in 1862–63). It seems that Green wanted to exhibit the connection with Victor's novel, since the two sisters there are called Eleanor and Mary, but the underlying model she is using in *The Leavenworth Case* is the very elaborate plotting, extending from amazing opening scene to final complete explanation that Gaboriau had offered in the early Lecoq novels like *File 113* and *The Mystery of Orcival*, which were rapidly translated and republished in America—including in pirate form—but were not widely available in London in English until the Vizetelly series began in 1881.

As Maida notes (6–7), Green separated her work firmly from the female romance writers of the period, including those like Louisa M. Alcott who merged into suspense, and while dealing with women characters in detail she wrote without any special gender alignment. Watson comments that Green follows Gaboriau in combining strong elements of romance with a final surprise (120), but there are also ways in which Green's novel feels quite different from Gaboriau's work. It quite lacks the long—sometimes very long—middle sequences that go back in time, usually to the aristocratic past, to find the origins of modern disorder—a pattern both Stevenson and Conan Doyle were to adapt in their early fiction like *The Dynamiter* and *A Study in Scarlet*. Green also rejects the hyper-elaboration of the detective's role through which Lecoq keeps appearing in bizarre disguises.

Green makes her detective a much less assertive character but one of subtle power. Ebenezer Gryce is less than heroic in name and person—described as a "portly comfortable personage" with a "totally unimpressive countenance" (5 and 2); he is so far from a multi-disguiser that he cannot, he ruefully tells Raymond, manage to improve his class status from painfully lower-middle towards that of a gentleman. Gaboriau is not completely offstage: though Gryce is unlike Lecoq apart from his attention to detail, he has characteristics not unlike Gaboriau's superseded elderly amateur detective Tabaret. There are also some resemblances to Inspector Bucket in *Bleak House,* both in his social status and his apparent uncertainty, as well as the way both play with their fingers and use side-glances, appearing to focus on anything but their object of interest (Panek, 33). It is equally possible that Sergeant Cuff is a model for Gryce's apparent inconsequentiality, and Mr. Burton in *The Dead Letter* is also active and busy but unheroic: the key element appears to be a deliberately antiheroic detective, looking forward to Christie's Poirot and no doubt linked to the author's gender—though Maida suggests that Green may well have drawn on actual detectives she knew through her father's contact with the New York police (7).

A major innovation by Green, compensating for Gryce's recessive quality compared to Lecoq, is the legal tone. The novel is subtitled *A Lawyer's Story,* and though Raymond himself seems to have little legal activity, the eliciting and considering of evidence is strongly legalistic. The opening inquest runs for a fifth of the novel and is procedurally very detailed; there is recurrent emphasis on the apparent importance, but then doubtful meaning, of pieces of evidence such as Eleanore's open door, the key, the fragmentary letter, the incompletely cleaned gun and the handkerchief with gun marks on it. In Mrs. Belden's house this pattern resumes, with the window writing, the box containing papers, and the complicated details surrounding Hannah's death. Related to all this data is a continuing set of misreadings of the evidence—that it was Mary overheard criticizing Eleanore at the start, that it was Eleanore who married Clavering, that Hannah made a confession, that the key and letter were in Eleanore's possession for a bad reason—even the whereabouts of Clavering himself.

In terms of structure Green either introduces or establishes in an effective and coherent context a remarkable range of major features of the classic clue-puzzle:

> A rich man has died and his will has some importance.
> The body is in the library.
> The room and indeed house are locked.
> There is a lengthy inquest.
> Someone is missing.
> The servants are involved in a range of evidence.
> Medical and ballistic evidence of importance is given.
> Minor items of evidence are found and hard to interpret.

Much stress is laid on documents, some of which are forged.
There is a secondary death.
Suspicion falls on major characters in turn.
A totally unsuspected person is revealed as the criminal.

As is noted by Alma Murch, the first critic to give Green a substantial place in the history of crime fiction, she not only offers this "assemblage of characteristic features" (162) but also (158–59) develops into a commanding conclusion the mystery-explanation that had been a late chapter in *Bleak House* and *The Woman in White* and rather more than that in the perhaps more influential 1870 *Checkmate* by Sheridan Le Fanu.

In the process of both mystery and explanation, the foregrounding of the unreliability of circumstantial evidence is a crucial feature of the novel, and this was apparently the basis for its reported use, or at least reference to it, at Yale Law School and evidently can be traced back to Green's father's occupation as a trial lawyer and her own highly intelligent interest in the profession. The key idea, that an apparent situation can be explained in a quite different way, will continue as a basic formation of crime fiction through Christie's bravura examples like *Murder on the Orient Express* through to the completely alternative outcome finally revealed in *The Girl with the Dragon Tattoo*.

Coupled with that technically elaborate and confidence-disturbing process of revelation is a feature that seems to be regularly overlooked in commentary on Green's novel: the real villain is a person the novel never lets you suspect, a quiet, unassuming, apparently totally reliable secretary. The central trick is very similar to that in *The Murder of Roger Ackroyd,* and Christie has in fact condensed in her murderous doctor the figures of the lawyer who is called in and the secretary who does the crime: in her *Autobiography* she records that her sister read this novel to the family when Christie was about eight (Watson, 123) and she was most impressed by it—as Lucy Sussex notes (169), in *The Clocks* (1963) Poirot would call Green's novel "an excellent psychological study." Where Poe was happy with a monstrous criminal, Gaboriau favored bad or fake aristocrats and Collins distrusted them as well as bourgeois hypocrites like Godfrey Ablewhite, Green was the first to create the secretly insidious enemy that no one would ever suspect, hidden in the woodwork of respectable life.

Another striking element of *The Leavenworth Case*, which has been swamped by floods of imitations, is the elevated context of the story. While Gryce may be painfully middle-class, the Leavenworths are from the New York upper set, at the high tide of American business and power, described by Maida as Green's focal topic (9–11). But the city itself is not the object of attention:

it is the complex interrelations among people with real money that occupy the story. The style of dress and behavior of the Leavenworth nieces is not that of diligent and intelligent new women like Green herself, and the characters' anxieties involve the difficulty of a moral and personally credible lifestyle in a world where, as Mary says, they "have been taught to love money so" (257)—finally she gives up the inheritance and tears the diamonds out of her ears to rely on her husband. Mr. Leavenworth hated the English because his dead wife was so badly treated by them, and this is another sign of modern America's self-awareness: Martha Hailey DuBose comments that Green "wrote about the distinctly American people, places and styles of life that she observed" (9).

The story connects with more than crime fiction, insisting on the possibility of human feeling and even love in this world of high finance, massive consumption, and internationalism—Green's world is in fact looking forward to those of Edith Wharton and Henry James, and this will continue in crime fiction to "S. S. Van Dine" and "Ellery Queen," though American crime fiction as a whole would later move decisively towards the West Coast masculine quasi-democracy of the private-eye writers.

The thematic innovations, multiple subtleties, and technical strength of *The Leavenworth Case* made it a great success. Wilkie Collins noted the potent mix of very detailed observation and stress on character in his comment in an 1883 letter about Green's "fine perception of the influence of events on the personages of the story" (quoted by Sussex, 170). Conan Doyle made a point of visiting Green in New York in 1894 (DuBose, 7). Green pursued the form, remaining largely faithful to Gryce and this kind of complicated, evidence-testing puzzle, though as Sussex notes, her stories continue to focus on "domestic tyrants" (181), which may well also be an inheritance from her father, since he strongly opposed her own marriage, at the age of thirty-eight, to Charles Rohlfs, not because he was younger but because he was an actor. He played the villain in the early stage version of *The Leavenworth Case* and went on to be a well-known Arts and Crafts designer—Sussex reports that considerable overlap was seen at the time between his work and Green's own detailed design in fiction (172–75).

It was not only the very young Christie who felt Green's influence. Carolyn Wells, in *The Technique of the Mystery Story* (1913), says Green was "one of the best constructors of a mystery story" (quoted by Sussex, 176) and turn-of-the-century American women crime writers like Mary Roberts Rinehart and Wells herself clearly felt Green was showing them a path. They tend to lighten her style and dilute the evidence obsession but maintained the element of a romance strand that would long continue and reach on into Christie, Sayers, Marjorie Allingham and Ngaio Marsh—and even return, in embattled form, in the feminist detective writers.

Another area where Green showed a path, though less confidently and less early than in intense puzzle creation, was with women inquirers. Commentators have noted that she was herself never a female activist—not in favor of votes for women, for example—but she did in 1897 with *That Affair Next Door* bring in the figure of Amelia Butterworth, a wealthy, well-born spinster who helps Gryce resolve his problems—looking forward to Ariadne Oliver in Christie's work—and then in 1915 published *The Golden Slipper,* a set of stories starring Violet Strange, a wealthy young woman about town who resolves puzzles with acuity and courage (and what Murch calls a "remarkably sagacious bloodhound," 164). In both cases Green is more bluestocking than feminist, but there is nevertheless an element of social innovation about her work, both in the unassertive character of Gryce and in the way in which in her novels, as Sussex notes (181), "domestic tyrants, husbands and fathers, recur."

Green crafted the first powerful example of the technically focused, puzzle-oriented mystery, but at the same time the strength of her belief in the positive values of her major characters and their deep loyalties underlies and dynamizes the sheer expertise that made her so influential an innovator and influence in the mystery novel.

References

DuBose, Martha Hailey. "Anna Katharine Green: The Lady and the Inspector," in *Women of Mystery: The Lives and Works of Notable Women Crime Novelists.* New York: Dunne, 2000, 5–17.

Haycraft, Howard. *Murder for Pleasure: The Life and Times of the Detective Story.* New York: Appleton-Century-Crofts, 1941.

Maida, Patricia D. *Mother of Detective Fiction: The Life and Works of Anna Katharine Green.* Bowling Green, OH: Popular Press, 1989.

Messac, Régis. *Le "Detective Novel" et l'influence de la pensée scientifique.* Paris: Champion, 1929.

Murch, Alma. *The Development of the Detective Novel.* Second revised edition. London: Owen, 1968.

Panek, Leroy Lad. *Probable Cause: Crime Fiction in America.* Bowling Green, OH: Popular Press, 1990.

Peterson, Audrey. *Victorian Masters of Mystery, From Wilkie Collins to Conan Doyle.* New York: Ungar, 1984.

Slung, Michele. "Introduction," in Anna Katharine Green, *The Leavenworth Case.* New York: Dover, 1981.

Sussex, Lucy. "The Art of Murder: Anna Katharine Green," chapter 9 of *Women Writers and Detectives in Nineteenth-Century Crime Fiction: The Mothers of the Mystery Genre*. London: Palgrave Macmillan, 2010.

Watson, Kate. *Women Writing Crime Fiction, 1860–1880: Fourteen American, British and Australian Authors.* Jefferson, NC: McFarland, 2012.

7
The Mystery of a Hansom Cab, Fergus Hume

Though the idea is familiar that crime fiction is a mass, world-wide form, it seems strange that the first true best seller in the genre was by an unknown author and set far away from London, Paris or New York, a now little-read novel whose much-discussed success the author never replicated. There is a good deal of contextual mystery about *The Mystery of a Hansom Cab,* first published in Melbourne in 1886.

Fergusson Wright Hume was born in England in 1859, son of a doctor, who immigrated to Dunedin in New Zealand. Hume studied law at the University of Otago and after graduating moved in 1885 as a solicitor's clerk to Melbourne, Australia, a city still riding high from the mid-century gold boom and thriving wool sales around the world: it called itself Marvellous Melbourne. He wanted to be a playwright but in his 1898 preface to the Jarrolds reprint of his major novel said he thought writing a novel would attract attention and was advised by a bookseller that the crime stories of Émile Gaboriau were popular—the London-based publisher Vizetelly had started a series of translations in 1881. Hume bought several, he said, and read and copied them. The result was *The Mystery of a Hansom Cab:* Hume himself published five thousand copies in Melbourne when local publishers showed no interest—his preface reported that they "refused even to look at the manuscript on the ground that no Colonial could write anything worth reading."

He also said the edition sold out in three weeks in October 1886 (Caterson, ix) and a reprint did well. It has become a very rare in book in Australia, though now more exist than the one long resident in the New South Wales State Library—four in all is the latest report. Then it was picked up in London and was published in mid–1887 by the specially formed Hansom Cab Publishing Company. They were registered at the same address as a firm named

"The Effective Advertiser" and seem to have mounted a good publicity campaign. Hume's later preface paid tribute to a favorable review in the mainstream London newspaper the *Daily Telegraph* by Clement Scott, a theater reviewer and forcefully opinionated writer. Bearing the subtitle *A Startling and Realistic Novel* and priced at one shilling, the novel's sales were unprecedented—copies survive with a banner on the cover saying "six hundredth thousand." Christopher Pittard cites evidence that three hundred thousand sold in less than six months and it kept selling at "a thousand copies a week" (29). It is generally agreed that within two years the novel had sold half a million copies, as well as the American sales through Munro—without making for Hume more than the £50 for which he sold the copyright, though he did keep the stage rights and did fairly well out of them in London and Australia. Another impact was indirect: in Melbourne quite a number of minor writers followed Hume into writing about crime in the city, and there may have been, in spite of his later-expressed contempt for the novel, some influence on the young Dr. Arthur Conan Doyle's career in crime fiction. Though he claims in his *Memoirs* to have finished his first Sherlock Holmes story well before Hume published his novel in Melbourne, its London success may at least have developed publishers' interest in crime fiction at the time.

That Hume had read Poe is suggested by one reference—a comic landlady has "a Poe-like appreciation of horror" (91)—but also by the shared use of newspaper reports, not a major feature of Gaboriau, though a likelier source is Green, as with the lengthy inquest. *The Mystery of Hansom Cab* opens with a statement from the *Argus,* a leading local paper, about a murder that seems reminiscent of a case by the creator of M. Lecoq: that "Gaboreau" is the spelling used twice suggests either Hume or the typesetter was careless. A hansom cab has been hailed late on a Thursday night by a man in a light coat helping a drunk. The driver is asked to take him to St Kilda, a semi-genteel suburb south of the city, by the bay. But as the drunk turns, the other man says, "You," drops him, and leaves. The driver helps the drunk in, then sees the light-coated man return and join him. But he stops the cab in St Kilda Road, says the drunk does not want his help and walks towards the city. When the driver stops for an address, he finds the passenger dead, with a handkerchief soaked in chloroform over his mouth. The next day the paper reports a second cab picked up a man wearing a light coat in St Kilda Road and dropped him in Powlett Street, in fashionable East Melbourne.

The inquest reviews this material, adding that both cabdrivers said the man had a diamond ring on his first finger. Samuel Gorby, a portly, red-faced police detective, finds the dead man is Oliver Whyte, not long out from England, who has recently argued with a tall, fair man who threatened to kill him. Gorby identifies the tall man as Brian Fitzgerald, a "heavy swell" (54), handsome and very close to Madge Frettlby, only daughter of "the wool king" Mark Frettlby; her mother is dead. Gorby tracks Fitzgerald down and finds he wore a light coat and was home late that night and had reason to think Whyte was trying to displace him with Madge. He arrests Fitzgerald for murder; the newspapers report there is a social sensation.

Frettlby engages a barrister, Calton, to defend Brian, and he employs a tall, lean, clever police detective, Kilsip. Brian admits he hailed the cab but says when he recognized Whyte he left and did not return. They find that Brian was actually visiting someone else, a woman, at the time of the murder, but he will not say who this was, as it concerns Madge. They know Whyte was carrying papers in a special waistcoat pocket, and as it is torn they assume the murderer took them. Hearing this, Brian says, "My God it is true after all" (129), and faints.

Calton and Madge find a burned letter at Brian's lodgings, which leads them to Mother Guttersnipe, a "repulsive-looking old crone" (183) living in a city slum. She tells them on the night in question a gentleman visited the "Queen," who was a friend of Oliver Whyte, but she has now died. Brian admits he was there but will not say what she said; the girl Sal who took him there is missing. After postponing the trial to try to find her, unsuccessfully, Calton defends Brian, and things look dark. Only the fact that he never wears a ring and apparently got home a little too early to have been in the second cab seems on his side. But suddenly Sal turns up—she has been ill and then with a Chinaman—she gives Brian an alibi, and he is found not guilty.

Brian realizes he must tell Calton what happened, but delays. A doctor tells Madge that Frettlby's heart is weak. Kilsip continues to investigate: he suspects Whyte's friend Moreland, who does wear a ring, and he will search for the light coat in the park near where the second cab dropped its passenger. Mother Guttersnipe, before she dies in a rage, throwing her gold around, tells them she is mother of "the Queen," who was Rosanna Moore, a dancer whom Frettlby married in Melbourne. She then went to London and reported herself killed in an accident so she could marry again.

At Frettlby's house Madge mistakes him for Brian when he is wearing a coat and hat; she tells Brian, who sees the point. There is a cry from Frettlby's study. Later Moreland is seen leaving it, but Frettlby stays there writing. Calton at his office discusses the case with Brian. Whyte had Rosanna's marriage certificate, and Brian thinks Frettlby did the murder. A telegram comes, and Calton says, "The Judgement of God!" (351).

Previously, at his house, Frettlby had finished writing "My Confession"; he had been brilliant at dinner, though the old Scotch nurse had said he was "fey" (fated) (359). Later he appears with the marriage certificate, sleepwalking. Madge sees it and screams; he wakes and dies. That was the news in the telegram.

Madge is very ill. Sal, now her maid, is managing things very well; she does not know who her parents were. Frettlby's executors, Calton, Brian and the doctor, read the confession and destroy it. They will not tell Sal anything if Madge is named as inheriting in the will. Kilsip has found the coat in the park and in it an empty bottle of chloroform that Whyte had bought.

The confession says that Frettlby came out to Australia before gold was found and did very well. He married Rosanna, but they drifted apart and she went to England and reported her death. He was told the child Sal was also dead. Then, after many years and another marriage, Whyte appeared, with Rosanna his mistress, and had the certificate. He wanted to marry Madge: Frettlby supported this but then gave in to Madge and Brian. Whyte called on the fatal Thursday, wanting money. Frettlby followed Whyte hoping to get the certificate when he was drunk; he saw him fall but when Brian appeared, went home. Now Moreland has seen Frettlby and admitted killing Whyte, knowing Frettlby cannot inform against him. Frettlby gave Moreland a check for £5,000 for the certificate.

Kilsip wants to arrest Moreland. Calton is reluctant because of the impact on Madge, but Brian insists—they are leaving Australia anyway. They learn Moreland is calling on Frettlby's solicitor as he cannot now cash the check and they arrest him; he resists, then confesses. Whyte had told Moreland about the scheme and he wanted the money for himself. He followed Whyte that night, also wearing a light coat, which he had taken from Whyte. Moreland saw Brian hail the cab and leave and went with Whyte. When Whyte resisted Moreland's stealing the certificate, he used the chloroform in the coat: he did not realize Whyte was dead. Moreland says "we are the puppets of Fate" (404). The doctor predicts he will kill himself.

Brian feels that Madge's name will be ruined, but Moreland hangs himself. They burn the confession; people assume some quarrel between Whyte and Moreland was behind the murder. Brian gives Kilsip enough money to retire, but he keeps detecting privately "from sheer love of excitement" (407). As the will leaves the money to Madge by name, they tell Sal nothing, not even that she is Madge's half sister. Sal will work to help fallen women. Madge has recovered and marries Brian. They leave on a ship "for the old world and the new life" (410).

In spite of Hume's report of his advice from a Melbourne bookseller and the two in-text (misspelled) references, Gaboriau seems far from a model. Neither police detective is anything like Lecoq and less like the elderly amateur Tabaret. Gaboriau's habit of going back in time to explain the present, while common in Collins, is quite foreign to Hume (as it is in Green): though the motivation does have distant origins, the revelations are in the present. Hume does at the end of the first chapter refer to Fortuné du Boisgobey's *Le Crime de l'omnibus* (1881: in English, *The Mystery of an Omnibus*, 1882) and as well as using a public conveyance as a site of murder a woman returns from a dubious past to disrupt wealthy respectability in both novels. A fuller familiarity appears with the local author Donald Cameron's *The Mysteries of Melbourne Life* (1873). This almost completely forgotten but rather effective short version of the earlier Mysteries format (see Knight "Mysteries Across the World" for a detailed discussion) is set between the city and St Kilda, involves young Melbourne city men ranging from those with rural wealth to slippery self-seekers, has female roles ranging from true wives through to decidedly corrupt but still courageous women of the city's night, and the less than authoritative police play a minor and mostly corrupt role.

If Cameron seems to have provided the contextual pattern for Hume, a clear structural model emerges from the fact that the handsome gentleman who will marry the heroine is absolved of apparently certain guilt about halfway through and there is a real surprise ending with an unsuspected character proving guilty and an important sleepwalking scene. *The Moonstone* very clearly provides those structural features, though it would be unwise to assume it also offers the idea that the base of the crime is a troublesome secret brought from overseas—that is common enough in Australian crime writing and early fiction in general. However it is tempting to suggest that the name Rosanna and the mix of policing, first banal and then incisive but in neither case authoritative, also derives from Collins, and Calton and Kilsip do combine rather like Blake and Cuff.

Other connections have been suggested: Pittard ("'A Strange Inverted World,'" 28) feels Hume combines the shape of a sensation novel, notably in the Madge-Brian anxieties, with a slum examination related to the late nineteenth-century English "social purity" movement—but in doing this Pittard places great stress on the fairly brief and relatively unemphasized scene in Mother Guttersnipe's unsavory house (see Pittard "From Sensation to the Strand," 108–9). A stronger link with sensationalism is the idea that threatening relationships from the past emerge to disrupt the present as in the Madge–Sal relationship. Robert Dixon also identifies a far from evident emphasis on slums in the novel, paying less attention to the novel than to Hume's claim in his preface that, as Simon Caterson reports (ix), he "passed a great many nights" researching in the Little Bourke Street city slum.

It is noticeable that although the two French crime writers are mentioned and Anna Katharine Green's *The Leavenworth Case* is cited in chapter 7 as comparable with Whyte's death, Collins is never referred to, though there are several—perhaps too many—references to Thomas De Quincey's essays on

"Murder Considered as One of the Fine Arts" (1827, 1839 and 1854). The De Quincey citations, however, fit with a substantial series of other references clearly offering the author as a man of some literary knowledge: in order through the novel, reference is made to James Payn (chap. 1), Disraeli (chap. 5), Poe (chap. 9), Marcus Clarke (chap. 15), Shakespeare (chap. 21), Browning (chaps. 22 and 23), Thomas Moore (chap. 24), Thackeray (chap. 25), William Dean Howells, (chap. 24), Byron (chap. 28), Cervantes (chap. 29), George Eliot, Faust, Shakespeare, and Justin McCarthy (all in chap. 30).

There is little sign that Hume is fitting in with the substantial element of Australian crime fiction that had been produced by his time. Hardly surprisingly for a country founded as a European jail and with substantial resistance to order by escaped and time-served convicts, Australian crime fiction (see Knight *Continent of Mystery*) goes back to the early nineteenth century, when the first formations were novels that represented the wrongs of people convicted in England for crimes they felt were forced upon them by social pressures as in Henry Savery's *Quintus Servinton* (1831) and novels that celebrated the resistant spirit of the bushranger like Charles Rowcroft's *The Bushranger of Van Diemen's Land* (1846). But as soon as stories and novels about puzzling crimes that needed special investigation became common in Britain—whose magazines and books were eagerly consumed in Australia— the colony developed its own versions, both detective-free crime stories like Ellen Davitt's *Force and Fraud* (1865) and the long-lasting and high-standard series by Mary Fortune, writing as W.W. (short for her usual non-crime pseudonym, Waif Wander), which used mounted trooper Mark Sinclair as a roving and usually rural investigator, starting with "The Dead Witness" of 1866 (see Sussex *Women Writers and Detectives*, chap. 7).

Hume brought into play a set of ideas and issues that were central to Australian crime fiction and long lasted as such. The idea recurs through mid-century Australian fiction that someone who has done well in Australia will somewhere have a dark secret that will through malicious hands return in the present to cause serious problems. Writers and readers were both settlers, and they all understood how much baggage can be carried in the process. In Marcus Clarke's major novel *His Natural Life* (1870–72) the unjustly convicted hero can through sheer nobility outlast his dark fate, but the negative complexities of his family and upbringing back in England will pursue him to a grim ending. In the melodramatically tragic version of the novel form he dies bravely at sea, but in the more elaborate earlier serial he carves out a postprison life in rural Australia only, much like Brian Fitzgerald, to be simply ground down by circumstances and hope for some peace at last.

The criminal past of Australian society is still resonant for Hume, a nineteenth-century visitor from England and New Zealand, and trouble stems unstoppably from both the past of racy gold-ridden Melbourne and the vile contemporary slum of Little Bourke Street, supervised by Mother Guttersnipe—the audience would not have missed the London criminal slang she uses: her past is surely one of transportation.

The dubious basis of Frettlby's riches is also part of the uncertainty of the settler consciousness, and the suspicion of the rich is by this time made moral, where decades before their wealth would have been shown to be based on avaricious land taking and very often brutal dispossession of the indigenous previous owners, who are in Melbourne by this time out of sight, out of mind. Frettlby here suffers heart trouble and sudden collapse, a reversal of the fate of Franklin Blake as a sleepwalker. But Frettlby's outcome might have been worse. In his 1898 preface Hume says that at first he had an ending that was too obvious and in this he made Frettlby the hijacker of the hansom cab—as is suggested when Madge mistakes him for Brian in a hat and light coat. But a last-minute decision enforced a more mysterious surprise ending—and one much more like Collins, and indeed Green, than Gaboriau, in bringing out the under-noticed Moreland as the ultimate criminal. All three authors are suggested in the evidence and the in-text printing of the discovered letter (found in Collins' *The Law and the Lady,* 1875), but the long opening inquest and newspaper quotations look very like Green.

The ways in which Hume had, either deliberately or just by cultural osmosis, fitted into a structure of Australian concerns about the threat of the overseas past and the values to be constructed across the classes in Australia seem a sound basis for the good sales he achieved in Melbourne, though the brisk writing, the literary flourishes—there are some effective "fine landscape" set pieces—and the crisp tone of the news and court reports in the first half of the novel all give good reason why the novel should have been successful in Melbourne. This was a book-hungry culture, reading about the world and itself, and it was then—and still is today—a society without the hosts of non-readers found in other countries around the world.

But that does not explain why the novel took off so sensationally in publication-drenched London in 1887. A short novel of not much more than seventy thousand words—half the length of *The Moonstone*—was itself of value in a market moving away from the bulky three-decker public library model to a program of brisk sales at one shilling each for popular novels. The marketing reasons for Green's New York success operate for Hume in Lon--don not long afterwards: Charles J. Rzepka reports (113) that the first single-volume mystery novel in London was George Manville Fenn's *The Dark House* (1885). The tone of Hume's novel matches that new situation: just as Conan

Doyle, read against the flatulent confidence of routine *Strand Magazine* prose, seems sharply modern, Hume's brisk, speedy style is quite different from the languid, even verbose approach of crime novelists like Gaboriau in English translation or Anna Katharine Green in leisured American style.

Caterson sees the novel as an early example of "cross-sectional representation of urban reality" (xiii) and the setting itself may have been an attraction. Melbourne had become well-known in English fiction and journalism as a place, after the 1850s gold rushes, for migrants to do very well, replacing the grimmer model of New South Wales or Tasmania as dark sites of convict suffering in earlier novels like Thomas Gaspey's *The History of George Godfrey* (1828) and G. W. M. Reynolds' *Mysteries of London* (1845), and this new image of prosperity was basic, if obscurely so, to Dickens' *Great Expectations* (1860). That new positive internationalism was an attraction: it is not well recognized how much English fiction of the period is aware of the wider world—the stories of Conan Doyle's first two novellas have their origins in America and India: the reach of British trade and population distribution had by the late nineteenth century become widely understood and was itself a subject for fiction.

The runaway success of *The Mystery of a Hansom Cab* even gave rise to parodies like the Melbourne-published *The Mystery of a Wheelbarrow* by W. Ferguson Humer. In London it was ideally placed to exploit the new single-volume mystery book market, and the 1887 subtitle, *A Startling and Realistic Story*; combined two modes that were, picked up in the *Illustrated London News* comment that it was "a realistic sensationalist tale of Melbourne social life" (see Pittard "'A Strange Inverted World,'" 108), suggesting that it combined the grand excitements of Collins and Braddon with new journalistic modernity. In accordance with that idea there were, Hume's preface reports, rumors that the story was in fact based on a real case. This transmission of the dark passions of mid-late-century sensational writing into the cooler control of detectives and lawyers may well be a crucial element in Hume's achievement and a major reason for his remarkable acceptability—it can be seen as a street-level version of what Holmes was about to do as a gentleman and scholar.

Hume lived in England from 1888 and kept publishing, with over a hundred novels by his death in 1932, but he never again had a real success. The lively *Madame Midas* (1888) is about a very wealthy woman gold-mine owner (who really existed and owned London's *Sunday Times*): Kilsip and Calton reappear, and this sold well at first, presumably on Hume's name, but it and its Melbourne-set successor *Miss Mephistopheles* (1890) are less sharply focused than *The Mystery of a Hansom Cab*. Little of Hume's later work had the fresh bite of this first success, but the short-story collection *Hagar of the Pawnshop* (1898) has considerable energy, being about a young gypsy girl who solves problems that come across her counter. He wrote other woman-focused stories, but they are, like *Lady Jim of Curzon Street* (1913), hardly radical. Hume became a theosophist, led a quiet rural life, and never again made contact with either the urban anxiety or the astonishing sales that had so distinguished and had made so intriguing *The Mystery of a Hansom Cab*.

References

Caterson, Simon. "Fergus Hume's Startling Story: Introduction," in Fergus Hume, *The Mystery of a Hansom Cab*. Text Classics. Melbourne: Text, 2012.

Dixon, Robert. "Closing the Can of Worms: Enactments of Justice in *Bleak House*, *The Mystery of a Hansom Cab* and *The Tax Inspector*." *Westerly* 37 (1992): 37–46.

Knight, Stephen. *Continent of Mystery: A Thematic History of Australian Crime Fiction*. Melbourne: University of Melbourne Press, 1997.

_____. "Introduction," in Fergus Hume, *The Mystery of a Hansom Cab*. London: Hogarth, 1985.

_____. "Mysteries Across the World: Donald Cameron's *The Mysteries of Melbourne Life*," in *The Mysteries of the Cities: Urban Crime Fiction in the Nineteenth Century*. Jefferson, NC: McFarland, 2012.

Pittard, Christopher. "From Sensation to the Strand," in *Companion to Crime Fiction*. Ed. Charles J. Rzepka and Lee Horsley. New York: Wiley, 2010, 105–16.

_____. "'A Strange Inverted World'; Sensation and Social Purity in *The Mystery of a Hansom Cab*," chapter 1 of *Purity and Contamination in Late Victorian Detective Fiction*. Aldershot: Ashgate, 2011.

Rzepka, Charles J. *Detective Fiction*. London: Polity, 2005.

Sussex, Lucy. *Victorian Blockbuster: Fergus Hume and The Mystery of a Hansom Cab*. Melbourne: Text, 2014.

_____. *Women Writers and Detectives in Nineteenth-Century Crime Fiction: Mothers of Crime*. London: Palgrave Macmillan, 2010.

Part II
Mainstream

8

The Adventures of Sherlock Holmes, Arthur Conan Doyle

Arthur Conan Doyle, creator of the best-known fictional detective, Sherlock Holmes, was born in Edinburgh in 1859 in a Catholic family; his father was Irish-English and his mother fully Irish. Arthur's father was an illustrator, producing plates for the first book version of *A Study in Scarlet,* but was also an alcoholic and died in 1893. One of Conan Doyle's uncles was "Dickie" Doyle, well-known illustrator for the London satirical magazine *Punch.* Arthur was educated at Stonyhurst, a Catholic private school, spent a year at a Jesuit college in Germany, and then studied medicine at Edinburgh, where he met both J. M. Barrie and R. L. Stevenson. After visiting the Arctic and West Africa as a ship's surgeon, Conan Doyle became a doctor in 1882 and then in 1886 an ophthalmic specialist just around the corner from Holmes' Baker Street.

Interested in writing, Conan Doyle felt strongly the historicist spirit of Walter Scott but also had an international viewpoint, admiring the American Bret Harte, and his early work has a wide range: in the Scotland-set "The Mystery of Uncle Jeremy's Household" a half–Indian governess is involved with Thuggee vengeance, but with some justification and finally escapes; "The Gully of Bluemansdyke," set in Australia, is resolved by an astute amateur inquirer from America. *The Parasite* (1894) was about an Edinburgh medical student who is controlled, in part sexually, by a mysterious woman from Trinidad—her racial origin is not clear—who drives him to the point of murdering his respectable fiancée.

In early 1886, when patients at Conan Doyle's eye-specialist practice were rare, he produced the first Sherlock Holmes adventure, *A Study in Scarlet,* a novella. As Ronald Pearsall notes in his book on Conan Doyle (28), it was sent to James Payn, editor of the prestigious *Cornhill Magazine,* and joined the list of world-famous rejectees (along with *Moby-Dick* and now *Harry Potter*) but then was sold for a miserly £25 (with the copyright) to *Beeton's Christmas Annual* for 1887, published by the husband of Mrs. Beeton of *Household Management* fame.

Conan Doyle had recently read Gaboriau's *Monsieur Lecoq* and was familiar with Stevenson's *New Arabian Nights* stories in *The Rajah's Diamond* and the Suicide Club series (1882), offering London-based adventures verging on crime supervised by the enigmatic authority Prince Florizel. But the essential model for Holmes and Watson is Poe's great detective Dupin and his faithful recorder. As Booth records (104–8), Conan Doyle's notes show him planning an intellectual and logically focused mystery solver. Conan Doyle's first thoughts have a doctor called Ormond Sacker—a weighty name that has led some to believe he originally planned a doctor-detective—and in his diary opposite the page where he records reading *Monsieur Lecoq* he sketched the history of an army doctor, also seemingly more than a mere narrator. But the other person in the "Ormond Sacker" note is "Sherrinford Holmes," to become Sherlock. Neither a policeman like Lecoq nor an amateur like Dupin, Holmes is both a gentleman (he has £400-a-year private income) and, crucially, for his modern impact, a skilled professional.

From the start the story combines melodrama—a hideous murder, with a message in blood—with analytic knowledge: the message says "Rache," and the plodding police think the murderer was disturbed when writing "Rachel," but Holmes knows "Rache" is German for "revenge." His persona is vivid from the start: Watson meets him beating a corpse as an experiment in bruising, and his actions are at times rapid and decisive, at other times strangely languid. He can seem bohemian, injecting cocaine for "relaxation"—not then illegal but very much against Watson's advice. Conan Doyle later identified his own teacher of diagnosis Dr. Joseph Bell as the model for the Holmesian method, and Stevenson recognized Bell's influence. *A Study in Scarlet* looks towards Harte in the American sequence explaining the vengeance that visits South London, but the structure of the story, with its middle section set back in time and place to explain all, seems derived from Stevenson's *The Dynamiter* (1885). The title itself may refer to Gaboriau's *L'Affaire Lerouge* (though Lerouge is actually the name of the murdered widow) and was a definite improvement on the banal original idea, "A Tangled Skein."

The story was published separately in 1888, and on that basis J. M. Stoddard, an editor from Lippincott's of New York, commissioned both Conan Doyle to write *The Sign of Four* and, at the same dinner, Oscar Wilde to produce *The Picture of Dorian Gray*—a rare triumph for publishing hospitality.

Wilde expressed admiration for Conan Doyle's work, and Conan Doyle remained friendly, later commenting that Wilde's problems with sexuality and the law were based on medical issues.

Researching historical fiction was Conan Doyle's major focus at this time: it was *Micah Clarke* (1888) about the 1685 Monmouth Rebellion that Wilde admired, but Lippincott's offer was too good to turn down and *The Sign of Four* appeared in 1890. This is primarily a reworking of Collins' *The Moonstone:* an Indian treasure has been stolen and brought to England by a British officer, but here the retrievers of it are not the Brahmins who dignify Collins' story but a humble soldier, the survivor of the four who stole the riches, and his pygmy assistant, armed with poison darts. The story is colorful and energetic, with a climactic chase on the Thames: Holmes gains new honor and Watson marries the girl who might have inherited the tainted riches.

The new model took off when George Newnes, a Canadian who started at Christmas 1890 the *Strand Magazine*, a new-seeming monthly magazine with an illustration on every opening, offered Conan Doyle £30 a story for a set of six. When the copy arrived it is said the editor ran into Newnes's office saying they had found the best short-story writer since Poe. The stories have fine illustrations of a lean, intense Holmes, looking equally capable of intellectual concentration and sudden action. They include surprises. The artist, Sidney Paget, was commissioned by mistake, Newnes wanting his brother, but then the brother was apparently used as the model for the Holmes illustrations. They noticeably lack the curved pipe and (almost completely) the deerstalker hat that became iconic. Paget's Holmes smokes a straight pipe and like any gentleman only wears a deerstalker and cape on rural journey (to Dartmoor in "The Mystery of Silver Blaze" in the second series). The curved pipe emerged with the American actor William Gillette, as it interfered less with his profile in photographs; he also popularized the melodramatic deerstalker.

In a letter to his mother as early as 1891, Conan Doyle said, "Holmes keeps my mind from better things." He no doubt preferred the historical fiction. His medieval *The White Company* (1891) had been well received and he dealt with the Napoleonic period in *The Great Shadow* (1892), worked up to it with *The Refugees* (1893) and went on to his biggest success in this mode, the English sporting novel *Rodney Stone* (1896). He raised his price for Holmes to £50 a story after the sixth, hoping for rejection, but Newnes paid up gladly. So at the end of the second dozen Conan Doyle famously killed Holmes off in "The Final Problem," sending him down the Reichenbach Falls struggling with Professor Moriarty. When Conan Doyle eventually gave in and resurrected Holmes, that further magnified his status: mythic heroes always return from the dead. But there was already enough for lasting fame. The basis of

Holmes' power is in the twelve stories collected in *The Adventures of Sherlock Holmes* (1892): they created the world-famous, still vigorous and immensely influential Great Detective.

The first short story, "A Scandal in Bohemia," has a sensational and international basis much like the novellas but a more local edge. Holmes is asked to protect the King of Bohemia against exposure and possible blackmail by a previous mistress, the opera singer Irene Adler, but shows some contempt for the king and comes to admire the lady's independence as well as her charm. The king is evidently the libertine Prince of Wales, but none of the other *Adventures* stories reach so high, though "The Noble Bachelor" shows a sturdy woman outlasting the manipulations of a lord and "The Beryl Coronet" has a titled villain. The other stories operate within the bourgeois social levels. They reach down to clerks ("The Red-Headed League") and up to a rich banker ("The Beryl Coronet") but often lack any formal crime: at the start of the seventh story, "The Blue Carbuncle," Watson says "of the last six cases which I have added to my notes, three have been entirely free of any legal crime" (202).

The dominant problem is financial greed and the temptations it places on ordinary respectable people. There is a professional thief behind the bank robbery in "The Red-Headed League," but he is a nobleman turned bad; "The Engineer's Thumb" is overtly about coiners, but they escape. The other stories turn entirely on the pressures felt, and yielded to, by respectable people: in "A Case of Identity," "The Speckled Band" and "The Copper Beeches" the money of a daughter/stepdaughter's substantial income is a temptation to a brutish father—sexual motives may be suggested by posting as a lover in the first and using a snake as a weapon in the second. John A. Hodgson ("The Recoil of 'The Speckled Band'") has pointed out the notable improbabilities of the very popular "The Speckled Band"—snakes are deaf, cannot climb ropes, and would not kill a big man so quickly (336)—but its meaning is potent. Rosemary Hennessy and Rajeswari Mohan elucidate the story as offering "the entangled encoding of the feminine and the orient as sexualised other" (400), with Dr. Roylott representing both a weakened aristocracy and imperialism as well as incestuous invasion. In "The Red-Headed League" and "The Man with the Twisted Lip" and "The Beryl Coronet" there operates the disruptive effect of financial greed on men. In "The Blue Carbuncle" a servant cannot resist greed (but avoid consequences) and in "The Engineer's Thumb" the coiners' love of money is very damaging to an employee. Farther afield, "The Boscombe Valley Mystery" and "The Five Orange Pips" show how past crimes, Australian bushranging and American Ku Klux Klan activities have a dark influence on the present.

Conan Doyle quite overlooks the dominant crimes of late nineteenth-century London, which were mugging, breaking and entering, prostitution and "baby farming" (incompetent, often dangerous, child minding). The problems in the first twelve stories, even for the nobility, are mostly family-based and financial disruption, matching the self-conscious aspirational uncertainty common to the audience of *The Strand,* which was primarily white-collar workers, who often bought the magazine at railway bookstalls—including at Baker Street Station. The audience was primarily male and Catherine Belsey argues that the stories show this, being "hounded by shadowy, mysterious and often silent women. Their silence repeatedly conceals their sexuality" (385).

The setting matches the characters and crimes: it is respectable London, the inner areas and sometimes the outer suburbs, occasionally the country areas where the upper bourgeoisie lived, commuting in on the trains to their city businesses: Holmes remarks in "The Copper Beeches" that "the smiling and beautiful countryside" in fact has a "dreadful record of sin" (277). The city is itself given a selective account: the story hardly ever goes offstage into the areas where the "dangerous classes" live; Holmes can visit as a brave emissary and will recount his exploits; the boys who form his "Baker Street Irregulars" appear to come from the lower classes as conscripts to respectability. This London is a busy, working city, with many small offices and thronged with hansom cabs, but there is hardly a mention of the proletarian horse buses that actually dominated the traffic. It is not inherently a mysterious, threatening city: the fogs that are now so strongly associated with the great detective are almost completely absent; the threats and uncertainties are inside the behavior of the people.

Holmes' personality and practices are complex. From the start we are told he has deep medical/scientific skills and has published on topics like the varying ash of cigars and cigarettes, but in fact there is nothing forensic about his detection. He keeps excellent records of crime and can liken a case to others from the past and right across Europe. As a clerical/scientific hybrid he is evidently a hero for the white-collar class. The most famous of his methods is what Conan Doyle calls deduction, examining people's appearances and clothing and from that understanding their past or behavior. Holmes knows Mary Sutherland in "A Case of Identity" is a typist because of a characteristic crease in her plush cuff. There is a link to Dupin's "thought-reading," but this is a much more material practice, apparently close to the diagnostic technique taught by Dr. Bell in medicine at Edinburgh. Philosophers would not call it deduction, which goes from established rules to confident assertions: all swans are white, so that black bird cannot be a swan. Rather, it is induction, working out a rule from the evidence: we have never (yet) seen a swan that is not white, so all swans are white. Martin Priestman points out that the method conservatively embodies "large-scale assumptions about unbreakable social rules" (320).

Memorable as it is, this Holmesian method is never used to solve a case: the detailed reading of the hat in "The Blue Carbuncle" has nothing to do with finding the jewel. The memorable displays are used as scene setting to make a statement about the hero and his methods: very clever, almost mysterious, he somehow understands the lives and problems of ordinary people. Solving a case is much more practical: he will sometimes do research in archives or go off on his own to examine people and places and also visit the scene of the crime with Watson and often sum it all up there. In spite of the tendency in films and television to finish a case back at Baker Street, only six of the original twelve end that way. It is curious that the three detecting techniques—archiving, sole detecting and joint inspection—never all appear in one story but always appear in that order, and this can cause oddities as in "The Boscombe Valley Mystery," where Holmes goes off at night to visit a prisoner so he and Watson can explore together the next day.

These are quite long stories—fifteen thousand words is normal, and in his memoirs Conan Doyle commented that each had enough plot for a novel. They are also quite varied: Holmes' long solitary silences are interspersed with hectic action and his physical ability can be asserted, as when he straightens the poker Dr. Roylott threateningly bent in "The Speckled Band." There is also irony: Holmes can be amusing at times and Conan Doyle entertains us, and himself, with wry titles of untold cases like "The Bogus Laundry Affair" or, famously, "The Politician, the Lighthouse and the Trained Cormorant"— but the actual cases have quite calm, unironic titles.

The story endings in general have a direct summary tone. At first they can be elaborate: the opening one has a lengthy summary; the next two look back to Poe with foreign references. Then they settle to being simple and unintellectual statements of outcomes. Only one of the first twelve stories ends in an arrest ("The Red-Headed League"), and usually Holmes' moral judgment is the key sanction, as when he threatens to beat the fake-lover stepfather in "A Case of Identity" or notes the ironic justice of death by snakebite of the money-crazed bully in "The Speckled Band."

Conan Doyle's growing dislike of the Holmes phenomenon may appear in two of the stories. "The Man with the Twisted Lip," the sixth, is about a missing man, thought murdered by a filthy beggar at a Thameside house. He was a journalist, named, rather nobly, Neville St Clair, who for a story spent a day begging in the city. His vile disguise and his witty sallies from a mouth with a twisted lip brought in that day much more than his wages, so he kept it up the practice, coming in on the train from the suburbs, like any *Strand* reader, and transforming himself each day in the riverside house into a beggar. In the climax, Holmes cleans his face with a sponge. It seems that the man represents Conan Doyle himself working for the *Strand Magazine* in popular disguise and through degrading use of his communication skills earning a fatefully large amount until he is purified. In a parallel way "The Engineer's Thumb" is about a skilled man who is involved with a press, used by coiners, people literally making money by crime. In escaping, his thumb is cut off, an event that might well be seen as symbolic castration.

The second set of stories, published as *The Memoirs of Sherlock Holmes* (1894), are broadly similar to *The Adventures,* though they include more stories dealing with the upper-middle class and can move toward the sensational— "The Cardboard Box" is about an extra-marital sexual liaison and was not reprinted until *His Last Bow* in 1917 (though it did appear in the first U.S. version of *The Memoirs*). "The Yellow Face" was unusual in finding Holmes completely in error—he never worked out that the strange face was a mask to hide a small boy who looked like his American black father. A fuller deferral of Holmes' authority was his death in the last *Memoirs* story, and Professor Moriarty seems to have been invented for this purpose.

In spite of being active with other work, including his visit to South Africa to report the Boer War, Conan Doyle finally gave in to Newnes in 1901 and produced *The Hound of the Baskervilles,* set back before the death. The novella has fine mood pieces about Dartmoor but lacks Holmes for a surprising amount of the action. It raised sales of the *Strand Magazine* so much that Conan Doyle, for the magnificent sum of £100 a thousand words, resurrected Holmes in a series of twelve stories beginning with the notably unenthusiastic title "The Empty House," which were published as *The Return of Sherlock Holmes* (1905).

Parallel to the modernity of Holmes was Conan Doyle's interest in science, with the Professor Challenger series of novels and short stories, starting with *The Lost World* in 1912, often seen as groundbreaking science-fiction adventures. Conan Doyle kept his hand in with a fourth Holmes novella, *The Valley of Fear* (1915), using Moriarty, so also set back before 1893. Structurally modeled on *A Study in Scarlet,* it explains an English mystery through a long sequence about the Irish-American Molly Maguires, here more a ferocious gang than semi-organized labor.

Conan Doyle produced more short stories—some were published in the *Strand Magazine* as "Reminiscences of Sherlock Holmes" and they were collected as *His Last Bow* (1917). There were to be more, gathered in *The Case-Book of Sherlock Holmes* (1927), and the later stories could often show more grotesque detail and sensational crime, as in "Charles Augustus Milverton," a blackmail and murder story, and the somewhat sadomasochistic "The Lion's Mane." Some also responded to the increasingly military nature of British politics, as Holmes worked in the national interest in stories such as "The Bruce-Partington Plans" and "His Last Bow." But to the end the stories showed no lack of invention or confidence of style: some of the latest are excellent, if quite melodramatic, like "The Blanched Soldier" and "The Veiled Lodger."

Well before Conan Doyle finished writing his cases, Sherlock Holmes had become iconic. There were two minor plays in the 1890s and then from 1899 William Gillette, a major figure of the American stage, used a script by Conan Doyle, playing Holmes as something of a dandy to great applause across America and in London in 1901—this may have caused Newnes' growing pressure on Conan Doyle to resume production. The first film was in 1900, with the great detective defeated by a burglar who vanished through the magic of the new medium. Evidence suggests Holmes is the most filmed character in literature, with over two hundred versions on the large screen, including fourteen starring Basil Rathbone in the service of the American effort in the Second World War, only two of them based on the stories by Conan Doyle.

At least seventy-five actors are recorded as playing Sherlock Holmes (including some surprises like John Gielgud and John Cleese). As well as the American war-propaganda series there have been notable adaptations to period: the 1970s saw a myth-testing and socially investigative ironic sequence, including Billy Wilder's inventive and mildly parodic *The Private Life of Sherlock Holmes* (1970), *The Seven-per-Cent Solution* (1976), based on Nicholas Meyer's novel where Sigmund Freud shows himself to be the greater detective, and *Murder by Decree* (1979), in which Holmes tracks Jack the Ripper close to the royal family. The more conservative eighties gave rise to the London Weekend Television series running from 1984 to 1994 of all the stories, starring Jeremy Brett as a dedicated and almost compulsively authentic version of Conan Doyle's hero, but the less respectful twenty-first century has seen TV versions featuring Benedict Cumberbatch as an up-to-date ironic, even postmodern Sherlock, with clear influence from *Dr. Who,* and this has been matched by *Elementary,* stories updated to the world and style of modern American television, with the British actor Johnny Lee Miller as a nervy Holmes and the Chinese-American Lucy Liu as a sometimes ironic female Watson.

Literary responses to Sherlock Holmes have long flourished. Conan Doyle's Canadian friend Robert Barr wrote "The Adventures of Sherlaw Kombs" in *The Idler* as early as 1892 and "The Adventure of the Second Swag" in 1904. Maurice Leblanc produced *Arsène Lupin contre Herlock Sholmès* (1908: in English, 1910, as "Holmlock Shears"), and there have been many pastiches, notably those by Conan Doyle's son Adrian and John Dickson Carr based on some of Watson's comic titles. Recently feminism has had an impact on the tradition with Laurie R. King's "Mary Russell" series about a young woman who becomes the aging Holmes' trainee and partner and also the "Irene Adler" detective series by Carole Nelson Douglas.

A parallel form of honor has been provided by the many people around the world who pay respect to the myth through quasi-serious Sherlock Holmes scholarship. The crime fiction author and expert Monsignor Ronald Knox was one of the first, and a major figure was Vincent Starrett, New York crime reviewer and bookman. Clubs were founded around the world, starting in 1934 with the "Baker Street Irregulars" and including the "Diogenes Club of Dallas" and "The Sydney Passengers," even "The Reichenbach Irregulars" in Switzerland. They and the Holmes scholars are playing elaborate games, but there are still some who take the hero in full seriousness: mail asking for his advice is still said to be received by the bank that now occupies 221B Baker St.

Conan Doyle's capacity in his fiction to probe people's greed and weakness and to shape a bravura mythic response seems to have no direct link to his direct, manly persona. He led a busy public life, being a very good sportsman and a patriot, and was a bastion of the English-Speaking Union, feeling like many at the time that the United States and Britain should patch up their differences and reunite. He reported sympathetically on the controversial British involvement in the Boer War—and believed this was the basis for his knighthood in 1902. In politics he was a committed liberal who twice stood for Parliament, was energetically involved in righting serious miscarriages of justice against two ordinary members of the public, strongly opposed Belgian mismanagement in the Congo, and had some sympathy, short of nationalist violence, with the Irish quest for self-government. He abandoned his family's Catholic religion and from early days was interested in spiritualism, more strongly after his son died in the war and his brother soon afterwards: his well-known faith in some photographs of fairies that turned out to be a hoax is even further from a Holmesian viewpoint.

His private life was beyond reproach. He married Louisa Hawkins in 1885 and they had two children, but before long she was seriously ill with tuberculosis. He was enchanted by Jean Leckie, whom he met in 1897, but they remained chaste, marrying after his wife died in 1906; they had three children. He died at his large country home in Crowborough, East Sussex, in 1930, age seventy-one; his tombstone reads: "Steel True, Blade Straight."

Holmes has been reinterpreted in many ways. Hodgson ("Arthur Conan Doyle [1859–1930]") has suggested Conan Doyle, especially in later stories, uses Holmes as a somewhat interrogative figure, testing English social values. Then the idea has been often floated that he and Watson are essentially a gay couple. But the force of the stories, and the dynamic, often ironic, figure of the great detective, seems to persevere through such redirections. The potent myth depends greatly on the complexities and subtleties of his persona and his relationship with his audience, and also on the skillful invention and variation of both plot and style that Conan Doyle brought to the stories that his publishers—and above all his public—insisted that he create.

References

Barr, Robert. *The Triumphs of Eugène Valmont*. New edition. Oxford: Oxford University Press, 1997.

Belsey, Catherine. "Deconstructing the Text: Sherlock Holmes," in Sir Arthur Conan Doyle, *The Major Stories with Contemporary Critical Essays*. Ed. John A. Hodgson. New York: St. Martin's, 1994, 381–88.

Booth, Martin. *The Doctor, The Detective and Arthur Conan Doyle: A Biography*. London: Hodder and Stoughton, 1997.

Conan Doyle, Sir Arthur. *Memories and Adventures*. London: Hodder and Stoughton, 1924.

Dickson Carr, John. *The Life of Sir Arthur Conan Doyle*. London: Murray, 1949.

Hennessy, Rosemary, and Rajeswari Mohan. "'The Speckled Band': The Construction of Woman in a Popular Text of Empire," in Sir Arthur Conan Doyle, *The Major Stories with Contemporary Critical Essays*. Ed. John A. Hodgson. New York: St. Martin's, 1994, 389–401.

Hodgson, John A. "Arthur Conan Doyle (1859–1930)," in *A Companion to Crime Fiction*. Ed. Charles J. Rzepka and Lee Horsley. New York: Wiley-Blackwell, 2010, 390–402.

_____. "The Recoil of 'The Speckled Band': Detective Story and Detective Discourse," in Sir Arthur Conan Doyle, *The Major Stories with Contemporary Critical Essays*. Ed. John A. Hodgson. New York: St. Martin's, 1994, 335–52.

Knight, Stephen. "'... A Great Blue Triumphant Cloud'—*The Adventures of Sherlock Holmes*," chapter 3 of *Form and Ideology in Crime Fiction*. Bloomington: Indiana University Press, 1980, 67–106.

Nordon, Pierre. *Conan Doyle*. London: Murray, 1966.

Pearsall, Ronald. *Conan Doyle: A Biographical Solution*. London: Weidenfeld and Nicholson, 1977.

Priestman, Martin. "Sherlock Holmes—the Series," in Sir Arthur Conan Doyle, *The Major Stories with Contemporary Critical Essays*. Ed. John A. Hodgson. New York: St. Martin's, 1994, 313–20.

9

The Murder of Roger Ackroyd, Agatha Christie

Agatha Christie is often referred to as "the Queen of Crime." Sales of her books around the world have been recently reported as over 4 billion: the most popular, *And There Were None* (previously known as *Ten Little Niggers* and *Ten Little Indians*), has apparently sold a hundred million copies. She is generally regarded as the leader, ahead of Dorothy Sayers and Margery Allingham, in the clue-puzzle form associated with the English-linked Golden Age of detective fiction. It also had major American voices like "S. S. Van Dine," Rex Stout and "Ellery Queen," and from an apparently pro–American position she and the approach were dismissed as over-conventional and under-realistic by Edmund Wilson in "Who Cares Who Killed Roger Ackroyd?" and Raymond Chandler in "The Simple Art of Murder."

In recent decades Christie's sales have in part depended on the regular use of her work in English-learning contexts—her style is straightforward in structure and simple in vocabulary, ideal for new readers—and to some extent they have benefited from the heritage values found in the British TV versions giving close attention to clothes, cars and décor. But the major basis for her success is as creator of mystifying puzzles that are resolved fairly and sometimes flamboyantly. More recently some commentators, such as Susan Rowland and myself, have argued against the negative views of Wilson and Chandler, claiming Christie deals quite searchingly with the social and personal anxieties of her period, especially issues dealing with gender and the secret interpersonal hostilities of allegedly respectable society.

Christie was born in 1890 to Frederick Alvah Miller and his wife, Clara: he was an American stockbroker working largely in Britain and she came from Northern Ireland, though her father was Captain Boehmer, suggesting German ancestry before his role in the British army. With an older sister and brother,

Agatha grew up in Torquay, a seaside town in the southwest of England. Educated at home, she excelled in music and arithmetic and only attended school for any period when she went to Paris at fifteen for several years of "finishing," which was largely musical study. She was a good pianist but was thought too nervous for a professional career—and music plays curiously little part in her fiction. Her father died in 1901 and though the family income was reduced they still traveled a good deal, spending time particularly in Egypt. When the war started in 1914 she married Archibald Christie, a colonel in the Royal Air Force—it then still had army ranks. She worked first as a volunteer and from 1916 on a small salary in the dispensary of the local hospital and returned to the same activity during the Second World War in London—she always had a professional interest in poisons.

Before the war Christie was interested in writing: her first novel was *Snow upon the Desert*, set in Egypt, and rejected by several publishers. Her sister challenged her to produce a mystery—they had been reading Gaston Leroux's classic locked-room puzzle *The Mystery of the Yellow Room* (1908 in English)— and in 1916 she started what became *The Mysterious Affair at Styles* (1920), itself rejected by several publishers before John Lane accepted it. A classic multi-suspect story with domestic detail and an effective surprise ending (the first person cleared of suspicion is the culprit), this was the first outing for Belgian war refugee and amateur detective Hercule Poirot and his friend, Captain Hastings of the British army. There are resemblances to Holmes and Watson—Conan Doyle was still writing: *His Last Bow* came out in 1917—but Poirot was neither heroic nor bohemian, a fussy figure operating far from Conan Doyle's conflicted London. It seems certain that Christie was familiar with the turn-of-the-century American crime writers like Mary Roberts Reinhardt and Carolyn Wells: the latter summarized their approach in *The Technique of the Mystery Story* (1913) and Christie perfected the clue-puzzle form in the context of English social and gender anxieties.

She would go on to produce thirty-three Poirot novels and twelve with Miss Marple, as well as many short stories involving them. She also used other detectives—Superintendent Battle, a fairly plain policeman; Mrs. Ariadne Oliver, a popular novelist with challenging hair, clearly a parodic version of herself; and, most surprising of all, a supernatural avenger of the dead named Harley Quin—evidently Harlequin: Christie always had an interest in the paranormal. She also, especially early on, produced thrillers, often with rather banal patriotic, even xenophobic, plots, focused on the heroics of a married couple, Tommy and Tuppence Beresford: Tuppence, the wife, was much more dynamic. Merja Makinen is one of the few critics to discuss these thrillers in any detail (424–25). There were also fairly serious romantic novels Christie published as "Mary Westmacott": *Absent in the Spring* (1944) includes thoughtful self-scrutiny.

The Poirot novels were through Christie's career the most popular and in later years she produced them less frequently, even somewhat grudgingly, having grown bored, perhaps even irritated, with her rather arch hero, especially compared with her favorite, Miss Marple—who has gained in popularity as time has passed and women readers have exerted their influence. While the later novels can weaken in focus, with characteristic planning and bravura during the war Christie wrote and put away the final adventures of Poirot (*Curtain*, 1975) and Marple (*Sleeping Murder*, 1976), the latter appearing after her death. Some of her novels are deliberately spectacular, offering what Robert Barnard called "outrageous coups" (47), notably *And Then There Were None* (1939), where the first apparent victim is in fact the murderer, and *Murder on the Orient Express* (1934), where all the suspects combine in a justifiable execution. The novel that first showed her powers to imagine a genuinely startling solution, and also deployed her plotting and writings skills so the shock was lucidly justified, was *The Murder of Roger Ackroyd* (1926).

Crime fiction depends on plot surprises that displace, and so euphemize, the reader's anxiety about the unexpected dangers of the ambient world. These surprises can be quizzical rather than threatening—Poe's Rue Morgue murders were done by an orangutan, not a crazed human; Mary Sutherland's missing fiancé was, Holmes discovers, actually her stepfather in disguise—or they can be genuinely alarming: Sayers' ultra-respectable solicitor in *Strong Poison* and the retarded girl of Chandler's *The Big Sleep* are deeply disguised crazy killers. Christie ramped up anxieties beyond expectation when she disrupted the central traditions of both social order and the novel itself: the murderer of Roger Ackroyd is the amiable, surely reliable, local doctor and—worst of all—the narrator of the novel. Reportedly there was consternation at this ultimate deception: a letter was written to the *Times* giving up Christie as a favorite author; the *News Chronicle* reviewer, presumably annoyed by the trick, called the novel "a tasteless and unfortunate let-down by a writer we had grown to admire" (Morgan, 122). In her autobiography Christie, noting that some people had thought she had "cheated," commented "if they read it carefully, they will see they are wrong" and added that Dr. Sheppard, as both narrator and murderer, "took pleasure in writing nothing but the truth, though not the whole truth" (342).

The book appeared early in 1926 and did quite well—of a print run of about five thousand (the precise details were lost with William Collins' records in the London bombing), some four thousand sold quickly. It was serialized, with illustrations, in the *Evening News,* under the title *Who Killed Ackroyd?* It also had behind it the weight of Christie's new publisher, William Collins, highly professional at publicity and attracting reviews. This was her third Poirot story, and they seemed quite varied. *The Mysterious Affair at Styles* (1920) is a complicated clue-puzzle, with elements of romance, featuring both Poirot and Hastings. *The Murder on the Links* (1923) took them to France and the context of the war, and *The Murder of Roger Ackroyd* brings Poirot, now retired, back to a rural village but without Hastings: the closest to a partner in investigation is Poirot's neighbor Dr. Sheppard. This change was evidently driven by the underlying plot. Christie later recorded that two people had suggested that a Watson could be a murderer. One was her brother-in-law James Watts, the other, from royal circles, Lord Louis Mountbatten, who also offered quite extensive plot advice, which she ignored: forty years later they corresponded about this. In her autobiography she added that her "mind boggled at Hastings murdering anybody" (342), and so Dr. Sheppard was conceived—including his evidently ironic name, a maladjusted shepherd in spirit as well as spelling.

He starts by telling us he has just visited the deathbed of Mrs. Ferrars; that evening he goes to dinner at the house of Ackroyd, her admirer, who wants to see him. She has posted Ackroyd a letter about her blackmailer, but he refuses to read it and Sheppard leaves his study at 8:50. He meets a stranger on the way home, who asks for the Ackroyd house. Later that night Sheppard is telephoned but when he arrives at the house is told no one made the call. Sheppard and the butler force the study door at about 10:30 and find Ackroyd stabbed. He was heard speaking, apparently about business, at 9:30. His niece Flora was seen by the butler leaving the study at 9:45. Footprints are found outside matching Ackroyd's nephew Ralph Paton, who has disappeared.

The police and the new neighbor, Poirot, become involved. Suspicions gather about the residents: The butler looks nervous, and is found to have blackmailed a previous employer. The housekeeper was seen inspecting the cabinet where the murder weapon was kept and is soon found to have an illegitimate son; the stranger Sheppard met, evidently a drug addict, is inherently suspicious. Ackroyd's sister-in-law is short of money and was searching his desk for a will (this scene was on the dust jacket of the original edition).

Her daughter Flora is very nervous and is eventually found to have only pretended to be leaving the study to cover the fact that she had been in Ackroyd's bedroom stealing money. The otherwise upright Major Blunt is known to have accessed money recently, perhaps an inheritance, conceivably through blackmailing Mrs. Ferrars. Ursula Bourne, a maid, argued with Ackroyd the afternoon of the murder, and her previous employer is evasive. This is in fact her sister: Ursula is wellborn but poor, forced into service, then in love with and married to Ralph—hence the row with Ackroyd. Ralph is the major suspect and remains elusive until he appears at Poirot's house at the final meeting of the suspects.

Sheppard has helped Poirot with minor inquiries, and the detective has enlisted the thoughts of Sheppard's sister Caroline, a keen gossip, sharp on most people, including her brother, whom she thinks essentially weak willed. Most of the action is local, in the village and the house, but Poirot makes one mysterious trip to the nearby town, claiming he has visited a dentist, and then he, Sheppard and Inspector Raglan go all the way to Liverpool to check on the stranger who visited the house.

Poirot focuses on a number of apparently minor things. A chair had been moved out of place in Ackroyd's study—the butler noticed, and it was then moved back by someone unknown. From the start Poirot knew Sheppard must have done something extra, as he took ten minutes between leaving the study and reaching the gate of the house: a map clarifies the issue. Poirot is very interested in the phone call apparently telling Sheppard of the murder, and his final piece of evidence is a telegram from a ship to confirm that a sailor, whom Sheppard saw that morning in his surgery, had been asked to ring him late that night. Sheppard pretended it was about Ackroyd so he could get to the study first and put back in his bag the key alibi provider, a dictaphone that he had set so Ackroyd's voice was heard at 9:30: he hid it behind the chair he moved out. After killing Ackroyd, he made the footprints outside with shoes he had stolen from Ralph's hotel that day, and he had then hidden Ralph in a nursing home, persuading him he was under serious suspicion of murder. Poirot's alleged dental trip was to find him there.

After Poirot talks to all the suspects and sends them home, saying the truth will be made public in the morning, he explains to the doctor that he must be the murderer. Sheppard takes this calmly, goes home, and finishes his manuscript, saying that he did blackmail Mrs. Ferrars, he did kill her with veronal, and to save his sister pain he will take the same way out himself.

Christie's self-defense on the charge of "cheating" is fair. Sheppard never tells a lie: he does not reveal what was in his bag when he visited Ackroyd and does not admit what he did between leaving the study and leaving the house—though he does indicate that ten minutes elapsed. We have as much to go on as Poirot, though when he reads Sheppard's account of the case—the manuscript we are also reading—he remarks on both Sheppard's accuracy and also his reticence. The situation is a classic, indeed a literal, instance, of Todorov's famous structuralist argument that there are two narratives in a clue-puzzle: one the fiction constructed by the elusive, fiction-generating murderer, one the true tale slowly assembled by the detective.

It is both a calm, mundane story and also in retrospect a deeply disturbing one, as we share the murderer's thoughts and practices throughout but are almost entranced to believe him. Poirot himself operates in a similarly banal but potent mode. Although when he first appears he is bizarre, throwing a marrow over the fence and speaking in his comic-foreigner mode, he is in action and speech diligent and courteous throughout and places high value on the plain-speaking and unsentimentally realistic Caroline Sheppard.

In crime fiction the detective's methods will always embody the key values that the reading community is encouraged to think can be functional against betrayals and threats, and Poirot's key knowledge, here and elsewhere, rests on careful observation of people, and especially their domestic habits. In a classic moment, when he finds a scrap of linen on a wooden chair in the summerhouse, he says "a good laundry does not starch a handkerchief" (131). It is from an apron: the maid Ursula Bourne has been there, to meet Ralph secretly. When he first appeared in *The Mysterious Affair at Styles,* a key piece of Poirot's detection was to notice that someone had rearranged fire-lighting spills in a jar on the mantelpiece, and here the displaced chair is of great importance.

Poirot's mastery of domestic detail, like his interest in Caroline's thoughts and information, is essentially gendered female. Susan Rowland commented that in *The Murder of Roger Ackroyd* "the reader is alerted to feminine modes of knowledge traditionally marginalized by the law" (22). It is not surprising that Miss Marple developed as Christie's second detective: she commented in her autobiography that Caroline Sheppard was probably the origin of the village gossip turned detective, and Ariadne Oliver later offered a more intuitive kind of female analysis—though she acted in company with Poirot in six of her seven novel appearances, alone just in *The Pale Horse* (1961). Makinen comments on Poirot's unmasculine aspects (418–21) and asks whether this feminizing is an essential critique of the heroic detective like Sherlock Holmes—and G. K. Chesterton had in Father Brown already offered a variant dissent to masculinist confidence. Makinen also notes Poirot's foreign aspect, and Christie also seems to offer through him some implied critique of Englishness. Usually Hastings represents the good-hearted, well-mannered national numbskull who needs the detective's European externalized subtlety to solve the problems he encounters. Here that position is represented largely by the naïve Ralph Paton, though also by the brave but limited Major Blunt, who does at least acquire Flora by the end (no doubt Christie thought the names made an amusing pair), and also by the evidently gauche Roger Ackroyd, manufacturer of wagon wheels and coming from the north, who was unable to gain or even defend Mrs. Ferrars while evidently in love with her.

It is easy enough to comment that while 1926 was the year of the Great Strike and its political tensions were strongly evident in the previous year as

Christie was at work on the book, none of that class-based politics enters this or any other of her novels. But it is also true that within the narrow social range of her work Christie does represent a substantial amount of social and personal anxiety. Makinen comments that Christie brings out "the deadly potential embedded in even the most mundane situation" (417). Her criminals are neither the insurgent foreigners of Sax Rohmer or John Buchan nor yet the lower class who often provide threats in Edgar Wallace. If a Christie villain is a servant, there will be some secret family connection, as in *Sad Cypress* (1940), where the nurse-murderer has links traceable through New Zealand: Georgette Heyer pointed to this tendency towards in-class villainy in her title *Why Shoot a Butler?*

Such evidence as exists about Christie's early readership indicates that public libraries were a major source of her dedicated readers, and these were largely used by lower-middle-class people, especially women, whose social aspirations were, like Conan Doyle's largely white-collar readers, also mixed with anxieties about threats that might be encountered along the path of social and financial self-improvement. Christie's victims tend to be well-established people who discovered some secret enemy to their continued success, very close to them but quite unrecognized. The fact that it is only an outsider, marked in many ways as not one of the tribe, who can resolve the issues of the anxiety is itself a testimony to the extent of the anxiety. Robert Barnard, himself a finely nervous crime writer, said in his conscious tribute to her work that "Christie saw evil in our crimes, our friends, the quiet circle of which we are a part. And perhaps thereby she made us sense it in ourselves" (133). Miss Marple will bring the detecting within the social circle, constructing a reduced tension that may help explain the continuing power of Poirot.

The banality of Poirot's method, like the village-based techniques of Miss Marple, is part of the unsensational, anti-heroic quality of the stories that validates a very English idea of reticence and also a social dislike of vulgarity. Those characteristics are supported by the very identifiable style of writing Christie uses, essentially simple, even banal, and so suggesting a set of values and meanings that are widely shared and available to all of good sense and shared decency. In "'... Done from Within'" I discuss the way Christie's language expresses "simple, shared evaluative categories about people" (123): Sheppard speaks in simple sentences with no attempt at variety of syntax or rhythm, and his comments use a familiar, even cliché-ridden vocabulary. An opening remark is: "To tell the truth I was considerably upset and worried. I am not going to pretend that at that moment I foresaw the events of the next few weeks" (9). He closes his narrative in a similar tone, saying, "And then— what shall it be? Veronal? There would be a kind of poetic justice. Not that I take any responsibility for Mrs. Ferrars's death. It was the direct consequence of her own actions. I feel no pity for her" (368).

The simplicity of language that has made Christie so popular with language learners is also an assertion of the shared values of the novels' observations—and for all his occasional foreignness, Poirot himself can speak in a very direct manner, especially at the crisis: when Sheppard asks, "Are you sure you've quite finished?" he replies, "Now that you remind me of the fact, it is true that there is one thing more. It would be most unwise on your part to attempt to silence me as you silenced M. Ackroyd. That kind of business does not succeed against Hercule Poirot, you understand" (363).

At once brilliantly imagined and dedicatedly banal, *The Murder of Roger Ackroyd* catches exactly both the anxieties and the complacencies of English respectable society. It remains the archetype of the clue-puzzle form, that immensely popular mode that offers fearful personal betrayals that can be traced by simple thoughtful observation. Knowledge is all: there is very rarely any clear punishment of the criminal—the police might finally and discreetly arrive, or as here the penalty may be intrinsic to the story. And equally, the audience's relief is only temporary: this is a serial form and operates as what Freud called a repetition-compulsion; like having the same anxiety-based dream, the readers would be impelled to consume more of the same—and Christie's diligent and steady standard of production fed those drives, and her ability to fulfill such needs made her both very wealthy and highly famous.

This particular novel had other distinctions: it was the first of her books to become a play, in 1928, as *Alibi*—its New York version had the title *The Fatal Alibi*—and then in 1931 it was the first Christie to be filmed. In both instances Charles Laughton played Poirot. Christie thought he was not her idea of the detective but was a very fine actor; in photographs he looks remarkably like Albert Finney in *Murder on the Orient Express*. Though filming Christie can be hard, as the understated clue is easily over-emphasized by the camera, here, when the murderer is no longer the sole narrator, the story comes across as more like her other major works. But it has always been seen as one of Christie's masterpieces: Julian Symons, both author and scholar of crime fiction, said it was "one of her must stunningly original plots" (28) and Laura Thompson described it as a "dazzlingly accomplished book" (157).

There have been other surprises attached to this novel. Unusually for her, Christie played the same trick again, though forty years later, with the low-level layabout narrator of *Endless Night* (1967)—and again completely fooled her audience. A reverse reversal was in Pierre Bayard's book, originally in French, *Who Killed Roger Ackroyd?* (2000), which argued that Christie finally fools us all and that the story clearly means the real murderer to be Caroline

Sheppard, who follows her brother, sees he cannot manage to commit the murder and kills Ackroyd to protect the family name. Sheppard then gives his life to save the sister he loved and back up Poirot's erroneous conclusions.

Equally sensational, and quite as puzzling, were the events of November and December 1926 when, after her husband left her for a woman called Nancy Neele, Christie went missing. Her car was found abandoned late at night, with her belongings in it. As she was the author of the much-discussed *The Murder of Roger Ackroyd,* the press was in a frenzy, and searches were widely held, ponds were dragged—whole pages offered nothing but photographs of the nationwide search, and even Conan Doyle was involved. Eleven days later she was discovered in a Harrogate Hotel registered under the name Teresa Neele, and her return to her family was also covered frenetically. The excitement was good for sales and the power of her long-lasting reputation: the events were covered, largely factually, in the film *Agatha* (1979). Christie was always reserved on the topic, just suggesting a nervous breakdown, but Jared Cade's recent study holds that she wanted her erring husband to be arrested for just the sort of murder she wrote about; the family finds this idea offensive.

Christie went on to vary her technique a good deal. A number of novels from her middle period had apparently playful nursery-rhyme titles (often changed in the United States), but they were still sharp accounts of human betrayals: several good critics feel *Five Little Pigs* (1942) is, though more conventional than *The Murder of Roger Ackroyd,* the finest of them all. She also went on to produce novels about wartime and postwar London, where young people had lives that were freer than in the past but also more shadowed by anxiety, as in *Hickory Dickory Dock* (1955) and *Third Girl* (1966). She married again, a distinguished archeologist, Max Mallowan, and they lived happily and busily, becoming that great rarity, a couple who were separately granted high honors, he Sir Max, she Dame Agatha. She had one daughter, Rosalind, and through her one grandson, Mathew Prichard, whose father, a major in the Royal Welch Fusiliers, was killed in France in 1944.

Christie gave the young Mathew in 1952 the royalties for her new play, *The Mousetrap,* which is, amazingly, still running, in the same London theater. He tends her memory with care and affection and is also a most generous supporter of charities and the public good. The spirit of social order, of responsibility in interpersonal duties, that is at the heart of Christie's fictional values is still observed through the tangible rewards of her astonishing success. The complete series of stories that has now been released by the BBC with David Suchet as a thoughtful, wry, and above all deeply human Poirot is only the present stage in the continuing reign of the Queen of Crime.

References

Barnard, Robert. *A Talent to Deceive: An Appreciation of Agatha Christie*. Revised edition. London: Fontana, 1990.

Bayard, Pierre. *Who Killed Roger Ackroyd?* Trans. Carol Cosman. New York: New Press, 2000.

Cade, Jared. *Agatha Christie: The Missing Eleven Days*. Revised second edition. London: Owen, 2011.

Chandler, Raymond. "The Simple Art of Murder." *Atlantic Monthly,* December 1944, reprinted in *The Art of the Mystery Story*. Ed. Howard Haycraft. Second edition. New York: Carrol and Graf, 1992, 222–37.

Christie, Agatha. *An Autobiography*. London: Collins, 1977.

Knight, Stephen. "'... Done from Within'"—Agatha Christie's World," chapter 4 of *Form and Ideology in Crime Fiction*. Bloomington: University of Indiana Press, 1980.

Makinen, Merja. "Agatha Christie (1890–76)," in *A Companion to Crime Fiction*. Ed. Charles J. Rzepka and Lee Horsley. New York: Wiley-Blackwell, 2010, 415–26.

Morgan, Janet. *Agatha Christie: A Biography*. London: Collins, 1984.

Rowland, Susan. *From Agatha Christie to Ruth Rendell: British Women Writers in Detective Crime Fiction*. London: Palgrave Macmillan, 2001.

Symons, Julian. "The Mistress of Complication," in *Agatha Christie: First Lady of Crime*. Ed. H. R. F. Keating. London: Weidenfeld and Nicholson, 1977.

Thompson, Laura. *Agatha Christie: An English Mystery*. London: Headline, 2007.

Todorov, Tzvetan. "The Typology of Detective Fiction," in *The Poetics of Prose*. Trans. R. Howard. Oxford: Blackwell, 1977, 42–52.

Wilson, Edmund. "Who Cares Who Killed Roger Ackroyd?" *New Yorker,* January 29, 1945. Reprinted in *The Art of the Mystery Story*. Ed. Howard Haycraft. Reprint edition. New York: Carroll and Graf, 1974, 390–97.

10

Strong Poison, Dorothy Sayers

Dorothy Sayers was born in 1893, the only child of the chaplain of Christ Church College, Oxford: her father was a scholarly man and her mother a strong and intelligent woman—her surname, Leigh, was Sayers' second name and she always insisted on it being used, if only as a middle initial. When she was four the family moved to a village church in East Anglia: educated at home, the gifted child was sent to an academically strong boarding school and in 1912 won a prized scholarship to Oxford's most intellectual women's college, Somerville. She loved the world of learning and female friendship and gained a first in modern languages in 1915—but though women were at the university, they were still not admitted to degrees, until 1920.

Sayers did some teaching, in both England and France, but had basically decided to be a writer and was intrigued by crime fiction—in 1920 she drafted a somewhat parodic version of a Sexton Blake adventure, including an aristocratic amateur detective (Reynolds, 171), and by 1921 was working on what became the first of the Wimsey stories, *Whose Body?* (1923). Brother of a duke, rich and languid-seeming, Wimsey might seem an English response to Agatha Christie's Belgian, who had just appeared, but he, too, was a real detective: the monocle also served as a magnifying glass.

This novel was hard to place but was first accepted in New York and Sayers followed with a character-rich but fairly thin mystery, *Clouds of Witness* (1926), focusing on Wimsey's less than intelligent brother. Her next books were more serious. Sayers had many women friends, both from Oxford and afterwards, and some of this experience went into *Unnatural Death* (1927), a rather bleak novel featuring a strong-willed lesbian murderer. In *The Unpleasantness at the Bellona Club* (1928) an old man's murder exposes rifts between those who have suffered war trauma—including Wimsey himself—and those who did not serve but pretend patriotism. Bellona is a classical (and female) god of war, and the title has, as is common in Sayers, ironic impact.

She also produced short stories, usually limited in scope and plot: twelve appeared in *Lord Peter Views the Body* (1928), the year when Sayers combined her crime fiction specialism with her learning. Victor Gollancz, a young radical publisher, wrote asking to become her publisher, and she keenly agreed. His first proposal was that she collect and introduce the best mystery short stories, and her long, scholarly introduction effectively started serious consideration of crime fiction, as well as casting light on her own contribution.

Sayers' approach to the genre is both historical and qualitative. She stresses Poe's role in establishing the patterns but also offers a full account of late nineteenth-century work, discussing many writers who have since been overlooked and laying special emphasis on Willkie Collins—Sayers was the first critic to admire him seriously, though T. S. Eliot would support her in this in his introduction to *The Moonstone* in the same year. Sayers sees crime fiction as a genre that studies the nature of evil, and she is bothered by two ways in which this can be diluted. One is the addition of non-functional romance: she feels a good mystery can be "marred by a conventional love-story, irrelevant to the action and perfunctorily worked in" (105). She also sees weakness in crime stories that are merely mechanical and only create characters to operate like robots in the plot and suggests that soon "the public will have learnt all the tricks" (108). Christie may be the main target of both charges, though a footnote praises *The Murder of Roger Ackroyd* as a tour de force (98).

The opposite to merely tricky and shallow crime fiction is Collins' *The Moonstone,* which Sayers describes as "probably the very finest detective story ever written," praising "its dove-tailed completeness and the marvellous variety and soundness of its characterisation" (89). Characterization seemed crucial to Sayers, and she suggests it holds the future of crime fiction: "A new and less rigid formula will probably have developed, linking it more closely to the novel of manners and separating it more widely from the novel of adventure" (108).

Sayers became, consciously like Conan Doyle, aware of the limits of her successful detective. Her first response was to work on a Wimsey-free mystery suggested by the doctor and author Eustace Robert Barton. This became *The Documents in the Case* (1930): though Sayers apparently wrote the whole text, she granted him, as "Robert Eustace," co-authorship, as he had shared with the earlier woman author L. T. Meade. Esme Miskimmin is one of the few critics to discuss this novel in detail (444–46): with a complex plot and completely written in letters, it looks back to the early novel and the multiple-narrator effect of Collins, but it seemed to reviewers somewhat flat against the lively wit and less detailed mystery plotting of the Wimsey novels, and she never repeated this experiment.

The second anti–Wimsey response was embodied in the plot of the next novel, *Strong Poison* (1930). Later, in her essay "Gaudy Night," she reports having "the infanticidal intention of doing away with Peter; that is, of marrying him off and getting rid of him" (210), seen as a less extreme version of Conan Doyle's response to the annoyance of Holmes. But the 1928 introduction also shows that she thought romance had a place in a novel if it was central and character was also emphasized— *The Moonstone* may, as will be discussed later, be a model for more than just the technical approach in *Strong Poison*. Her epigraph to the novel (not always reprinted) signaled a different connection, quoting from an early English ballad: clearly dying, the son says, "I dined with my sweetheart, Mother, make my bed soon, I am sick to the heart and I fain wad lie down," and she replies, "O that was strong poison, Lord Rendal my son."

As *Strong Poison* opens, Harriet Vane, a mystery novelist, is on trial for murdering her former lover Philip Boyes, also a novelist but writing more prestigious modernist fiction. The prosecution claims that when he visited her for coffee late one evening after dining with his cousin she gave him arsenic. Wimsey watches the trial, apparently because the case was investigated by his friend Inspector Charles Parker: it is a coincidence that Miss Climpson, who runs the informal women's detective agency he supports, is on the jury. He is very impressed by Harriet Vane, who is handsome rather than beautiful, and determinedly truthful, even when it seems to go against her. The judge clearly thinks any woman who would take a lover is a potential murderer, and the defense has to rely on lack of actual proof of where and how he was poisoned—Harriet did buy arsenic, but she insists it was to help her with the plot of a novel.

Like Wimsey, Miss Climpson is convinced by Harriet and holds out against the pressure of other jurors, with some timid support from two others. Wimsey says to the defense barrister "she is a tough, thin, elderly woman with a sound digestion and a militant High-Church conscience of remarkable staying-power" (41–42). As the jury cannot agree, a retrial is ordered, and he visits Harriet in jail to offer his services—but ends by saying suddenly "when all this is over, I want to marry you, if you can put up with me and all that" (49). She says dismissively this is the forty-seventh proposal she has received, and the difficult romance is under way.

Wimsey makes sure Miss Climpson and her staff are available and encourages his friend Chief Inspector Parker to undertake inquiries to see what else Philip Boyes did that night. He visits Boyes' father and hears about his mother's aunt, a notorious actress called Cremorna Garden. Then he tries to visit Boyes' cousin, a lawyer named Urquhart, but he is away visiting a sick relative. As

Wimsey obtains his address from the office he hears a secretary has just left. In this novel Wimsey uses a lot of detective assistance: he sends his manservant, the all-competent Bunter, round to chat to Urquhart's women staff, suggests Miss Climpson install an employee in Urquhart's office and engages his friend the sculptor Marjorie Phelps to take him on a tour of bohemia on the track of Boyes.

The tour allows Sayers to be somewhat satirical of the bright young cultural people of the period, but the women tend to be positive and sturdy spirits, hostile to Boyes and very supportive of Harriet. Bunter discovers that the dinner Boyes ate with his cousin Urquhart was entirely shared and the staff also ate it, except for a jam omelet Boyes himself made at the table and they finished between them. Urquhart has taken considerable care to make sure nothing at the meal was tainted in any way—later, Wimsey calls it "a suspicion-proof meal" (263). He also hears that the rich aunt Mrs. Wrayburn was a former actress who only had time for Mr. Urquhart, hence his visiting her now.

The police have found that Boyes went into a pub after leaving Harriet and while there did take a mysterious white powder, which he left behind but is now lost and is being looked for. At his office, Urquhart tells Wimsey Mrs. Wrayburn had no contact with the Boyes family and he is her only legatee. It is Miss Climpson's colleague Miss Murchison who brings the deed box, but the will is not there—he says he remembers leaving it at home. The next morning Wimsey visits him and reads the will.

The story starts to unfold. Miss Murchison writes to say that Urquhart lost a lot of money in the collapse of the Megatherium Trust recently; Wimsey notices her letter uses the same typewriter as the will, and she ascertains it was bought three years ago, though the will is dated eight years back. After Christmas with the family (when he asks more about his sister's feelings for Inspector Parker and is told by his foolish-seeming but financially skilled friend Freddie Arbuthnot that Urquhart was indeed in the Megatherium Trust), Wimsey in a lengthy and comic scene takes Miss Murchison to the East End to learn lock picking from an ex-burglar he knows. The burglar is now a keen evangelist and hymns are required before the lesson. After a daring piece of burglary, she discovers a letter from the rich aunt Mrs. Wrayburn, formerly Cremorna Garden, giving Urquhart money to invest.

Then Miss Climpson goes to Westmorland and with daring and skill obtains Mrs. Wrayburn's real will, which shares the money between Urquhart and Boyes: in the process Miss Climpson fakes séances with complete conviction. A last piece of female detection has Miss Murchison find Urquhart's secret office safe, with papers showing how he appropriated the money to his own use and lost it—and also a small packet of white powder. The pub has found the powder Boyes took. It is merely stomach medicine, but Wimsey shows Boyes' symptoms over time were linked to visits to Urquhart's and (with Bunter's scientific expertise) that the powder in his safe is arsenic. But how did Urquhart do it?

Wimsey says, "Give me the statutory dressing-gown and ounce of shag" (261) and he sits up thinking in Holmesian mode. In the morning he tells Bunter he has solved it: he has been reading about the Florence Maybrick trial, some toxicology books and A. E. Housman's *A Shropshire Lad*. Wimsey invites Urquhart to his flat and explains how he established resistance to arsenic and then ate without any problem the omelet laced with arsenic. He denies it, and Wimsey says he has just eaten Turkish delight dusted with arsenic powder. Urquhart believes this and tries to escape: Parker arrests him, and soon enough the prosecution withdraws the case against Harriet—but she still refuses Wimsey.

Probably because of her interest in character and tone, Sayers' plots tend to be rather narrow, tending to turn on one device, often medical in origin, like the hemophilia in *Have His Carcase* (1932) or the circumcision in *Whose Body?*, and the clues are not always as well signaled as in *Strong Poison*. Urquhart's hair and skin with potential signs of arsenic eating are noted early, and Harriet's plain-spoken friend Sylvia both stresses them and suggests him as the murderer, feeling he is "too sleek to be true" (101).

Apart from the murder, the other major significance is the Harriet–Peter romance: Sylvia also predicts they were meant for each other. But in their final scene, when Harriet knows she will be cleared, she refuses again to marry him, and so they separate—but romance is not entirely abandoned, Wimsey has spoken sternly to Parker: he and Peter's sister Mary definitely love each other, but he has felt too socially inferior to act. In the last pages Wimsey hears they are to be married. His friend Freddie is also marrying Rachel Levy, whose father, Sir Reuben, was murdered in *Whose Body?*—and the last words of the book are Wimsey telling his brother, after breaking the news about Mary and Parker, that he himself is planning to marry "the prisoner" (282). In her later essay "Gaudy Night," Sayers commented that her plan to use romance to dispense with Wimsey did not work because "I could find no form of words in which she could accept him without loss of self-respect" (211)—Catherine Kenney comments that "she had unwittingly put the young woman into a degrading situation" (156).

This indicates that because Sayers paid serous attention to characterization, as she valued in Collins' work, the idea of marrying Peter off was exposed as simplistic. However, there is in *The Moonstone* a stronger model for the Peter–Harriet pairing. Franklin Blake, the very wealthy young man who is custodian of the stone, is not himself an aristocrat (though his father had gone to law arguing his right to a dukedom) but is a predecessor to Wimsey, being a gentleman who inquires into a mystery and is in love with a suspect (the only other, rather dubious, candidate being E. C. Bentley's Philip Trent from *Trent's Last Case*). When Rachel Verinder is suspected of stealing the Moonstone Franklin vows to investigate and does so with some success, and Harriet's discomfort at Peter's affection seems parallel to, if less than, Rachel's self-agonizing fury over Franklin. The romantic outcome for Harriet and Peter will also be a good deal more complex than Collins' immediately resumed delight, as it will take two more joint investigations, the rather distant one in *Have His Carcase* (1932) and the decidedly romantic interaction of *Gaudy Night* (1935), before Harriet accepts Peter.

Another encounter between a clever young woman and a noble suitor seems behind *Strong Poison:* her own situation and surprise at the overture suggests Elizabeth Bennet's rejection of and slow reconciliation with Darcy in *Pride and Prejudice*. Kenney has noted the similarity in attitude between the two couples (169–70). Other, less far-reaching, literary sources are made explicit as Wimsey solves the mystery by Holmesian overnight thought. A. E. Housman's *A Shropshire Lad* would have provided a reminder of Mithridates, the ancient ruler who protected himself against poison by ingesting sub-lethal doses over time. Wimsey also consults the case of Florence Maybrick, an American whose older English husband was an "arsenic-eater": she served fourteen years for poisoning him, on slender evidence, before returning to America in 1902—she, like Harriet, had bought arsenic, which Florence said was for cosmetic use.

Most readers see Harriet Vane as what Reynolds calls "in many respects a projection of the author" (230): not until *Gaudy Night* will her brilliant Oxford background be revealed, but from the start she is a successful writer of mystery stories, living just around the corner in Bloomsbury from where Sayers owned a flat. Harriet's uncompromising honesty, as well as an element of self-deprecation, might also have been seen as autobiographical features, but a more searching connection arises from her strained relation with Philip Boyes. His idea of modernity expected sex and domestic support without marriage: eventually her feelings for him made her consent. When he later sought to marry her, she was outraged at what she saw as a betrayal.

Sayers was not keen on modernist fiction, but she had a much more personal model, having become fascinated with John Cournos, a Russian of Hasidic Jewish family who both was a flamboyantly modernist writer and made sexual demands on her that she was unwilling to fulfill without marriage. He went to America in 1922, and when in 1924 he himself became married Sayers was both deeply hurt and angered by his irritating inconsistency.

Reynolds comments that Cournos "was revealed as an empty theorist" and Sayers, like Harriet Vane, "had been made a fool of" (131). The presentation, and indeed disposal, of the man she named Boyes—surely implying his lack of manly maturity—seems a novelist's way of responding to such treatment.

B. J. Rahn has linked Wimsey to the novel's quasi-feminist theme as "a model of enlightened male behavior" (54), but some commentators have found him less impressive. Harriet's interest in, and eventual acceptance of, him is often taken as simply a conservative fantasy; Lee Horsley sees "snobbish conservatism" behind the figure (109). In a 1936 New York essay, "How I Came to Invent the Character of Lord Peter Wimsey," Sayers spoke of him as a fantasy reversal of her own poverty, saying, "It relieves the mind and does no harm to anybody" (Reynolds, 230–31). She gave a more sophisticated account in the essay "Gaudy Night," where she agrees he is a "wish-fulfilment" but denies any social or sexual element, claiming that "the essential Peter is seen to be the familiar figure of the interpretative artist, the romantic soul at war with the realistic brain" (219). She goes on to say "Harriet, with her lively and inquisitive mind and her soul grounded upon reality, is his complement—the creative artist; her make-up is more stable than his, and far more capable of self-dependence" (219). Sayers evidently sees herself as a mix of the two and notably resolves their amatory difficulties in the context of her higher educational ideals, in *Gaudy Night*'s Oxford.

Not all have shared this positive understanding of Wimsey. Julian Symons said, "It would be charitable to think that [he] was conceived as a joke" (123) and ultimately sees him as "a portrait of what might be thought an unattractive character" (124). The American Edmund Wilson found him "the dreadful conventional English nobleman of the casual and debonair kind with the embarrassing name of Lord Peter Wimsey ... I had to skip a good deal of him" (392).

The acceptance of a lord as an authority certainly links Sayers back to an earlier world that matches her reverence for both the Anglican church and the mystique of Oxford, but there are ways in which her work responds to the present. The agency that Miss Climpson runs is supported by Wimsey to both target predators on women and also make use of the energy of what appeared "surplus women," the many who worked with skill and energy during the war and were replaced by returning men, and also those were unable to find partners simply through the massive loss of male life. Charles Rzepka sees in this material "the feminist themes of social usefulness and dignity" (162).

It is notable that in *Strong Poison* to free one unjustly treated woman both Miss Climpson and Miss Murchison are brave and resourceful and Wimsey does little more than reflect on their discoveries. This is not a deeply radical position—Miss Climpson is the Anglican church personified and in *Gaudy Night* Miss Murchison is reported as happily married; while Sayers mounts an effective critique of spiritualism, a movement supported at the time by Conan Doyle among others, and mocks religious enthusiasm at the house of the burglar turned lock picker, both critiques come from the heights of her Anglicanism. Less elevated in origin is the evident interest in exposing modern malpractice: Robert Kuhn McGregor and Ethan Lewis explain that the Megatherium Trust would have been a readily identifiable mix of two financial scandals of 1927 and 1929 (82–83).

Religion and learning would become dominant in Sayers' later work, though she did not immediately yield her interest in and power to produce crime fiction. After *Strong Poison* she produced her most classical puzzle in *Five Red Herrings* (1931, in the United States titled *Suspicious Characters*). In Scotland a painter is murdered and his last painting faked after his death—the outcome turns in clue-puzzle fashion on a tube of white paint. Miskimmin suggests this was a response to reviewers who found *Strong Poison* drifted away from the clue-puzzle (443). This lacks Harriet, but in the following *Have His Carcase* (1932) the pair enjoy something of a standoff, and then Sayers produced *Murder Must Advertise* (1933), filled with amusing and interesting details relating to her work from 1922 to 1929 in a London advertising agency and featuring Wimsey as an undercover employee there, again without Harriet, and *The Nine Tailors* (1934), which is for some Sayers' richest work. Still lacking Harriet, it is an effective mystery providing the basis for a rich tapestry of village life, bell ringing and East Anglian drama including a mighty flood—but Edmund Wilson found it "one of the dullest books I have ever encountered in any field" (392).

Sayers followed with *Gaudy Night* (1935) and her final crime novel, *Busman's Honeymoon* (1937), where a rather strained mystery is largely sidelined by the married life of Harriet and Peter. There were some more short stories to come, and a number of letters from the Wimsey family appeared in *The Spectator* in 1940, where Peter is on secret service in Europe—in them Sayers writes war propaganda for the beleaguered British. She did more work in religious mode, including writing plays, which never matched the lucid power or the large audience of those of T. S. Eliot. But she also turned, in both religious and scholarly mode, to her much-admired translation of most of Dante's *Divine Comedy* into supple, coherent and lively poetry, using the difficult rhyme scheme Dante had employed—it was completed after her death by her friend and biographer Barbara Reynolds.

The fine scholarship and vivid writing of the *Divine Comedy* translation are, in their different modes, consistent with the Wimsey stories. The two achievements have left Sayers a major place in both fields, and she has, through her remarkable energy, wit and generosity of spirit, left a strong model for clever, engaged and artistic women—in a centenary essay Carolyn G. Heilbrun, both a professor of English and, as "Amanda Cross," an important crime writer, spoke of Sayers' "great intelligence, the devotion to craft, and above all, the sense of vocation that rings, bell-like, through her writing" (1).

Sayers led a very busy life of remarkable success and often considerable difficulty. The failure of the John Cournos relationship seems to have left her with limited ambitions in personal life, and soon after that she became pregnant by a married man of limited capacity. She told no one at work or at home but in late 1923 took two months off, had a boy, and arranged for him to be raised well by a relative: he also went to Oxford and remembered her fondly. She then married in 1926 an entertaining but hard-drinking journalist, who had been damaged by the war—some of him appears in Wimsey—and with him led a sometimes difficult life until he died in 1950, but kept on working productively.

Sayers' traditionalism and love of a lord have not pleased everybody, and her casual command of deep and wide learning has sometimes been felt ostentatious. She has even been accused of anti–Semitism, notably by her biographer James Brabazon (216–19), but this seems unfair. While her characters can use casually racist language at times, she deeply loved a Jewish man, published happily with Victor Gollancz, and made the trials and courage of the Levy family central to her first novel—Wimsey welcomes one as wife of his closest friend.

A woman of many friendships, notably with clever women, Sayers was probably the most scholarly and the most amusing person to write major crime fiction, and she did a great deal to widen its acceptance. She died in 1957 aged only sixty-four, and while there is probably enough of Peter Wimsey, and even of Harriet Vane, for public consumption, the absence of the life of Wilkie Collins Sayers long planned to write will always be felt by admirers of both these great crime writers.

References

Brabazon, James. *Dorothy L. Sayers: A Biography*. New York: Scribner, 1981.
Heilbrun, Carolyn G. "Dorothy L. Sayers: Biography Between the Lines," in *Dorothy L. Sayers: The Centenary Celebration*. Ed. Alzina Stone Dale. New York: Walker, 1993, 1–13.
Horsley, Lee. *Twentieth-Century Crime Fiction*. Oxford: Oxford University Press, 2005.
Kenney, Catherine. *The Remarkable Case of Dorothy L. Sayers*. Kent, OH: Kent State University Press, 1990.

McGregor, Robert Kuhn, with Ethan Lewis. *Conundrums for the Long Week-End: England, Dorothy L. Sayers and Lord Peter Wimsey*. Kent, OH: Kent State University Press, 2000.

Miskimmin, Esme. "Dorothy Sayers (1893–1957)," in *A Companion to Crime Fiction*. Ed. Charles J. Rzepka and Lee Horsley. New York: Wiley-Blackwell, 2010, 438–49.

Rahn, B. J. "The Marriage of True Minds," in *Dorothy L. Sayers: The Centenary Celebration*. Ed. Alzina Stone Dale. New York: Walker, 1993, 51–65.

Reynolds, Barbara H. *Dorothy L. Sayers: Her Life and Soul*. London: Hodder and Stoughton, 1993.

Rzepka, Charles. *Detective Fiction*. Cambridge: Polity Press, 2005.

Sayers, Dorothy L. "Gaudy Night," in *Titles to Fame*. Ed. Denys K. Roberts. London: Nelson, 1937, reprinted in *The Art of the Mystery Story*. Ed. Howard Haycraft. Second edition. New York: Carrol and Graf, 1992, 208–21.

_____. "Introduction" to *The Omnibus of Crime*. London: Gollancz, 1928, reprinted in *The Art of the Mystery Story*. Ed. Howard Haycraft. Second edition. New York: Carrol and Graf, 1992, 71–109.

Symons, Julian. *Bloody Murder: From the Detective Story to the Crime Novel: A History*. Revised second edition. London: Pan, 1992.

Wilson, Edmund. "Who Cares Who Killed Roger Ackroyd?" *New Yorker*, January 29, 1945, reprinted in *The Art of the Mystery Story*. Ed. Howard Haycraft. Second edition. New York: Carrol and Graff, 1992, 390–97.

11

The Yellow Dog,
Georges Simenon

Georges Simenon is the only non–English-language author who has achieved major world status as a crime writer, with sales challenging those of Agatha Christie. He produced seventy-five novels and twenty-eight short stories about the famous Jules Maigret, over a hundred other detective-free crime novels, which he calls *romans durs,* "tough novels," and around two hundred minor pulp stories, mostly written before he settled in 1930 to be a serious crime writer.

Born in Liège, Belgium, in 1903 and retaining Belgian citizenship all through his wandering life, he left school early, took a range of jobs and settled to work as a reporter, then a writer of pulp fiction, or what he called *littérature alimentaire,* commercial or "food-producing" literature, in both magazines and books. Much of this writing was forms of crime fiction, which was booming in France at the time (Shorley, 36–39) and he used many pseudonyms, a favorite being Georges Sim (which some thought his real name), and perhaps he referred to French crime tradition when he produced a comic newspaper column, "From the Hen Roost," as M. Le Coq (Becker, 32). He enjoyed social life, especially in bars and clubs, and moved to Paris, where he worked busily at both journalism and writing (he produced thirty-four novels and novelettes in the year 1929) and also played hard—including an affair with the newly famous American exotic dancer Josephine Baker.

By 1930 he had used the name Maigret for occasional characters, and when he decided to settle to write something more serious—he called it "semi-literary fiction"—he used that as the name for a police *commissaire*: "chief inspector" is the closest English equivalent. Porter suggests Simenon had in mind Louis Lépine, chief of Paris police before 1914, who "projected an image of efficiency with a genial face and a touch of the common man" (206). As Patrick

Marnham describes, Simenon had difficulty getting these more serious novels accepted (129)—when the publisher Fayard saw the first Maigret, *Petr-le-Letton (The Case of Peter the Lett)*, he said it had "no really good characters, no really bad ones, no leading man, no heroine," and he would lose money, but agreed to publish it (Assouline, 89). Four Maigrets came out together in February 1931, the first books under his own name, and were very successful, so that his income trebled.

In March 1931 he wrote *Le Chien jaune* (The yellow dog), a fine example of how Simenon creates his detective, the people he encounters, and the way in which crime is a deep-seated and largely psychological element in the people of France. It also shows how though he would later locate many novels in Paris, Simenon was always concerned with the whole of the country—Marnham comments that none of the first nineteen novels were entirely set in Paris (134). Here Simenon focuses on a small seaport in Brittany, where he had spent a period writing in the winter of 1930–31. It acts as setting for a conflict primarily of social forces, both invoking the troubled spirit of the time and also involving, as is common in French writing past and present, the mixed promise and threat of America.

The story starts late on a windy November night as a man leaves the café of the Admiral hotel in Concarneau. To light a cigar he steps into the doorway of a deserted house: there is a shot and he falls dead; a large yellow dog comes and sniffs him. A customs guard calls an ambulance. The man is the wine dealer M. Mostaguen, who has been drinking with friends at the Admiral. No one recognizes the dog.

Commissaire Maigret, on assignment for a month at Rennes, arrives the next day with a young inspector and meets Mostaguen's fellow drinkers, Servières, a journalist, Le Pommeret, an aristocratic-looking man, and Dr. Michoux, actually a property dealer, with "a cold hand" (9). Suddenly Michoux refuses to drink and makes the waitress Emma ask the pharmacist to test the Pernod bottle—there is strychnine in it, and later he finds strychnine in the calvados. The doctor seems scared and stays at the hotel. Maigret interviews Emma, who is twenty-four, quite plain but with "glints of pride" (18). She reports that Michoux demands sexual services from her and Le Pommeret does occasionally. She denies poisoning the drink and says Michoux has also asked her that.

Maigret and young Inspector Leroy visit Michoux's vulgar house and see paw prints, traces of enormous boots and remains of food. Back at the hotel the yellow dog is lying at Emma's feet. Servières—whose real name is Goyard—is missing, and the *Brest Beacon* sensationally reports bloodstains in his car, also the yellow dog and a huge man. Paris journalists begin to ring up. Maigret goes to

Servière's house: his wife knows nothing. A teacher tells Maigret people have asked if they have the right to shoot the giant the paper reported.

Leroy tells Maigret the mayor is angry, and Maigret reads Leroy his notes—Michoux is "a degenerate type" (38), Le Pommeret a "Big shot" (39) with little money, Servières a skilled journalist. Then Maigret looks at Leroy's notes: the shot man was a mistake; the poisoning was aimed only at the drinkers; the dog knows the café. Maigret compliments Leroy. The mayor keeps phoning; the yellow dog has been found, shot in the leg; the Paris journalists arrive. The mayor appears, "a very well-groomed elderly man" (49); Michoux seems ill. Le Pommeret is found dead, poisoned with strychnine. The dog has been taken from the hotel.

The next morning people are nervous: the police find the giant, but he breaks the handcuffs and escapes. The mayor demands an arrest and Maigret locks up Michoux. The mayor says, "Bluffing" (62). As Maigret leaves the café, he taps Emma on the cheek. The local superintendent tells Maigret the mayor knows Michoux well, and the two police go to the old tower where the giant was found. He had "SS" tattooed on his hand but was only armed with a knife. At the jail Michoux says Maigret is only doing this to protect him and Maigret says, "Yes indeed" (70).

Michoux says he had a card reading recently: he would die a violent death and should beware of yellow dogs. He is nearly frenzied about the danger he is in, but Maigret sits like "a monument of placidity" (71). Leroy reports Servières has been seen in Brest; Maigret seems unsurprised. Leroy has researched Le Pommeret—his brother is a manufacturer, but he liked "to play lord of the manor" (80). Leroy finds a note in Morse code in his room telling him to come to the roof at 11:00 p.m. with a gun and say Maigret has left for Brest.

From the roof, in the bitter cold, they see, in the empty house, the giant asleep. Emma arrives with a chicken: she and the giant argue, then make up, kiss and leave. The police hear the customs guard has just been shot in the leg. Maigret checks that Michoux is still in jail and then is told Servières has been arrested in Paris. That night at the mayor's fine house, where Maigret "seemed to have the awkward manner of a petit bourgeois" (101), he describes the crimes: tonight's he thinks just a deliberate wounding. For the others, Michoux is a candidate, but Maigret imagines another criminal for all of them called Monsieur X. A nearby house belongs to Michoux; his mother returned today. When Maigret and Leroy reach the hotel Madame Servières is there, saying her husband was misled by the others. She asks if Maigret believes that and he replies, "I never believe anything" (112).

The next morning Maigret, in "very good spirits" (113), searches Emma's room and finds a letter from "Léon" saying he has bought the boat and they will soon be married. Maigret searches Michoux's room and finds blotting paper revealing a letter in Emma's writing arranging a meeting, signed "E." At the jail Michoux says he is ill. Servières arrives, and Mme. Michoux: then the police bring in Emma and the giant; Maigret calls him Léon.

With them all gathered Maigret asks the police to find out what happened to the boat *Belle Emma*, but the mayor says he knows. It belonged to Le Glerec: one day it sailed away (with the young yellow dog aboard) and two months later they heard it was seized off New York, carrying cocaine. Maigret asks Léon Le Glerec to explain what happened. He wanted to pay off the bank loan quickly and marry Emma, but times were bad. Servières, Michoux and Le Pommeret offered him a cocaine shipment to America. After they were taken, he served two years and then more in lieu of the huge fine. A friend he met in jail knew the three had informed against him for a large reward. He was freed and returned, still with the dog, to frighten them, especially Michoux. Michoux says this all has no legal standing.

Maigret says Emma did not know Léon was back or recognize the grown dog. Michoux made her write a letter signed "E"—his name is Ernest—and tied it on the dog's collar, but instead of shooting Léon when he came in response, by accident he shot the wine-dealer. When Maigret arrived he thought the three were frightened and says he put poison in the drink to check that. Servières checked Michoux's house, saw Léon had been there and, before he faked his disappearance, wrote the piece for the *Brest Beacon* hoping people would panic and shoot the giant—but it was just the dog. Le Pommeret was frightened and likely to go to the police, so Michoux poisoned him. Maigret guesses rightly the dog is now dead: Maigret understood Léon wanted to provoke Michoux to attack him and so have him suffer jail, as he did, so Maigret arrested Michoux—who put on the fortune-telling act. On her return, Michoux's mother shot the customs guard thinking that would clear Michoux. Léon met Emma and they went away together. Servières has committed no real crime, and Maigret says he has no charges against Emma and Léon. Michoux will not speak without a lawyer.

After lunch Maigret borrows the mayor's car, takes the pair to a railway station and gives them 200 francs—from his expense account, he says. Emma asks why he claimed to have put the poison in the bottle when she did it, knowing Léon was back and they were after him. "Just an idea" (148), Maigret says; after he drops them he "shrugged his shoulders three times, like a man with a strong urge to make fun of himself" (149). The trial took a year; Michoux defended himself with many arguments and claimed to be dying. He was sent to Devil's Island; his mother served three months. Now Léon is a fisherman and Emma is having a baby.

The figure of Maigret is central to the Simenon phenomenon through his presence and personality, more than his remarks or methods: Pierre Assouline sums him up as: "Plebeian, stable, intuitive, apolitical, suspicious, chaste, neuter, reassuring," and his behavior is not dramatic or heroic: "He likes to eat, drink, and smoke his pipe. He is gruff, discreet, sedentary and not very sociable" (92). It is a paternal image, though Maigret has no children and there are rarely any in the novels: it is the confused citizens, among them always a criminal, whom Maigret supervises in his understanding way. Assouline comments, "Simeon's characters are often second-rate people ... they are rarely optimistic" (345).

Through the stories Maigret tends mostly to watch and listen, occasionally examine rooms, and question people in a relaxed manner. He may at times get advice from specialists, but as Christopher Shorley notes, Maigret "steers clear of technical operations" (43) and "his actions will often seem inconsequential, even incomprehensible, before a conclusion" (44). His ultimate achievement is to identify the criminal by understanding him or her: Assouline notes that "it is by climbing into the suspect's skin that he tracks him down" (93). In this process Maigret uses "intuition rather than logic" (Assouline, 93) and, as Simenon's first major commentator, Thomas Narcejac, said, Maigret "lives the mystery of others, and allows us to live it with him" and he "reads the mentality of the criminal in the tragedy of his solitude" (17).

This is a pattern of crime fiction quite different from that which was proving so successful from Agatha Christie: Bill Alder comments that the Maigret stories offer "exemplary social and psychological portraiture rather than focus in on a 'puzzle' to be solved or an action" (9). Simenon does not follow the British clue-puzzle tradition in completely focusing on a mystery, nor does he just tell a story that reveals all finally in action, the pattern of the American private-eye mystery. Maigret's career is almost contemporaneous in origin with Chandler's detectives, and Dennis Porter comments that both writers combined "an insider's knowledge of the countries they represent with the distance of the outsider" (202).

While there is clearly some overlap between Maigret and Simenon himself—certainly in the pipe smoking and it would appear in the benign but aloof response to human behavior—a key element in the new detective method is that it derives from the French system of justice, and especially the different process of criminal investigation in France. The French legal system dealing with crime is what is called inquisitorial: there will in a major crime such as murder be an "examining judge," like a magistrate or a district attorney who manages the early inquiries, employing police to gather all the appropriate data. This judge will then make a decision on whether the case should go to court, on the basis of a full understanding that includes historical, social and psychological features, not just evidence about the crime. The British and American systems, though having their differences, are both based on an "adversarial" system, where the police and the defendant face each other before a completely neutral judge and jury—and to convict a person there is almost complete reliance on specific, often physical, evidence of guilt.

It is not, as has sometimes been suggested, that the French system assumes guilt and works to prove it: a full understanding of the criminal and the crime is seen as the appropriate activity for the inquirer, and Simenon has filled this role with considerable and innovative power. Pierre Weisz comments that Maigret is "a striking antithesis to the great aesthetes of detective fiction" (176). Large, steady, imperturbable, he is evidently paternal, but he also has the personal and reliable authority that had long been associated with a priest. He sees all, understands all, is not shocked, can always sympathize, and yet also brings people to the final judgment they deserve. The resemblance to the role of the Catholic father is unmistakable, and charitable understanding is a key feature: Weisz comments further: "Every Simenon novel shows that the line is thin between criminal and victim" (182).

But there is also a social meaning, more overt than the underlying priestly function. All of the novels are aware of class distinctions, and it is clear that Maigret, for all his authority, is not from the upper or indeed the upper-middle classes. Assouline's first word to describe him was "Plebeian," of the people, and later he develops this, saying that Maigret is "firmly attached to the social layer from which he had come. Jules Maigret would always be more touched by the distress of the humble than by that of the rich" (93). In *The Yellow Dog*, he is acutely aware of the posturing of the town "notables": the mayor is genuinely upper-class and at his house Maigret behaved with "the awkward manner of a petit bourgeois" (101), not only feeling but also insisting on revealing his sense of not belonging there.

Obviously related is Maigret's sympathy with the hardworking and exploited waitress Emma. He will also treat her giant lover with respect, but Emma is especially important: Maigret comments that there was from the start "one face that appealed to me and I never let go of it" (114). The first English translation of 1939 used this statement for its title: *A Face for a Clue*. His empathy extends to the criminals whom he works out through both his insight into character and his power of observation. When he and Leroy compare their notes, Maigret's are more psychological, calling Michoux "a degenerate type" and Le Pommeret a "Big shot," while Leroy's are about facts, like the dog knew the café. He compliments Leroy because from the start Maigret observes and then psychologizes: as Weisz comments, "the intuitive element does not replace logic, it is part of it" (180).

This process is central to the novel. Maigret knew all the time Emma had poisoned the Pernod and also that the three "notables" were frightened. He saw she was against them; then when the dog that was at the shooting scene came to her and he saw its prints appear with the huge footprints he knew whom they were frightened of. They responded variously in their fear, Servières by faking absence, Michoux by killing Le Pommeret. Maigret presumably locks Michoux up not in fact to protect him from Léon but also to stop Michoux from killing Emma's man, the dog's master.

This process is not in fact as far from Christie as it might seem. In *The Murder of Roger Ackroyd* Poirot's understanding of Ralph's position and his role in Sheppard's plotting is similar to Michoux and Léon (and Michoux is also a criminal doctor); the way Maigret moves towards the proof is also Christiesque—as with the blotting paper and the trick, when because Michoux and Emma share an initial she thinks she is signing for him, but Léon reads it as from her. The final assembling of the participants in the set of crimes is also like the final scene in a classic mystery, though by being in the town jail it does have a professional sense that is wholly appropriate for the police rank and role that Maigret never forgets.

So what can be read as a complicated and strained plot—Stanley G. Eskin finds it "implausible and grotesquely involuted" (87)—actually has an inner coherence arising from Maigret's ability to sense and then trace the falsity of the "notables" who first were cocaine dealers and then set Léon up to enhance their income. Faithless to their fellow Frenchman, they imported American criminality—which an American criminal, Léon's friend, remedied. These notables are well-known in the town as exploiters of the people, chasing ordinary girls other than Emma.

There is also a secondary plot, which commentators seem to not have noticed, concerning the mayor. He is never named, as though his social role is his real identity. He only telephones at first but then calls, takes Maigret to his house, and is present in the final scene—without any crime-linked reason. For some time it is implied that as Michoux's neighbor and colleague in the property business the mayor is the mastermind of the strange activity. But this use of him—like Eddie Mars in *The Big Sleep*—is a distraction: the mayor is a true noble, who has deserved his modern wealth, and his real concern is only the tranquility and order of the town.

Alder has discussed the way in which *The Yellow Dog* explores both the general social and economic tensions in France of the period and also particular difficulties in the region (33–35), and as in much of Simenon's work, especially as he grew older, the mystery plot is used to identify weakness and criminality that are closed related to the modern situation—and through Maigret and figures like the mayor there is a sense that the order of the old days is what is needed again.

The force of that message is borne by the strong simplicity of Simenon's style of writing—something he also shared with Christie, though for Porter "Simenon's deceptively unadorned narrative style [is] like Hammett's and Chandler's" (207). Simenon estimated his own vocabulary as about two thousand words (Marnham, 142): this was originally linked to the needs of his journalism but was also a self-concept of comprehensibility. The simplicity was directly encouraged by popular fiction editors: among his many famous acquaintances was the writer Colette, who was in 1923 editing fiction for the newspaper, *Le Matin*. She liked his work but insisted it should not be "too literary," frowning on adverbs and elaboration (Assouline, 62). Simenon was conscious of his approach, using the term "substance-words" for the language he preferred. Assouline sums up his views:

> Simenon prided himself on using words that ordinary readers could understand. The deeper his art became, the more he strove for simplicity and sobriety, in a kind of quest for purity.... He liked concrete worlds, "table" instead of "furniture," "rain" instead of "shower." He considered these the most effective way of reducing the distance between author and reader [349].

Weisz comments, "Whether it is dialogue or description, a Simenon text seems deceptively simple" (178), and that mix was often evident in the early titles, underlining a key feature as in *The Yellow Dog* or suggesting a key mood as in *The Chinese Shadow*—though, especially after the war, publishers preferred putting Maigret's name in every title, including *Maigret and the Yellow Dog*.

Simenon also routinely established from the start a mood that was caught in a few phrases and often focused by Maigret's response. Assouline comments, "In many of his books climate and ambiance combine with smells to constitute what surely must be called an atmosphere" (344). Simenon was highly aware of this technique and linked it to the French artists just becoming famous in his youth: "What the critics call my 'atmosphere' is nothing but the Impressionism of painting adapted to literature" (Assouline, 344).

Simenon worked methodically and hard: he would draft a novel in eight days, take a few days' break, then revise it in three days. He would fill his pipes and sharpen his pencils before starting each day, to avoid breaks in the writing, then, in what he called "the Simenon factory," would draft up to eighty pages in small handwriting a day. With this approach, between 1930 and 1934 he wrote nineteen Maigrets in what critics call "the first cycle." These remain some of his finest work, covering France and its many concerns and dealing with the life and crimes of ordinary people. As Lucille F. Becker notes (42 and

44), there are very few professional criminals in his novels and Maigret very rarely appears in court—when he does so, much later, the title emphasizes it: *Maigret aux assises* (1960, in English *Maigret in Court*, 1961).

While *The Yellow Dog* is a powerful evocation of a small provincial town, Simenon often dealt as searchingly with human interrelations in Paris. Porter says, "In the Maigret novels, Paris appears mellow, generous, forgiving, a home for millions of very ordinary people as well as for criminals, and is also the capital of civilization" (211). Among the first set is *L'Ombre Chinoise* (The Chinese shadow), best known in translation as *Maigret Mystified* (though it also appeared as *The Shadow in the Courtyard*). Set almost entirely in the Place des Vosges where Simenon and his wife had been living, it charts complex relationships among a group of people in the same apartment block and in their past lives, and the outcome is, as common in Simenon, based on a set of coincidences and misunderstandings that only Maigret can penetrate and comprehend.

After this varied and lastingly powerful set of novels he paused in 1934, concentrating on the more ambitious *romains durs* in a period when he still worked for newspapers, traveled widely, and spent the large sums he was earning for Maigret. In the last of the first phase, simply titled *Maigret* (*Maigret's Return* in English), as he has Maigret retired he probably planned an end to the series, but the *commissaire* reemerged in 1939. This was perhaps to ensure income as the war approached and Simenon now had a son—though Narcejac sees a deeper reason: "In age and experience he had caught up with his hero" and "he had realised that Maigret was really his own self" (118). This new work did not appear until 1942 and 1944, and the difficulties of wartime publishing led him to concentrate on drafts of his largely autobiographical novel *Pedigree* (1948), about which the great French writer André Gide advised him.

Simenon and his family sought to live quietly in occupied France, but this was not easy: on one occasion he was harassed by the authorities who thought his name was really Simon and so Jewish—his mother managed to find documents disproving this. There have been several reports that he was accused of, even found guilty of, collaboration, linked to either local accusations or his involvement with a German-run film company, but Marnham's well-researched biography firmly denies this (218–19), arguing that if Simenon was concerned about anything in 1945 it was the new vigor of the communist-led left. Whatever the detailed reasons, he was not comfortable in postwar France, and left for America in 1945 and did not return for twelve years: in this period he produced another eighteen Maigret titles, starting with *Maigret in New York* (1947), and many other non–Maigret novels.

He also separated from his wife, Régine, and married a French-Canadian, Denise, from whom he would split with some hostility by the 1970s. However much they shared central values, Simenon's personal life was the opposite of Maigret's. The character lived quietly with his calm wife, valued a pipe and beer, and hoped to be home in time for dinner, but his author loved social life, plenty of drink, and also women. His two sons, one by each wife, seem to have coped satisfactorily, but his daughter seemed fixated on him, led a troubled life and eventually shot herself. Apparently to resolve some of these conflicts Simenon was drawn more and more into autobiographical writing and formally abandoned fiction in 1972: he said he had been a slave of his characters, but "now, I am trying to understand myself" (Becker, 34).

When he died aged eighty-six he was one of the great names in crime fiction: he had been spoken of in France for the Nobel Prize, but that went to his friend and mentor, and author of literary fiction, Gide. But Simenon's status survives. Apart from the massive sums earned from his writing, the huge number of titles, and many associated films, he gained the honor of bringing into the present world with maturity and literary power the long-standing tradition of French crime writing.

The strength of French crime writing today, one of the most sophisticated and politically incisive versions of the international genre, owes a great deal to the man who both was and was not Maigret and who showed that disciplined, unostentatious writing about human beings and the ease with which they can drift into crime was a way of both fascinating many people and making a fine career as an author.

References

Alder, Bill. *Maigret, Simenon, and France: Social Dimensions of the Novels and Stories.* Jefferson, NC: McFarland, 2013.
Assouline, Pierre. *Simenon: A Biography.* Trans. Jon Rothschild. New York: Knopf, 1997.
Becker, Lucille F. *Georges Simenon.* Boston: Twayne, 1977.
Eskin, Stanley G. *Simenon: A Critical Biography.* Jefferson, NC: McFarland, 1987.
Marnham, Patrick. *The Man Who Wasn't Maigret: A Portrait of Georges Simenon.* London: Bloomsbury, 1992.
Narcejac, Thomas. *The Art of Simenon.* London: Routledge, 1952; as *Le Cas Simenon,* Paris, Presses de la Cité, 1950.
Porter, Dennis. "The Case of Simenon," chapter 10 in *The Pursuit of Crime: Art and Ideology in Crime Fiction.* New Haven: Yale University Press, 1981, 202–15.
Shorley, Christopher. "Georges Simenon and Crime Fiction Between the Wars," in *French Crime Fiction.* Ed. Claire Gorrara. Cardiff: University of Wales Press, 2009, 36–53.
Weisz, Pierre. "Simenon and 'Le Commissaire,'" in *Art in Crime Writing: Essays in Detective Fiction.* Ed. Bernard Benstock. New York: St. Martin's, 1983, 174–88.

12

The Big Sleep, Raymond Chandler

Raymond Chandler was born in Chicago in 1888. His father, Maurice, a hard-drinking railway engineer, left the family when Raymond was seven. His mother, Florence, from a professional Protestant Irish family, took him to London when he was twelve, and his uncle paid for Raymond's education at Dulwich College, a high-quality private school. Especially good at mathematics, when in 1907 he sat for the British civil service examination he came third overall and top in classics—to do this he had taken British nationality, which his mother had retained. He joined the Admiralty but disliked it and left after six months. He worked briefly as a journalist and also sold poems, essays and reviews to London literary journals: the poems are basically late romantic "Georgian," but Tom Hiney's biography printed one in brand-new modernist style with prophetically ironic realism.

In 1912 Chandler borrowed money from his uncle to return to the United States; his mother soon joined him in Los Angeles, where he was deploying his math skills as a bookkeeper. He was less than settled and after the United States entered the war in 1917 joined the Canadian army: he said he felt at home in a British uniform, and it was the Gordon Highlanders, with kilt. He served in the trenches, became a sergeant and on at least one occasion was buried after an explosion. Apart from the rather different history of Terry Lennox in *The Long Goodbye,* these experiences do not enter Chandler's fiction, though Tom Hiney links the explosion to Marlowe's frequent unconsciousness in the stories and also suggests this was the start of Chandler's serious drinking. After returning to America he worked as an accountant, was promoted to a lucrative position as an oil company executive, and met Cissy Pascal, seventeen years older but extremely attractive and vivacious. After Cissy divorced her husband, Chandler's mother, who was living with him, opposed their marriage, but after she died in 1923 they soon married. He was involved in some major activity in the oil business, but he eventually attracted trouble for drinking and absenteeism, both apparently including female colleagues. In 1932 he was sacked and took up writing fiction—even taking a prose-writing course, though he never stopped writing poetry. He started publishing for *Black Mask* magazine, where Dashiell Hammett was one of the leaders of what is routinely, and naively, called "tough-guy" private-eye writing.

This tradition in America goes back a good way, to J. B. Williams' 1865 stories about "Jem Brampton the New York detective" and crime adventures published under the name Allan Pinkerton, beginning with *The Expressman and the Detective* (1874). By 1900, crime stories appearing in "dime novels" had become very popular, with heroes like Nick Carter, whose adventures were still being published in the late twentieth century. This figure is often seen as being an urban version of the frontier and cowboy hero: he was usually engaged in fighting some form of corruption, though elements of sexism and racism were also prominent. After the war *Black Mask*, started in 1920, was the leading example of monthly serials, selling for as little as 15 cents, which specialized in fast-paced action stories, with simple, dramatic illustrations. Joseph Shaw, known as "Captain," was from 1926 the editor, famous for liking work to be direct. In "The Simple Art of Murder" (1944) Chandler talked of Hammett as "giving murder back to the people who commit it," as if he were a social realist, but also finding the detective's response heroic: "Down these mean streets a man must go who is not mean, neither tarnished nor afraid" (234). Chandler saw this as both admirable and truly American, while the English-style clue-puzzles were stagey and unrealistic, mocking especially the fairly soft target of A. A. Milne's only crime novel, *The Red House Mystery* (1922). In a later essay, "Casual Notes on the Mystery Novel," Chandler found the English form based on "a fluky set of events" and said that at her best, in *The Murder of Roger Ackroyd,* Christie offered "dishonesty," albeit "rather cleverly explained" (63 and 67).

When he was out of work in 1932 Chandler apparently split his time between driving around California and slowly writing drafts of Hammett-style stories—though at this time, he later said, he also synopsized and rewrote an Erle Stanley Gardner story to work out the way he handled plotting. His first published piece was "Blackmailers Don't Shoot" (1933), a complicated narrative about tough but also honorable guys. The detective's name, Mallory, connects with King Arthur (as written by Sir Thomas Malory) and also seems close to Marlowe, as well as predicting the knight-linked opening of *The Big Sleep* and the general "knight-errant" character of Chandler's version of the Californian private eye. Commentators have also noted that Dulwich College's most famous early graduate (with now a schoolhouse named for him) was Shakespeare's contemporary Christopher Marlowe. But early on Chandler used a range of heroes, with several appearances by John Dalmas and Carmady, more Hammettesque than the talented and always somewhat sensitive Marlowe: Chandler also, as Leroy Lad Panek records (407), used other names that seem playful, like Delaguera (of the war?) De Ruse (a joke?), Anglich (English?) and even the Marlowe-like Malvern.

The plots of Chandler's early stories deal primarily with corruption in the mode of Hammett, whom he only met once, at a 1936 *Black Mask* dinner. But fairly soon the crimes and the motives become more a matter of personal betrayals, often by younger figures, usually women, and the older male figures tend to be corrupt or unable to control events, in need of the detective to restore order and punish the guilty. Julian Symons found the early stories rich in cliché and the real wit a later product (26), but they still read very strongly, being wry, dramatic and substantial—almost all well over fifteen thousand words.

There is a direct link between the short stories and the novels because Chandler very unusually created all but one of his early novels from combining short stories. This was a careful and very effective process, which, with characteristic irony, he called "cannibalization." *The Big Sleep* (1939) starts up reusing "The Curtain," about a rich woman's missing husband, O'Mara; her son, his stepson, is the murderer. This is interwoven with "Killer in the Rain" about a troubled young woman named Carmen who gets involved with a blackmailer: her father will finally be killed trying to rescue her. In the novel Carmen leads both plots, taking the role of the murderous stepson in "The Curtain." There are also single Vivian Sternwood scenes taken from "Mandarin's Jade" (her visit to Marlowe's office) and "Finger Man" (winning at the casino). The novels that rapidly followed and built Chandler's reputation, *Farewell, My Lovely* (1940), *The Lady in the Lake* (1943) and *The Little Sister* (1949), all used this "cannibalization" process, the exception being *The High Window* (1942), which only used one early story, perhaps why it is comparatively dull. The more extended *The Long Goodbye* (1953) is original, after its opening sentence from "The Curtain," and *Playback* (1958) was originally written as a film script without Marlowe and was quite late reworked to include him—but strangely is the only Chandler novel never filmed.

The "cannibalization" method has been taken to support the myth that Chandler was not very interested in plotting, because he said himself he focused on character, and critics continue to feel that it was a sign of plotting weakness (Panek, 409). But Chandler valued structure: he thought *Farewell, My Lovely* his best because "the bony structure was much more solid" (in a letter to Dale Warren, his Boston publisher, see Chandler, *Raymond Chandler*

Speaking, 224) and of *The Little Sister* he said critically "there is nothing in it but style and dialogue and characters. The plot creaks like a broken shutter in an October wind." (letter to Hamish Hamilton, his UK publisher, *Raymond Chandler Speaking*, 270) The "cannibalization" method itself tends to make the plots more multiple, with many switches of action and location that add to the density effect.

Chandler published *The Big Sleep* in 1939 with Knopf, Hammett's publisher. It was a prestigious-looking hardback, not in any way "pulp" fiction, though they did link it in their advertising with Hammett and James M. Cain, the two major crime writers they had published in the recent past. It sold moderately well, about ten thousand copies in a year. Only one reviewer, from California, really liked it, and of the first four reviews Chandler saw, as Philip Durham reports, two found in it "depravity and unpleasantness" (33). It was in fact a challenging novel, with some drugs, a youthful sex addict/mad killer, and a gay pornographer/blackmailer. Yet it is hard to see how so many people missed the style and authority the novel exudes from the start as Marlowe is calling on a million dollars up above their oil wells.

Rusty Regan has disappeared, allegedly with the wife of casino-owner and gangster Eddie Mars. Regan was a former IRA commander and experienced bootlegger, known always to carry $15,000 on him: General Sternwood misses his lively company and Rusty's wife, the beautiful and demanding Vivian, asks Marlowe if finding him is why he was hired—he won't say. In fact, the general has received IOUs for gambling debts for his other daughter, Carmen: he paid before, to Joe Brody, and asks Marlowe to look into it.

This is the plot of "Killer in the Rain," but with a Carmen who is now young and fake innocent: she has already pretended to faint in Marlowe's arms. He goes to the bookshop run by Geiger, the debt holder: a dumb blonde and a good-looking boy are there. Marlowe sees it runs a pornography racket and, later, at Geiger's house finds him shot and Carmen drugged and naked, giggling in front of a camera missing its plate holder. He returns her home and the next morning is called to see a Sternwood car driven off a pier: the family chauffeur is dead, with a bruise on his head, as if he has been sapped.

The next day, in heavy rain—a famous Los Angeles scene—Marlowe revisits the shop to find the books being moved out to Joe Brody's apartment. Vivian is waiting at his office with nude photos of Carmen and a demand for $5,000. When Marlowe visits Geiger's, Carmen is there and Eddie Mars arrives—he owns the house. Marlowe won't tell him who has the books.

The blackmail-pornography plot moves fast. At Brody's flat, Marlowe finds the bookshop blonde, Agnes. Carmen arrives and, assuming rightly Brody is behind the photos, tries to shoot him in revenge. Marlowe gets her gun and chases her off. Brody says he saw the chauffeur leave after shooting Geiger, sapped him, and took the plate holder from him—the chauffeur then drove off to the pier. The bell rings again; Brody opens the door and is shot dead. Marlowe (who now has the photos) chases the shooter, the boy from Geiger's shop, who thinks he has avenged his lover Geiger. After a fight Marlowe rings the police, turns the boy in, and explains it all as two linked murders, without mentioning the Sternwoods. Next morning's papers are also silent about the family but praise the police highly. The general's butler rings, thanking Marlowe and promising a check for $500; but Marlowe says he is not finished. The Regan case is still open; Marlowe has already visited Missing Persons and is also being tailed.

That night he goes to the casino to see Mars, who says he is not tailing him, and Marlowe rejects payment for keeping him out of the Geiger case. Vivian is there winning heavily. Outside, Marlowe sees a Mars henchman steal the money back and sticks him up for it, pretending his pipe is a gun. He and Vivian go for a drink, kiss, and argue; he leaves her at home and at his apartment finds Carmen naked in his bed: he dresses her and turns her out, angry and hissing.

The next day, still in the rain, Marlowe stops the car tailing him. It is Harry Jones, who knows Brody and is now with Agnes: she knows where to find Mona Mars, who has been linked to Regan. When Marlowe comes to an office to buy the information, he hears Canino, Mars' hit man, is there. Harry gives Canino Agnes' address (a false one), then accepts a drink and dies of poison. Marlowe meets Agnes and gives her $200 for Mona's location. He drives there, in Realito, and when right by the house bursts two tires; at the nearby garage is Canino, who knocks Marlowe out. He wakes handcuffed and tied, with Mona Mars. She wears a silver wig, as she cut off her hair to prove her love to her husband. After a while she frees Marlowe, except for the handcuffs. He waits outside for Canino and shoots him. Mona undoes the handcuffs and they separate; she kisses him with cold lips.

At the DA's office Marlowe explains; they think Eddie killed Regan. Marlowe hears the general wants to see him. It is only five days since Marlowe first went there; he has Carmen's gun with him. The general offers him $1,000 to find Regan. Carmen asks for a shooting lesson. She and Marlowe go down to the oil sump and he sets up a target. She shoots at him, hissing. But he has put blanks in the gun, and she faints, wetting herself. Back at the house, he tells Vivian that when Carmen shot Regan, also for rejecting her, Mars, at Vivian's request, hid the body, probably in the sump. Mars sent the IOUs to see if the general knew about Carmen's crime; as he didn't react, Mars had been waiting for Vivian to inherit the money to make a big hit. She offers Marlowe

$15,000—the Regan pocket amount—and seems attracted to him. He refuses both her and the money and tells her to institutionalize Carmen. Vivian agrees; he leaves, thinking of the old man soon to join Regan in "the big sleep" (220). Marlowe has a few drinks and thinks about silverwig but never saw her again.

In "The Simple Art of Murder" Chandler offered Hammett and the American private-eye story as postwar realism, exposing real crime on real streets. But in *The Big Sleep,* though blackmailers like Geiger and Brody and gangsters like Mars prey on women and the wealthy, the ultimately criminal force is the crazed Carmen, much darkened from the mildly wrongdoing lead in "Killer in the Rain." Later novels would show glamorous, sexually active women as a deadly force, from torch singer turned millionairess Velma Grayle in *Farewell, My Lovely* through to the manipulative murderer Eileen Wade in *The Long Goodbye.* They threaten the detective, both in person and also because he seems in a substantial way a double for the victims—Rusty Regan has a manner like Marlowe and the general likes them both; Moose Malloy in *Farewell, My Lovely* chooses him as a drinking partner and is shot in Marlowe's bedroom; in *The Long Goodbye* Roger Wade is a Chandleresque drunken novelist who sees Marlowe as his only friend.

Joyce Carol Oates, writing in the *New York Review of Books* in 1995, thought the pattern of female killers unacceptably misogynist, but an American school of male thought accepts the "corruption as theme" reading. Peter Rabinowitz argued that the women killers offer only incomplete solutions to the plots and the novels still realize the pressure of crime and corruption. If so, why do the gangsters have benign-sounding names like demigod Eddie Mars or, in *Farewell, My Lovely,* Laird Brunette, musical-comedy-style? Sean McCann has argued that *The Big Sleep* is "an allegory of economic predation" in which "the vernacular energy of the white ethnic falls prey to the economic elite" (166), and he sees the thrust of Chandler is "the New Deal liberating a form of populist democracy" (152). This patriarchal patriotism seems less than convincing when you reread about Carmen hissing and cutting loose with a pistol: as Lee Horsley comments, the "forces of urban criminality operate more as background than foreground" (*The Noir Thriller,* 39).

More widely recognized is the novel's power to realize the space, sprawl and conflicting forces of the first modern megalopolis. Marlowe drives everywhere–chapters often start with an elaborate Angelino address as Chandler projects Hammett's close reading of San Francisco over greater distances. In *City of Quartz* Mike Davies recognizes this influential reading of the developing social agglomeration of southern California but also, tucked away in a note, says that "Blacks, Asians, [and] 'greasers'" are a "target of Marlowe's dislike" (91, note 42). It may be fairer to say that Chandler represents the racially separate worlds of the huge city rather than consciously down-values some of the citizens: in *Farewell, My Lovely* there are positive African Americans and also cautious ones, none of them as malevolent as the white criminals, and by *The Long Goodbye* Chandler is presenting with some vigor the Latin element of the region.

Less severe than Oates on gender is Gill Plain, with a view shared by numbers of women readers: she sees Chandler as producing "narratives of besieged masculinity," which outline "the paradoxical vulnerability of men in patriarchal society" (57). Plain's reading can recycle the highly wrought qualities of style that women readers usually admire at least as much as men—including Oates in her otherwise negative account—and explains, perhaps a little generously, how dangerous sexualized women seem to the story and, it appears, to Marlowe: he tends to like well enough less up-front females like helpful secretaries and librarians.

The confident, self-assertive style is a major feature, from the start of Chandler's writing career, and that of *The Big Sleep*. Symons implicitly criticized the approach by calling it "basically sentimental aestheticism" (23), but most have been impressed by Chandler's power to interweave a poet's insights with vigorous action. In *The Big Sleep* he first realizes the double voice of the hero: clipped and defensive to other characters, insightful and sensitive to himself, so shaping perfectly the double consciousness of the all-feeling, all-resisting hero of tough fiction and film. Panek outlines the richness of the similes that Marlowe uses in his private voice (410–11) and also suggests that he is "more psychological than physical" (408) and suffers more harm than he causes. In all, he is a very sensitive kind of tough guy.

In spite of its richness, the novel brought in little more than the stories. Hiney estimates an income of $2,000 from eighteen thousand copies sold, far less than Hammett and Cain had been making. *Farewell, My Lovely* came out in 1940 and sold less well—Blanche Knopf thought its title too weak for crime fiction. It was received in general with reviewing indifference, as was *The High Window* in 1942. Knopf still believed in Chandler's quality and was not willing to sell his work to the pulp publishers as too degrading, but when they finally did that in 1943 *Farewell, My Lovely* took off and sold nearly half a million at 25 cents. Presumably linked to this, in the same year *The Lady in the Lake* did much better than the previous two hardbacks—and then a major financial corner was turned for Chandler.

Paramount were looking for someone to script James M. Cain's *Double Indemnity* for Billy Wilder's direction and selected Chandler, at $750 a week. With his mix of irony and arrogance he fitted poorly into studio life but is credited with making *Double Indemnity* the first film to challenge the timid

Production Code, which banned sex, drinking and even criticism of authority, by implying through its dialogue a real, sensual adult world. He worked on some very minor films, then produced his original script for *The Blue Dahlia,* a searching story of returned-soldier trauma, which he insisted on doing at home, with great quantities of drink, though this may have been in part a deliberate tease. He left Hollywood to return to novels in 1946 but in 1948–49 produced on commission a thriller script, *Playback,* without Marlowe and in 1951 was lucratively invited back to work on Highsmith's *Strangers on a Train,* though he and Hitchcock found it hard to agree.

Commentators feel Chandler had a major influence on the development of film noir, the dark but also witty and self-confident crime action style that still reverberates today, so it is appropriate that one of its major events was the 1946 Warner Brothers film of *The Big Sleep* starring Bogart and Bacall, directed by Howard Hawks, with a script by William Faulkner and Leigh Brackett, a rare woman scriptwriter and interesting crime fiction writer. Chandler thought Bogart was an excellent Marlowe, saying he "can be tough without a gun" and had "a sense of humour that contains that grating undertone of contempt" (Hiney, 162). There is a "Chandler-couldn't-plot" myth: much favored by journalists, that Hawks and Faulkner contacted Chandler to find out how Owen Taylor, the chauffeur, died, and Chandler said he couldn't remember. The novel is quite clear: after shooting Geiger, Taylor was sapped by Joe Brody and then drove to the pier to kill himself; it seems very likely Chandler, in the script business himself, felt Hawks and Faulkner might earn their huge salaries by reading the novel to find out.

The film was ready by 1945, but Warners was keen to get all its war movies out to the public before it was too late and waited till 1946 for release, when it also inserted some scenes wavering between comedy and sexiness, featuring Bacall in particular, to exploit her now-public relationship with Bogart—Vivian has more positive action with Marlowe in the film and is less dubious a figure. Chandler's story was already in any case quite heavily censored. In the film there are no drugs or nudity, Geiger is not gay, the book business is not clearly pornographic and most of all the final blame is not placed on the youthful murderess, Carmen, but—as many in the novel suspected wrongly—on Eddie Mars, who is finally shot by his own men. A different form of closure affected *Farewell, My Lovely:* late in the process the studio decided that Chandler's title sounded like a musical, so they foisted on the rather convincing Dick Powell as Marlowe the feeble title *Murder, My Sweet* (1944), though Horsley calls this the "most canonically noir" Chandler film (*The Noir Thriller*, 35). Chandler was less lucky with the earlier version of *Farewell, My Lovely,* which just dropped Marlowe and used the plot about George Sanders as "the Falcon" in

The Falcon Takes Over (1942); *The High Window* was also weakly filmed twice, as *Time to Kill* (1942) and *The Brasher Doubloon* (1950).

Chandler's views of Hollywood survive in the ironic, even bitter, *The Little Sister* (1949). His last major novel, *The Long Goodbye,* was published in 1953. This is longer than previous ones and is widely held to be more "sentimental," especially in Marlowe's friendship with the weak but interesting Terry Lennox and late fling with rich beauty Linda Loring. But the sentimental can carry introspection: Terry Lennox, who has had war trauma, and Roger Wade, the hard-drinking novelist, seem projections of Chandler himself, and for the first time there are both bad and good women who are highly sexualized, not the mix of harpies and good dull girls of the earlier novels.

In the 1950s Chandler spent time back in Britain: his first visit was a difficult month with the now aged and fragile Cissy; then after her death in 1954 he spent longer periods there, when he was much feted, including by famous writers (Stephen Spender, Ian Fleming, Evelyn Waugh) and literary women—Natasha Spender (the poet's wife), Sonia Orwell (widow of the great man), Helga Greene (former wife of Graham's brother). Chandler fell in love, or perhaps romance, with those three and others. He came close to marrying both his secretary, Jean Fracasse, and his agent, Helga Greene, but finally withdrew to La Jolla. Though ill and drinking heavily, he was still writing: his last Marlowe story, "The Pencil," appeared in 1957, he turned *Playback* (1958) into a Marlowe novel, the sparest and least misogynist of all, and started *The Poodle Springs Story* about Marlowe's married life with Linda Loring. Robert B. Parker, a major follower and understanding critic, made a good job of completing it in 1989.

Though he still had loyal friends and now held a high position in terms of wealth and prestige, being a major figure in world literature rather than just crime fiction, especially in England, Chandler's last couple of years were largely uncertain and unhappy, though he still wrote to many people his wry, witty, learned letters. He drank more and more and was involved in at least one bungled suicide attempt, with a gun, and he died early in 1959.

Chandler's unusual mix of a very powerful, idiosyncratic prose voice and a very narrow range of subjects and settings—Jane Austen and Ivan Turgenev may be the only real parallels—has made him a potent force in the world of literary fame. Very many writers have followed his approach, the best of them with significant areas of innovation like Ross Macdonald's insertion of deep family psychology or James Lee Burke's transmutation to a resonant New Orleans setting. Chandler's novels continue to be filmed, though never reaching the bravura level of *The Big Sleep* or even the calm menace of *Murder, My Sweet*. Most abiding of all is the image of the "tough guy" arises more potently from his stories than those of its originator, Hammett, as iconic as that of Sherlock Holmes: the trilby hat tilted forward, the trench-coat collar turned up and—in the past at least—wreaths of cigarette smoke rising past Chandler's great gift to world culture, the tense profile of the intelligent, courageous, witty, morally focused private eye.

References

Chandler, Raymond. "Casual Notes on the Mystery Novel," in *Raymond Chandler Speaking*. Ed. Dorothy Gardiner and Kathrine Sorley Walker. Reprint edition. Berkeley: University of California Press, 1997, 63–70.

_____. *Raymond Chandler Speaking*. Ed. Dorothy Gardiner and Katherine Sorley Walker. Reprint edition. Berkeley: University of California Press, 1997.

_____. "The Simple Art of Murder." *Atlantic Monthly*, December 1944, reprinted in *The Art of the Mystery Story*. Ed. Howard Haycraft. Second edition. New York: Carrol and Graf, 1992, 222–37.

Davies, Mike. *City of Quartz*. London: Verso, 1990.

Durham, Philip. *Down These Mean Streets a Man Must Go: Raymond Chandler's Knight*. Chapel Hill: University of North Carolina Press, 1963.

Hiney, Tom. *Raymond Chandler: A Biography*. London: Chatto and Windus, 1997.

Horsley, Lee. *The Noir Thriller*. Second revised edition. London: Palgrave Macmillan, 2009.

_____. *Twentieth-Century Crime Fiction*. Oxford: Oxford University Press, 2005.

McCann, Sean. *Gumshoe America: Hard-Boiled Crime Fiction and the Rise and Fall of New Deal Liberalism*. Durham: Duke University Press, 2000.

Oates, Joyce Carol. "The Raymond Chandler Case." *New York Review of Books*, December 21, 1995.

Panek, Leroy Lad. "Raymond Chandler (1888–1959)," in *A Companion to Crime Fiction*. Ed. Charles J. Rzepka and Lee Horsley. New York: Wiley-Blackwell, 2010, 403–14.

Plain, Gill. *Twentieth-Century Crime Fiction: Gender, Sexuality and the Body*. Edinburgh: Edinburgh University Press, 2001.

Rabinowitz, Peter. "Rats Behind the Wainscoting: Politics, Convention and Chandler's *The Big Sleep*." *Texas Studies in Language and Literature* 22 (1980): 224–45.

Symons, Julian. "An Aesthete Discovers the Pulps," in *The World of Raymond Chandler*. Ed. Miriam Gross. London: Weidenfeld and Nicholson, 1977, 19–30.

13

The Talented Mr. Ripley, Patricia Highsmith

Patricia Highsmith was described in 1972 by Julian Symons as "the most important crime novelist at the present time" (205). Her work is both highly finished and intrinsically disturbing; the Irish writer Brigid Brophy spoke of it as "excellent" and "a persistent challenge" (Klein 170). Highsmith remains very highly regarded in Europe but still has relatively little fame in America, though her novels brought to a head two important variant traditions of crime fiction whose strongest examples were American, the crime novel and the psychothriller.

Always in essence an outsider, Highsmith was born in Texas in 1921 but moved six years later to New York with her family. She grew up feeling distant from her mother and stepfather and close to her bookish grandmother (Highsmith, 22–23). From an early age she was only attracted to women, and she soon left America, returned several times, and then from 1963 made her home in Europe. With a strong, even eccentric personality, she combined rudeness and generosity to her many friends, preferred animal to human company, and loved her work as a writer, keeping notes of feelings and ideas in her *"cahiers"* (notebooks). She produced twenty-two novels and eight books of short stories (one of each posthumous), and there are many other early stories and unpublished drafts.

As a child she read widely, including her grandmother's books on human identity and early psychology (Thomas, 326). She found *Moby-Dick* captivating and would at times call herself Ishmael, the outsider—and survivor—who tells that story. Highsmith studied at Barnard College, mostly literature and writing, and for five years worked as a writer of superhero comic books. She wrote and published successful stories starting from her college days and in 1946 won a prize in *Harper's Bazaar.* Her first novel, *Strangers on a Train*

(1950), was developed under the advice of the young Truman Capote and finished at the New York State writers' center at Yaddo—to which she left most of her wealth, $3 million. Rejected, Highsmith said, by six publishers (Reynolds, 99), the novel was well reviewed and sold quite well, but the crucial breakthrough was when Hitchcock bought it—she later complained for too little; Bran Nicol reports the figure as only $7,500 (504)—and, after Raymond Chandler worked on the script, the film appeared to great acclaim in 1951.

The novel set out Highsmith's lifelong challenge to conventional attitudes. Two men meet on a train, the respectable Guy Haines and the disreputable Charles Bruno (for some reason critics, and Highsmith herself, use the latter's surname, the former's first name). They discover they would both like to be rid of someone: Haines' wife and Bruno's father, so Bruno suggests they should murder each other's problem and no one will ever connect them. This mix of casual events and complete lack of conventional morality will recur through all of Highsmith's work. Haines thinks it is a joke, then his wife is killed, and he goes through with the bargain. Finally, Bruno is drowned and Haines gives himself up; the film was weaker in that Guy did not commit murder, but against the bland morality of Hollywood even the euphemized version seemed powerful, and Highsmith's career path was set.

Her agent urged her to write something similar; what she produced was *The Price of Salt* (1952), the story of a lesbian love affair that had a happy ending—this was innovative at the time, and the book sold well, under the pseudonym "Claire Morgan"; it was in 1984 republished as *Carol* under Highsmith's name. She continued her determined originality by not writing any more about women in major roles, important though they were to her as friends and lovers. One of her most remarkable achievements among women writers was to present male attitudes and anxieties with complete conviction. She turned back to murder in the potent context of accident and amorality, but having used a nervy dissenter from suburban society to imitate a murder in *The Blunderer* (1954), she then condensed the villain and the naïve figure into one person, in a lighter but not less testing spirit, as the basis for her first creation of her one recurrent hero, with whom she apparently felt a real bond, Tom Ripley.

The Talented Mr. Ripley (1954) is not a mystery in the conventional sense: as Margaret Caldwell Thomas comments, Highsmith "owed practically nothing to the great puzzle-makers and their detective heroes" (329). We know what is done, and by whom: the issue is both why did Ripley do all that and what will happen to him as a result, if anything? The crime novel is usually seen as part of American postwar realism. James M. Cain's *The Postman Always Rings Twice* (1934) explores the development of a crime, but its sympathy is firmly contained by the story being presented as a convicted man's reminiscences. In his *Double Indemnity* (1943), based on a real murder, the same process of intriguing attraction and recurrent sense of wrong is offered, though here the killers end in a suicide pact. When Hitchcock bought *Strangers on a Train* he no doubt saw the connection with this tradition—especially as *Double Indemnity* had been a very successful film, with a script by Raymond Chandler.

The Cain style of crime novel may empathize with the criminal but also imposes some form of law. Overlapping with Highsmith is a stronger pro-criminal voice, Jim Thompson. In *The Killer Inside Me* (1952) a troubled but also resourceful criminal seems to act out the audience's sadomasochistic fantasies as well as his own dark plans, which include some Ripley-like fakery; he is not caught, but his own sanity starts to fail. If Highsmith was attracted by a story that foregrounded the criminal, she did not imitate the brutality and near pornography that Cain and Thompson relished but developed the psychological, identity-focused complexity evident in the sub-genre, as Malmgren shows in his discussion of this as a crime novel (160–63).

Julian Symons values Highsmith as what he calls a "crime novelist": he had special interest in what is sometimes called the "whydunit," or, better, the psychothriller. Its first major author was Anthony Berkeley Cox, an Englishman working in the 1930s, who would describe the murder in the opening chapter and then steadily explain it all. The psychothriller pattern was developed by the American Margaret Millar: after three entertaining mysteries with a detective called Paul Prye, she produced *Wall of Eyes* (1943) and *The Iron Gates* (1945). The first unfolds a past murder using a police detective but also placing considerable weight on psychology, and the second moves into the mind of a woman who has murdered her husband's first wife, grows more and more tormented by the memory, and eventually kills herself. These are very unlikely not to have been noticed by the young Highsmith, but she takes the pattern in a calmer, more satirical direction. Preferring to write about men and adding to Millar's model the Henry James–like idea of an American leaving for Europe, in 1954 Highsmith produced *The Talented Mr. Ripley*. It took only six months: she said, "No book was easier for me to write, and I often had the feeling Ripley was writing it and I was merely typing" (Highsmith, 76). She did, though, elaborate the plot: it originally started with Ripley murdering the older Greenleaf and in an early draft he wanted to travel from Italy to Paris with coffins full of drugs, but such casual melodrama was removed (Schenkar *The Talented Miss Highsmith*, 341–42).

The novel opens with Tom, twenty-five years old, drifting about in New York without plans for life. He amuses himself by writing to people on Tax Office paper he took while briefly working there, pretending they owe a modest amount. He does not try to cash the checks they send, but when a man seems to be following him at night he assumes he is about to be caught. But from the start chance is kind to him: it is the father of a casual acquaintance, Dickie Greenleaf, who wants Tom to go to Europe and persuade Dickie to return to a useful life in the family factory. Tom instinctively lies to suggest he knows Dickie better than he does, flatters the family, and is soon on his way to Italy, expenses paid.

Tom is basically asocial but would like contacts: he is horrified by the large party that farewells him on the ship, then weeps to receive a "bon voyage basket" from the Greenleafs. In the ship's library he looks, unsuccessfully, for Henry James' novel about a young man sent to Europe on a mission to persuade someone to return—Tom misnames it *The Ambassador*, not *The Ambassadors*. He writes to his aunt, his only relative alive, and recalls how she mocked him as "a sissy" (36). He belongs nowhere; he has no masculine confidence.

After an enjoyable boat trip and train trip through Europe, Tom eventually finds Dickie in Mongibello, south of Naples (based on Positano): he is with a girl called Marge and is rather distant, but Tom slowly manages to becomes friendly with him. Marge suggests Dickie is too interested and that Tom is probably gay. Dickie is handsome and charming, in a facile way, wears ostentatious rings and is a poor but ambitious painter. The two men travel about together: a trip to Paris is planned, and skiing in Cortina. They are the same size and alike in appearance and Tom buys clothes similar to Dickie's. One night when they take a cab, as Tom pays, Dickie says to him, "Thank you, Mr. Greenleaf," and "Tom felt a little weird" (59).

Tom exchanges letters with Mr. Greenleaf, who is cross that Dickie is not returning at once, and Marge grows more irritated with Tom. When he sees the pair kissing one day he goes up to Dickie's room, dresses in his clothes and pretends to be strangling Marge. Dickie comes in and is angry. He calms down, but when Tom proposes they should go to Paris in two coffins that an acquaintance is sending—the third will be full of dope—Dickie rejects this as stupid and Tom sees in his eyes "nothing more than he would have seen if he looked at the hard bloodless surface of a mirror" (78). They go to San Remo and take a boat: Tom feels Dickie has no interest in him now, realizes they are completely alone, and kills him with an oar, weights his body with an anchor, and, after nearly drowning himself, sinks the bloodstained boat with stones.

He has removed Dickie's rings and goes back to Mongibello, telling Marge that Dickie is in Rome, wants to stay for the winter and has sent him to fetch his belongings. Tom takes all Dickie's clothes and his typewriter and in Rome forges a letter to Marge saying he, Dickie, is working with a painter and wants a break; she replies affectionately. Tom writes to Mr. and Mrs. Greenleaf as

Dickie, has a very good time in Paris, dressing and behaving like Dickie, takes a flat in Rome in his name, signs for his allowance and puts Marge off in another letter. One day, as Tom has just packed Dickie's cases and clothes to go to Majorca, Freddie Miles turns up at the flat, the man whose ski party Dickie did not attend. Tom has previously realized he should have forged a letter of apology. He says Dickie is out to lunch: he worries Freddie might recognize Dickie's clothes, then sees him looking at Dickie's silver identity bracelet on Tom's wrist. He kills Freddie with a heavy ashtray, then supports the body, as if he is a drunk, to the car—a man sees them—and dumps the body on the Appian Way.

The police call and ask Tom, as Dickie Greenleaf, when Freddie left the flat, and there is news coverage. The police have now found the bloodstained boat and think Tom Ripley may be dead, but he, still as Dickie, says he has seen him since then in Rome. Marge arrives and he manages to avoid her. He feels he can alternate between being Dickie and Tom and escape: "It all seemed simple and safe. All he had to do was weather the next few days" (153). The police allow him to go to Palermo: he plans to travel on to Greece. Marge writes to Dickie there, saying she realizes he is avoiding her and she is giving him up and returning to the United States. He forges a long, dull letter to Dickie's mother and enjoys Palermo, though he begins to feel lonely.

The police come looking for Tom in Palermo, with no result. Dickie's bank doubts some signatures and when the Rome police demand he, as Dickie, return to answer questions about Tom "This was the end of Dickie Greenleaf, he knew. He hated becoming Tom Ripley again, hated being nobody"(164). He sends Dickie's things to American Express in Venice and heads there himself—only keeping the rings. He buys a car and spends a night in it, so he can say that was what Tom has been doing. He sees in the Venice papers that the police are seeking Dickie about the disappearance of Tom Ripley, so he buys a pair of glasses and goes to the police as Tom, explaining he has been traveling around since late November and did not know they were looking for him.

Next he decides to forge Dickie's will, leaving everything to him: "Now that was an idea" (182). As Tom, he writes to Marge and Mr. Greenleaf to tell them Dickie was depressed and may have killed himself. Both of them come to Venice: Mr. Greenleaf is easily persuaded Dickie may be dead, and Marge eventually is—especially when she finds his rings in Tom's house. He thinks he is going to have to kill her and gets a shoe "to use the wooden heel of it as a weapon," but she decides Dickie "either killed himself or changed his identity—didn't he?" (216). Mr. Greenleaf has hired a detective, but he is not very skillful and speaks little Italian. Tom has made friends in Venice and with one of them, an Englishman named Peter, upsets himself through imagining traveling back with Dickie and becoming good friends with Mr. and Mrs. Greenleaf.

When Dickie's bags are found in Venice and the fingerprints match those in the flat in Rome. Tom expects to be arrested, as happens frequently in the novel. But the flat was in Dickie's name, the police are sure the prints are his, and he packed the bags and shipped them from Palermo to Venice himself: the police have no reason to take Tom's fingerprints. So he heads off for his long-planned journey to Greece, and when he calls at American Express in Athens there is a letter from Mr. Greenleaf acknowledging Dickie's will is in Tom's favor. He takes a cab and when the driver asks in Italian where to go the novel ends: "'To a hotel please,' Tom said. 'Il meglio albergo. Il meglio, il meglio!'" (249)—"'The best hotel. The best, the best!'"

This happy ending to a story of death and deception epitomizes Highsmith's challenge to and fascination for her readers—and explains why she can be too strong a taste for those dependent on conventional morality. Crime fiction rarely has a happy outcome as here: if there is some final comfort, as for Franklin Blake and Rachel Verinder in *The Moonstone,* there is also a grimly miserable one to match it for the criminal Godfrey Ablewhite. The crime novels of Cain and Thompson end in a regretted but nevertheless firm assertion of law and order in some form.

Ripley, whose talents are celebrated in the title and whose pleasures are carefully detailed, is someone whose anxieties and successes we are made to share and approve: a later novel will be simply called *Ripley's Game* (1974). Highsmith does not present him for simple reader identification in the first person; rather, she subtly merges the narrator's perspective with his, so that, as with the essential vulgarity of Dickie and Marge or the appeal of southern Europe, we experience things simultaneously with him and can hardly avoid sharing much of his view of life, including conventional morality. As Kathleen Gregory Klein puts it, Highsmith "draws her readers into recognizing themselves in most of the character's action and behavior" (195). At the same time, as Nicol comments (508), the calm, reportage nature of the style makes us assent to what happens and instinctively empathize with the in fact shockingly disruptive Ripley.

Himself, he swings between fearing capture and manifesting an unrealistically calm confidence, but circumstances absolve him and he never suffers the pangs of conscience. His only grief is lost pleasures, as when he nearly weeps to think of not being able to have a pleasant time with Dickie and his parents—not noticing this is because he has killed one and deceived the others. Behind the text is Highsmith speaking as a recurrent and persistent dissenter. At conservative Barnard College she was interested in communism but soon found it a limiting code; she rejected most aspects of American naïve self-belief, being particularly dismissive of both consumerism and neo-imperialism, and felt Europe was freer and more cultured.

Just as she had felt Ripley wrote the book, Highsmith shared his detachment from banal normality: occasionally she signed herself as Ripley (Wilson, 194). At one level his antics amused her: she said "to mock lip-service morality and to have a character amoral, such as Ripley, is entertaining" (Reynolds, 101), but she could also see the conflict more seriously, writing in her "cahier" for 10.1.54 that her purpose was "showing the unequivocal triumph of evil over good, and rejoicing in it. I shall make my readers rejoice in it too" (Schenkar 2013, 206). This is not pure anarchy but a determined interrogation of the basis of value: Klein comments that "she does not accept the legalistic notion of justice" (172) and in his introduction to her first book of short stories, *Eleven* (1970), Graham Greene found she created "a world without moral endings" (Thomas, 329).

Highsmith was always a deep reader and serious thinker and her conception of Ripley can be understood in philosophical and psychological terms. She read about identity very early among her grandmother's many books (Thomas, 326–27) and around 1950 (Wilson, 158) studied Kierkegaard's account of the human ego being constructed only through external responses, just like Ripley's ideas of culture and value. This idea evidently appealed to Highsmith's evaluatively restless mind and responded to her experience as someone who fitted poorly into the conventional world of family, gender and employment. In this respect she worked in parallel to the French existentialists—which might in part explain her later success in France and Germany—and she was aware of how Camus and Sartre represented the embattled persona in a world where consumer objects and naïve beliefs had replaced the previously dominant structures of religion. Andrew Wilson suggests a direct link with this culture (91–3) in her knowing the French-American Julian Green's novel, *If I Were You* (1949, in French 1947), in which a young man changes bodies with the person of his dreams. Highsmith certainly knew his earlier work, saying in her 1943 diary, in French, "I sense an exceptional friendship with J. Green ... I almost recognize my own thoughts" (Wilson, 91), but Joan Schenkar's biography challenges the idea she knew this particular novel (*The Talented Miss Highsmith*, 170).

The instability of the ego, the serious basis for Ripley, can also be read in psychological terms. Ilana Shiloh suggests that Marge and Dickie play for Tom the role of mother and father (and that Highsmith may advert to this sexually in Dickie's name) but more searchingly proposes that the scenes when Ripley looks into a mirror, either real or metaphorical, and finds his identity merging with Dickie respond to Lacan's account of developing what passes for identity. This is more elusive than the simple idea of setting free his deeper urges: as Tony Hilfer notes, Ripley's behavior is "not the triumph of the id but the evasion of the superego" (128). Some have felt Tom is schizophrenic in his assumption of Dickie's identity, but he is both more elusive and more negative than that—he is essentially a sociopath to other people in general and in private a psychopath, with all the uncertainty that brings.

This blurring of identity links with Highsmith's idea of the limits of American social values: Ripley's developing sense that European culture is richer and deeper than that of America is strong and was certainly shared by Highsmith. Shiloh even suggests that Dickie's murder is presented as a version of a brave American frontier-style self-defense (70): Horsley more generally sees "his rebirth as a 'true American,' another parodic version of the American success ethic" (117), and argues that "Ripley's ability to be another self brings into focus the falsity and superficiality of the social judgements that confer status and respectability" (118). Most commentators would agree with Schenkar that "Highsmith invested her creative capital in the dark side of the American Dream" ("Patricia Highsmith," 200). Where Henry James' Lambert Strether eventually returns to America better at making moral judgments through his European experience, Ripley remains loose, out there in Europe, inventing schemes and deceiving people and living the life of an apparently highly successful modern man.

The writer Highsmith most admired, all through her life, was Dostoevsky (Schenkar *The Talented Miss Highsmith*, 170 and 258), who also wrote crime fiction from the viewpoint of the criminal and without imposing any social constraints. She did not use the same kind of angst and intensity, but his concept, most fully realized in *Crime and Punishment*, that the criminal mind is worth exploring and may in some ways be an admirable alternative to dull and repressive normality is something that she brought to life a century later.

Highsmith produced eighteen more novels after *The Talented Mr. Ripley*, though rather surprisingly she reports in her book on suspense fiction that she often had to rewrite substantial elements of them and some were even rejected: almost all of the difficulties seem to have been with editors in America. Most of her later novels represent the ease with which normal-seeming people can slip into crimes, usually murder, though they lack the strange charm of Ripley, as if Highsmith censored her imagination somewhat. She still usually focuses on men, but *Edith's Diary* (1977) explores a woman whose distaste for banal morality leads not to murder or crime but to becoming an obsessive diarist, like Highsmith herself. At times she would let her novelist's respectability slip and burlesque human folly in extravaganzas like *Little Tales of Misogyny* (1974), in which women are represented as cruel brutes and treated in appropriately savage ways, or *The Animal Lover's Book of Beastly Murder* (1975), where each story celebrates an animal who sends a human to a well-deserved death—*"Beastly"* in the title is finely ironic. Reviewers often found these stories unacceptably dark, just as friends sometimes thought Highsmith's behavior wildly erratic and disturbing—and not only when she had been drinking.

She remained intermittently faithful to Ripley and relocated him in *Ripley Under Ground* in 1970 as an apparently successful American businessman, married in a routine way to a Frenchwoman and living in comfort in her country. But he is operating a major art scam: the fine painter Derwatt has died, so Ripley employs a forger and puts out that Derwatt has become a recluse in Mexico. When people become suspicious, Ripley either kills or outwits them, recurrently appearing as other people, including Derwatt himself. There were three more of these novels at intervals, and the fifth, *Ripley Under Water* (1991), was the last she saw published—*Small g: A Summer Idyll* (1995), which returns both playfully and ironically to the gay world, was just posthumous. Ripley's later outings remain startling, if not as challenging in terms of identity as the original novel: Symons feels Ripley's "exploits verge on the ridiculous in the later books" (208), but the series remains teasingly interrogative—Ripley hangs a real and a fake Derwatt on his wall and prefers the forgery—and also a serious celebration of the resemblance between criminality and success in the modern world.

Highsmith remained in Europe till her death in 1995, though she retained her American citizenship, however much she criticized her country. She was finally recognized in the United States as a major writer, but her sales there never matched those in Europe: this is usually assigned to her rejection of conventional morality, though she also would not engage in American publicity. Twenty films have been made of her work and after the initial *Strangers on a Train* they were all outside America. *The Talented Mr. Ripley* was filmed in 1960 as *Plein Soleil* ("Full Sun," in English *Purple Noon* and other titles) in 1960, with Alain Delon as a Ripley who is extremely handsome (he seduces Marge) and was admired by Highsmith, though she disapproved the police finally catching up with him. He eludes capture in the 1999 film directed by Anthony Mingella, which had distinctly glamorized characters, and Ripley both sleeps with and kills the Englishman from Venice. Wim Wenders' *The American Friend* (1977) reworked *Ripley's Game* with Dennis Hopper, whom Highsmith did not like, as Ripley (Schenkar *The Talented Miss Highsmith*, 345), and the Italian Liliana Cavani filmed it under its own title in 2002, relocated to Italy and much altered in plot: not a great success, it was never released in American cinemas.

Admired by major writers such as Graham Greene and Brigid Brophy and friends with incisive social critics such as Arthur Koestler and Gore Vidal,

Highsmith was a major figure in many ways. Her life seems a mix of personal upheavals and totally dedicated commitment to the art of writing. As Klein commented, Highsmith's art is "challenging the readers' self-image of safe innocence and protective, benign behavior" (196). Nobody has combined credible social detail and underlying moral chaos as she has done, and nobody in crime fiction has written so complete and compelling a critique of the everyday conventions of the morality and social order that so much of the rest of the genre unquestioningly supports.

References

Highsmith, Patricia. *Plotting and Writing Suspense Fiction*. London: Poplar, 1983.
Hilfer, Tony. *The Crime Novel: A Deviant Genre*. Austin: University of Texas Press, 1990.
Horsley, Lee. *The Noir Thriller*. Second revised edition. London: Palgrave Macmillan, 2009.
Klein, Kathleen Gregory. "Patricia Highsmith," in *And Then There Were Nine ... More Women of Mystery*. Ed. Jane S. Bakerman. Bowling Green: Popular Press, 1985, 170–97.
Malmgren, Carl. "The Pursuit of Crime: Characters in Crime Fiction," in *A Companion to Crime Fiction*. Ed. Charles J. Rzepka and Lee Horsley. New York: Wiley-Blackwell, 2010, 152–63.
Nicol, Bran. "Patricia Highsmith (1921–1995)," in *A Companion to Crime Fiction*. Ed. Charles J. Rzepka and Lee Horsley. New York: Wiley-Blackwell, 2010, 503–9.
Reynolds, Moira Davison. "Patricia Highsmith," in *Women Authors of Detective Series: Twenty-One American and British Writers, 1900–2000*. Jefferson, NC: McFarland, 2001, 98–103.
Schenkar, Joan. "Patricia Highsmith," in *The Cambridge Companion to American Novelists*. Ed. Timothy Parrish. Cambridge: Cambridge University Press, 2013, 199–208.
_____. *The Talented Miss Highsmith: The Secret Life and Serious Art of Patricia Highsmith*. New York: St. Martin's, 2009.
Shiloh, Ilana. "Subversive Doubles: Patricia Highsmith's *The Talented Mr. Ripley*," chapter 3 of *The Double, the Labyrinth and the Locked Room: Metaphors of Paradox in Crime Fiction and Film*. New York: Lang, 2010, 57–75.
Symons, Julian. *Bloody Murder: From the Detective Story to the Crime Novel: A History*. Revised second edition. London: Pan, 1992.
Thomas, Margaret Caldwell. "Patricia Highsmith: Murder with a Twist," in *Women of Mystery: The Lives and Works of Notable Women Crime Novelists*. Ed. Martha Hailey DuBose. New York: Dunne, 2000, 326–39.
Wilson, Andrew. *Beautiful Shadow: A Life of Patricia Highsmith*. London: Bloomsbury, 2003.

Part III
Diversity

14

Cotton Comes to Harlem, Chester Himes

Chester Himes is a major American author of crime fiction, but he only turned to the genre in mid-career, at the suggestion of a French editor after moving to Paris. Other surprises emerge. Essentially a Californian, Himes made his reputation as a writer about crime in Harlem, New York; a radical black writer, he dealt in aggressive comedy and satire, including about black people; he was for long more famous overseas than in the United States: Stephen F. Soitos comments that Himes was "largely unknown to American readers during most of his lifetime" ("Chester Himes [1908–84]," 475).

Himes was born in 1909 in Jefferson City, Missouri, to basically middle-class parents, both involved in education: as James Sallis describes, they moved a good deal, had serious disagreements, and eventually divorced. After being expelled from Ohio State University for misbehavior, Himes turned to crime and at nineteen was jailed for armed robbery. He started writing in prison, he said as a way to gain respect from guards and fellow prisoners, but it was still a very tough life—including being involved in the deadly Ohio Penitentiary fire in 1930. He began to publish stories and after he was paroled in 1936 worked in California, including in a shipyard, and kept writing. With the help of the Harlem Renaissance writer Langston Hughes, Himes wrote novels about the black situation, starting with *Black Sheep,* which almost reached publication in 1939 but was ultimately rejected and did not appear, in rewritten form, until 1952 as *Cast the First Stone* (Muller, 7): this was a cut version, and the full text did not appear until 1998 as *Yesterday Will Make You Cry* (Soitos "Chester Himes [1908–84]," 476). In this period Himes continued to suffer racial hostility and his work was often poorly received. A 1947 review of *The Lonely Crusade* said the main character and the author were both psychotic (Soitos *The Blues Detective,* 132), and he was increasingly unhappy about racism in

America (Margolies and Fabre, 73). After *The Lonely Crusade* was translated into French and highly praised, he sailed for France in 1953, knowing that black writers and musicians lived there in a relatively non-racist context.

The French respect for American crime fiction went back to Poe, with lively interest in the tough twentieth-century fiction and film they called *noir*, "black." The publisher Gallimard had a successful Série Noire, which mixed French writers with American private-eye and crime novel authors, and Marcel Duhamel asked Himes late in 1955 for a novel, with a $1,000 advance. Crime fiction was new to him, but the money was attractive. Soitos suggests this proposal also answered Himes' need to work in a new form, not just as a protest writer (*The Blues Detective*, 127), and he rapidly produced a Harlem story—Duhamel suggested the location (Milliken, 209–10)—full of scams, crimes and deceptions. In the first drafted segment there was no detective, and on Duhamel's advice (Soitos *The Blues Detective*, 143) Himes created his famous heroes, Grave Digger Jones and Coffin Ed Johnson, big, tough, streetwise, alive to the racism that oppressed their people but also scornful of the follies and crimes the Harlem folk resorted to in an unequal world.

Himes' working title was *The Five-Cornered Square*, published in French as *La Reine des Pommes* (1958)—"The Queen of Apples" or, colloquially, "The Queen of Squares." It appeared in English as *For Love of Imabelle* (1957) but later had the more political title *A Rage in Harlem* (1965): in 1958 it won a national French prize for the best detective story. Himes would continue to write freestanding stories and autobiographical work, but from then on his major contribution was the eight-book Harlem cycle, the last he completed being *Blind Man with a Pistol* (1969).

For Love of Imabelle focuses on the ever-faithful, ever-foolish Jackson (the square of the working title), an undertaker's assistant duped out of $1,500 in a scheme to change (in an oven) bills from ten to a hundred dollars. In the hectic action criminals pretend to be police, his beloved Imabelle constantly changes allegiances and stories (and moves her trunk allegedly containing gold ore for another scam), and the two detectives chase information, control riots and observe amazing events. Early on Jackson's twin brother dressed as a white-haired nun sells one-dollar tickets to heaven, but he finally turns up with his throat cut underneath Imabelle's trunk in the hearse Jackson is driving. Outlining both the massive impact of racism and the innate, excitable resistance to it, the novel is a tidal wave of events, inventions and richly invigorated language both realizing and threatening to be overwhelmed by the chaos of Harlem life.

As Soitos comments, crime fiction "proved to be a perfect vehicle for Himes's sardonic and absurdist view of American culture" ("Chester Himes [1908–84]," 476); his achievement is best exemplified in a more integrated novel, the seventh in the Harlem series, where he balanced most fully his riotous imagination and his technical skill. This is *Cotton Comes to Harlem* (1965—in French *Retour en Afrique*, 1964—Himes' working title was *Back to Africa*), where the crimes, the responses to them, and the position taken by the police, including the white police, all bear powerfully on the situation of the African American people in mid-century America. Andrew Pepper finds the novel a "more fitting culmination to the Cycle" (215) than the very dark *Blind Man with a Pistol* (1969) or the extreme, unfinished *Plan B*.

As the novel starts, Rev. Deke O'Malley is signing people up to return to Africa. Eighty-seven families have paid $1,000 each, put in an armored truck with two guards. Black and white police are watching. A meat truck arrives and white men emerge brandishing guns. Deke's assistant is shot and the money taken. The white cops are looking for black criminals, so the meat truck escapes. In the chaos, the black police drive into the barbecue pit and the armored truck chases the meat truck, which swerves, and a bale of cotton falls out. The white men speed off after shooting a black guard dead.

Grave Digger Jones and Coffin Ed Johnson are at the police station. To white Lieutenant Anderson "they looked like two hog farmers on a weekend in the Big Town" (13). He tells them to be careful, especially with violence. "And let the criminals go," replies Ed (14). They are to watch Deke O'Hara, anti–Syndicate police informer, recently released from jail, now Deke O'Malley of the Back-to-Africa scam. They hear about the robbery.

A little back in time, on the street a man discusses Jesus with a religious woman while his accomplice cuts away her skirt at the back to reach the purse between her legs. She slaps him; he runs away and is killed by the speeding meat truck. A junk man called Uncle Bud asks her to help him get the bale of cotton on his cart; she refuses angrily. A policeman asks Bud if he saw anyone suspicious, helps him with the cotton, and says he should take it to a station.

Back at the rally, Deke's other assistant tells the detectives there were four white robbers and one in the meat truck behind something. Deke, who has disappeared, got the idea from Marcus Garvey's Back-to-Africa movement. He needs his pistol and documents, so he rings his girlfriend Iris; she tells him the police are there and Grave Digger slaps her heavily. The lieutenant rings and sends them to the truck crash. Iris vows to have them sacked and punches Ed: "That makes us even," he says (30).

The police inspect the shot guard and the dead purse thief, find cotton strands inside the truck, and hunt the thief's partner. Meanwhile Deke rings the wife of the dead guard, hides there, prays with her, contacts his associates, prays some more, and has sex with her. With some difficulty the two police find the dead thief's accomplice at a brothel, but he knows nothing. The police report to the lieutenant, "He understood why colored people were mean and rough: he'd be mean and rough himself if he were colored" (54). He tells them to go home: they live on the same street on Long Island. Their car has been stolen.

The next morning the Back-to-the-South movement office opens, led by Colonel Calhoun, alleged southern gentleman. Deke offers to sell him his own subscriber list, so the families can be compensated with the $1,000 bonus the Colonel is offering. There is a sign up, "Wanted: a Bale of Cotton." Uncle Bud had slept with his cotton-loaded cart near the Triborough Bridge. Two cops asked if he has the $87,000 and what he would do with it—buy a new wagon and go to Africa, he says. He sells the cotton bale to junk dealer Mr. Goodman for $25. There is a demonstration outside Back-to-the-South: the Colonel says it is good publicity; then Josh, from Goodman's yard, offers him the cotton for $100.

Iris induces her white police guard to strip for sex, then escapes with only a coat on, learns where Deke is, fights with Mabel, grabs Deke's revolver and shoots her. Deke runs and is lost in Harlem. Grave Digger and Coffin Ed hear their car is found and that Iris is being held for murder. She is badly bruised (by Mabel) and wants them to catch Deke and prove Back-to-Africa is a scam. Finally they observe Deke meeting the Colonel, who comes in a black limousine, to give him the list. The Colonel asks where the cotton is and shooting breaks out. Deke's men kill a couple, one of his men is shot, and Deke is arrested.

Iris accuses him of Mabel's murder, and Grave Digger and Coffin Ed worry where the money has gone. They go to eat at Mammy Louise's, the barbecue of a woman descended from runaway slaves. Anderson calls to say a man is dead in Goodman's junkyard: it is Josh and there is a space in the yard. They get Goodman, who says a bale of cotton was there: he is a little sympathetic about the "poor colored man" (107). They hear Bud's cart has been found: Anderson says the Back-to-the-South movement is "legitimate" and the Colonel has "influential friends" (109).

On Sunday the papers carry the story of the Back-to-Africa robbery and Deke's church is full. His assistant, ironically named T. Booker Washington, leads the service, praising Deke and collecting $597 for him. Though the detectives usually rest on Sunday, they meet, drive through Harlem and see a Black Muslim parade, with approaching it a Back-to-the-South demonstration. With guns and threats they separate the groups. Lieutenant Bailey is pleased and knows "that colored cops had to get tough in Harlem" (117).

The next morning Deke has escaped and two white police are dead. As he was taken to court there was a demonstration and gunmen dressed as police freed him. Grave Digger and Coffin Ed are given a free hand to catch him. They want Iris released, but the captain won't cover that. Grave Digger says,

"I wouldn't do this for nobody but my own black people" (122). They make the light-skinned Iris use dark makeup and free her in exchange for an arrested Back-to-Africa woman. She is to tell Deke she knows where the bale of cotton is: they trace Iris to a meeting she has with Billie, an exotic dancer; then the police have a chili-laden dinner and notice in the paper the Colonel's advert seeking a bale of cotton. Their allegedly blind informant gives them a photograph of the Colonel with Josh in his black limousine. The two detectives explain they are "on the lam" (135) to other police, who have now been reassigned. Iris leads them to a church: Deke is in the vault imprisoned by his own gunmen who after freeing him now want the money. The detectives get into the church and when Iris comes back they hide. She goes down to the vault: the gunmen ask her about the cotton; they hear movement and go up to the church.

In a major gun battle the detectives' tracer bullets break off one man's leg and set fire to another's hair and then the whole church—both police burn their feet. In the vault Deke and Iris are tied to chairs but fight brutally. Upstairs the police kill the second gunman but can't break into the vault: firemen do, and Iris tells them Billie is dancing with the cotton.

At the Cotton Club Billie dances almost naked around the cotton bale, then auctions it to the Colonel for $1,000. The detectives break in to his office and wait. There is nothing in the bale and the Colonel seems frenzied. They threaten to arrest him for Josh's murder and demand $87,000 to let him go. The next day the Colonel has disappeared: the police tell the commissioner they now have the money, as well as Deke and Iris, and have shot the police killers. They find Billie bought the cotton from Bud for $50, to dance with. She rang the Colonel over his advert and told him to come to the club for it: Iris must have heard her.

A week has passed: the story has been widely covered. The Colonel is in Alabama free from extradition, as there "killing a Negro did not constitute murder" (157). Grave Digger and Coffin Ed get a citation for bravery but no raise. The undertaker is so busy his chauffeur Jackson gets a bonus and can marry his fiancée, Imabelle. The police have a drink together: Anderson says when the Colonel hid the money in the cotton it was "a symbol" (158). Grave Digger and Coffin Ed claim they found it there and returned it to the people. At Mammy Louise's, over a baked opossum dinner, they wonder about Bud. Air France confirms an old colored man named Cotton Bud has flown to Dakar via Paris. Dakar telegraphs he has bought five hundred cattle and exchanged them for one hundred wives. "'At least Uncle Bud got to Africa,' Coffin Ed said" (159).

American commentators have felt Himes was in the tough-guy tradition—Sean McCann titles his chapter on Himes "The Slow Death of New

Deal Populism" (251–305), seeing him breaking the popular liberal tradition McCann claims started with Hammett and included Chandler. However, Himes rejected any connection with the private-eye tradition and commented in a 1969 interview with John Williams that "in some of Raymond Chandler's crap out there," namely *Farewell, My Lovely,* Los Angeles racism was "very authentic" (205). It is striking that Himes makes his black detectives part of the police, which, suggested by Duhamel, may link to the success of Maigret, also with Gallimard in the 1950s. But the police connection is shared by many later African American writers, perhaps because a black policeman has been less unlikely than a black private eye, at least until Walter Mosley's Easy Rawlins' first appearance in *Devil in a Blue Dress* (1990).

There was a tradition, if slender, of black crime writing in America, outlined by Stephen Soitos in *The Blues Detective* (1996). Himes certainly knew (and references in *Run Man Run,* 1960) Rudolph Fisher's *The Conjure Man Dies* (1932), a subtle mystery with black police in Harlem, which sophisticated the naïvely comic *Florian Slappey* detective stories (by the white southerner Octavius Roy Cohen) and the little-known earlier serialized novels *Hagar's Daughter* (1901–2) by Pauline Hopkins and John Edward Bruce's *The Black Sleuth* (1907–9). In Paris Himes knew well, and long remained friends with, the groundbreaking African American novelist Richard Wright and had also met the young James Baldwin, but where like them his earlier novels—and others to come—focused on how racist America distorted the lives and hopes of able young black people, in his crime novels a quite different note was struck from the start.

Soitos comments that Himes' "novels as a whole are satires of white and black behavior" (*The Blues Detective*, 162). The scenes are dense, furious, comic and chaotic, whether about whites intruding into Harlem or black people responding to the pressures of everyday life with crime, political resistance, or even celebration. Extreme scenes abound from the start, from the fake nun selling tickets to heaven to a hearse as a getaway vehicle. The language is strong, sometimes euphemized, like "mother-raper," but still asserting the alterity and emotive dynamism of Harlem life. Postcolonial theorists call this process "abrogation," the way in which colonized writers disrupt "normal" language and so, in terms of the meaning of the word "abrogate," "avoid" or preferably "abolish" it. This can also be read, as Soitos does (*The Blues Detective*, 159–60), as the use of "signifyin' language," a discourse directly expressing the ideas and issues of African Americans. The sheer energy of Himes' language and action is a statement, through form itself, of the value of the social culture it represents: the English critic Julian Symons responded positively to the technique and the message, saying Himes' detectives make "exhilarating black comic comment on the activities of all other policemen," and felt he "recorded the activities of these fierce thugs in a world more thuggish still in rattlingly vigorous prose and with equal feelings for violence and comedy" (245).

Deke O'Hara is a man whose energy, verbal and sexual, is seriously misplaced, but at least he is undertaking a scam that is inherently sympathetic to the plight of the Harlem people, rather than the Colonel's ludicrous scheme to repatriate them to the South. In the same way, while Grave Digger and Coffin Ed turn very readily to the threat of violence to keep order on the streets or to force information from unwilling people, there is some socially responsible rationale behind their actions, unlike the white gangsters who are simply after the money. Grave Digger certainly brutalizes Iris, slapping her to the ground, but when she ends by punching Coffin Ed on the nose he recognizes that they are "even" (30).

Several commentators have felt that Himes' world is completely dark— Lee Horsley speaks of his "refusal to promote positive images" and says that "naturalism combines with absurdism to produce an inversion of all redemptive possibilities" (*Twentieth-Century Crime Fiction*, 209 and 210–11). There were many liberals and African Americans who felt his approach was too negative and not likely to help the process of integration: as Soitos notes, Himes "tended more to revolution than assimilation" (*The Blues Detective*, 155), and this is clear from his angry comments through the letters and interview exchanged with John Williams.

Some see Himes as nothing but negative. McCann believes that by *Cotton Comes to Harlem* Himes accepts "an ideology of violence" and the burning church at the end of the novel represents "an implicit awareness of the debasement it signifies to the virtually spiritual ideals Himes and his protagonists seek to defend" (291). However, as Pepper comments:

> Much of the criticism on Himes's crime fiction has overlooked the subtlety inherent both in the way he manages to bend, without entirely breaking, the genre's codes and conventions, and in his politically and culturally ambiguous depictions of black culture(s) and identities [213].

Horsley, in a noir-focused book, felt "in his earlier novels Himes' tone of edgy comedy enables him to end off in a positive way without sentimentalism" (*The Noir Thriller*, 181) and sees this still appearing at the end of *Cotton Comes to Harlem*. There is an element of restitution in the novel: the detectives squeeze out of the Colonel the money to repay the Back-to-Africa investors and there is finally a six-hog barbecue as "an outdoor testimonial" to the detectives (157). It is possible to read Uncle Bud's fabulous departure for Africa and a hundred wives with their original $87,000 as a form of fantasy positive, much as Jackson the undertaker's assistant is always faithful to Imabelle and, at the end of *Cotton Comes to Harlem,* in a surely affectionate, as well as ridiculous, Himesian moment, there are so many dead men he is able finally to afford to marry his totally undeserving beloved.

These patterns could hardly be seen as positive through the lens of practical, liberal, moralized white writing. But Soitos provides a different way of reading the text by drawing attention to what he calls the four tropes of black crime fiction—the "Blues detective" tradition of his title. Developing from theories of black sensibility, he identifies the four as: a black vernacular; the detective persona as trickster; double consciousness; and hoodoo. The first two are fairly obvious, as the text is full of Harlem speech and description and the detectives are constant tricksters, whether in the $87,000 scam they reverse or simply turning Iris into a quiet dark-skinned lady. More subtle is the way in which, like other African Americans (and colonized people in general), they tend to measure themselves in doubly conscious terms, through the eyes of the oppressor, or react aggressively or through tricksterism to throw off that perception system—the calm weekend domestic men Jones and Johnson become, as detectives, like actors playing black ogres. The last and most elusive of the terms is "hoodoo," voodoo made readily available, which is the set of beliefs, faiths and credibilities that are common to the Harlem people—the obsession with numbers is one, which can extend into buying one-dollar tickets of entry to heaven. As Soitos notes (*The Blues Detective,* 142), hoodoo is often used satirically by Himes, but it can also be viewed as extending upwards to the value of dreams and symbolism.

The whole story is a hoodoo-imbued symbolic fable of cotton, that motor of slavery, in Harlem, a place that for all its miseries is the opposite of Southern slavery. The cotton functions in satirical ways, from the opening holdup, through Uncle Bud's cart, to the famous nightspot the Cotton Club itself. When the detectives wonder why the Colonel put the money in the bale, Lieutenant Anderson, who is through the series a sort of side-stage commentator, says, "It was a symbol" (158).

Himes' later work became increasingly ferocious. *Blind Man with a Pistol* is in theme as in title about directionless hostility—though it is in fact based on a real blind man cutting loose with a pistol (Muller, 100)—and the unfinished *Plan B* (finally published in 1993), part of which was worked into the eighth Harlem novel, is based on the notion of race-based revolution in America, an apocalyptic political version of the episodic violence of the early novels in the Harlem series. It is the earlier novels where Himes, without giving up his aggressive tone and unyielding hostility to white racism, manages to mix comedy and vision with a dense and detailed plot—Gilbert H. Muller is one of the few critics who have appreciated what he calls Himes' "fine formal control" in *Cotton Comes to Harlem* (98). The bale of cotton is not only a mobile symbol of oppression and exploitation: it is also a key clue in the plot. We might well work out that after Uncle Bud sold it to Mr. Goodman he met Billie, who made him a better offer, so he stole it back for her $50. Meanwhile Josh had offered it to the Colonel in response to his advert (or perhaps the notice in his office) but was unable to find it, so the Colonel killed him. The wily Bud, familiar with cotton bales from the South, spotted the rip in the covering probably when, with police help, he manhandled it onto his cart and so he was able to depart, with in fact $87,075 to spend on wives.

Finished and energetic at every level, verbal, mechanical, satirical, political and mythical, *Cotton Comes to Harlem* is the finest work of, as Soitos says, the first African American writer "to break the color barrier in detective fiction on both sides of the Atlantic" (*The Blues Detective*, 143). Himes left for Europe in 1953, crucially, as Horsley argues (*Twentieth-Century Crime Fiction*, 204–8), before the 1954 Little Rock school judgment that began the very slow process of integration. The deep hostility he felt as a result of his life's experience, as a child, an adult, and a writer, would not be shared by all African Americans in the years to come: his politics were, as Soitos comments, basically revolutionary ("Chester Himes [1908–84]," 486) and he was quite hostile to the inherently benign position of Martin Luther King, which he felt pro-white (Williams, 130–31 and 212). For others, as Sallis comments, the "Black urban rebellions of 1964–8" (223), coming directly after Himes wrote the novel, helped to make people realize his importance as a writer.

Himes himself led something like a doubly conscious life. In France he mixed with American black writers and local authors and artists, including Picasso, whom Duhamel suggested as the artist for a comic strip version of *La Reine des Pommes* (Margolies and Fabre, 120). After a range of partners, Himes settled with Lesley Packard, a white Anglo-Irish woman who cared for him, both in his writing and later during his illnesses. After Sam Goldwyn bought several novels for filming in 1966 Himes was financially comfortable till his death in Spain in 1984—*Cotton Comes to Harlem* was the second to be filmed, in 1970, essentially as a "blaxploitation" film, replacing the Colonel with an ordinary white crook. But Himes never wanted to return to the United States or changed his views of what racism meant and how totally he responded to it.

So inventive a writer—and in his austere way so compassionate and affectionate a chronicler of his own people, their passions, their follies and their capacity to endure—has had a major inheritance. His own name grows consistently stronger, and the sub-genre he effectively began, black crime writing, has become a normal part of world writing. In the United States Walter

Mosley's Easy Rawlins is the best known, who can himself be read in terms of Soitos's four tropes, if less melodramatically or sensationally than the mighty Grave Digger and Coffin Ed. But there are also black women detectives like Barbara Neely's inspired amateur Blanche White (a name Himes might have been proud of) and the lesbian policewoman Marti MacAlister created by Eleanor Taylor Bland. The concept of being a socially responsible detective without being white has spread widely, to the Native Americans of Tony Hillerman and Dana Stabenow, the indigenous Australians of Paul Mclaren and Nicole Watson, many new detectives in South Africa and India, and even returning to French in the ex-colonial work of Raphaël Confiant and Patrick Chamoiseau.

A Parisian editor who did well through Simenon and admired the American tough-guy writers had the wit, and the luck, to stimulate a new type of writing that owed nothing to either model but has helped substantially to extend the breadth, the relevance, and the enduring richness of crime fiction through the brilliant, and important, work of Chester Himes.

References

Horsley, Lee. *The Noir Thriller.* Second revised edition. London: Palgrave Macmillan, 2009.
_____. *Twentieth-Century Crime Fiction.* Oxford: Oxford University Press, 2005.
Margolies, Edward, and Michel Fabre. *The Secret Lives of Chester Himes.* Jackson: University of Mississippi Press, 1997.
McCann, Sean. *Gumshoe America: Hard-Boiled Crime Fiction and the Rise and Fall of New Deal Liberalism.* Durham: Duke University Press, 2000.
Milliken, Stephen F. *Chester Himes: A Critical Appraisal.* Columbia: University of Missouri Press, 1976.
Muller, Gilbert H. *Chester Himes.* Boston: Twayne, 1989.
Pepper, Andrew. "Black Crime Fiction," in *The Cambridge Companion to Crime Fiction.* Ed. Martin Priestman. Cambridge: Cambridge University Press, 2003, 209–26.
Sallis, James. *Chester Himes: A Life.* New York: Walker, 2000.
Soitos, Stephen F. *The Blues Detective: A Study of African American Detective Fiction.* Amherst: University of Massachusetts Press, 1996.
_____. "Chester Himes (1908–84)," in *A Companion to Crime Fiction.* Ed. Charles J. Rzepka and Lee Horsley. New York: Wiley-Blackwell, 2010, 475–86.
Symons, Julian. *Bloody Murder: From the Detective Story to the Crime Novel: A History.* Revised second edition. London: Pan, 1992.
Williams, John A., and Lori. *Dear Chester, Dear John: Letters Between Chester Himes and John A. Williams.* Detroit: Wayne State University Press, 2008.

15

Indemnity Only,
Sara Paretsky

Paretsky is acknowledged as the first major feminist crime fiction author, consciously reversing the sexual politics of the "tough-guy" private-eye stories. There had long been women writers in the genre with some sense of gender independence, such as Anna Katharine Green and, to some extent Agatha Christie, but it was not until the 1960s, before the groundbreaking feminist literary criticism of Kate Millett's *Sexual Politics* (1970) and Germaine Greer's *The Female Eunuch* (1970), that a New York English professor, Carolyn G. Heilbrun, writing as "Amanda Cross," with *In the Last Analysis* (1964) started a series where another woman, Professor Kate Fansler, solves murders with gender issues prominent.

Inherently more challenging, because not an amateur and not an academic, was the central figure of *An Unsuitable Job for a Woman* (1972) by P. D. James, whose earlier mysteries centered on a distinguished senior policeman. The young Cordelia Gray inherits a very small detective agency from its male owner and investigates with skill and courage a family-gone-wrong murder in Cambridge. James' series character Dalgliesh appears finally, as if to sanction Cordelia's innovation, but permitting a mother to execute the son-murdering father brings a new quasi-feminist edge. Although the novel was applauded, James took years to remobilize Cordelia, and then in a distinctly traditional role in *The Skull Beneath the Skin* (1982)—Priscilla Walton and Manina Jones call it a "conservative transformation" of the earlier novel (18).

A firmer step towards feminist detection was Marcia Muller's *Edwin of the Iron Shoes* (1977), where Californian Sharon McCone moves from legal investigator to sole professional detective: she is determined, though often less than confident. The form itself was not an instant success: Muller's second, *Ask the Cards a Question,* waited until 1982. Similarly, the American-born

London-based Liza Cody began her Anna Lee series with *Dupe* in 1980, but her second, *Stalker*, did not appear until 1984. Sue Grafton's long series focused on the independent-minded Kinsey Millhone started in 1982 with *A Is for Alibi* and appeared steadily. The strongest and most overtly feminist of these initiators was Sara Paretsky, who in 1980 completed, after "about eight years of false starts" and some rejections from publishers (Reynolds, 139, 140), *Indemnity Only* (1982), the first of a series that has become for many the flagship of feminist crime fiction.

Paretsky was born in 1947 in Iowa in a family of Polish origin and grew up in Kansas: her father was a scientist and her mother a librarian. She took a degree in political science from the University of Kansas and worked in Chicago in community service and then for ten years in insurance marketing, not leaving that until after her third novel. Involved in Chicago feminist activities, especially the abortion rights campaign, she continued to study, earning both an MBA and a PhD in history at the University of Chicago, with a dissertation on early American philosophy.

Long devoted to crime fiction, reading it obsessively when waiting for her PhD orals (Reynolds, 140), she had a special interest in Ross Macdonald, the now somewhat overlooked 1950s and 1960s private-eye writer specializing in the psychological origins of crimes and family disruption (and husband to the fine psychothriller writer Margaret Millar). Paretsky also took a course at Northwestern University with the crime writer Stuart Kaminsky, to whom she dedicated her first novel.

In her 1990 foreword to *Indemnity Only* Paretsky comments that she invented V.I. Warshawski while working in insurance for an unappealing male boss, and from the start she interweaves skepticism about male assumptions with special knowledge about business, as well as the city she had made her home. As the story starts, V.I. drives through Chicago to her office at night to see a tough-looking client, who gives her a card for "John L. Thayer, a senior banker." He wants her to find Anita Hill, girlfriend of his son Peter: he is doubtful about a woman PI but provides a $500 deposit.

The next day, after her morning run, she finds at the university no student called Anita Hill but acquires an address for Peter Thayer. V.I. picks the lock to find a young man shot in the forehead. Anita McGraw shares his room: he works for Ajax Insurance. V.I. calls the police, then at home she showers and changes to "clean elegant" clothes (21). At Thayer's bank, she sees from a photo in the prospectus her employer was not Thayer. At Ajax Insurance she interviews Masters, Peter Thayer's boss and friend of his father. When she searches Peter's desk Ralph Devereux checks on her, and they go for a drink: he disbelieves she's a PI, then describes Peter's work. Ralph is divorced; he and V.I.

15. Indemnity Only

have an Indian meal and more drinks; she arrives home alone at 1.00 a.m. and collapses into bed.

At 8.00 a.m., the police arrive, led by Bobby Mallory, a friend of her policeman father, who disapproves of her being a private eye. He knows she was at Thayer's flat; she says she was seeking Anita and does not mention Ajax. Mallory feels the murder is linked to organized crime. V.I. suddenly realizes her father knew an Andrew McGraw of the Knifegrinders Union and Anita must be his daughter: she guesses he came to her thinking V.I. Warshawski was a man.

V.I. goes to the Knifegrinders office to see McGraw. A female secretary abuses her as "a whore" (48). The real Thayer is there, shouting at the man who hired her—McGraw. Thayer asks what she is doing for McGraw: she refuses to say, and he leaves. She asks McGraw about Ajax and possible corruption. He rejects the idea but gives her another $500 to keep seeking Anita. Ralph has left V.I. a message that Peter was not working on anything important and Ajax has little to do with unions. She looks for Anita at the university; a left-wing tutor refuses to help and calls her Philip Marlowe. She hears students discussing Anita and the University Women's Union.

V.I. is attacked on the stairs at home, bundled into a car and taken to Earl Smeissen, a minor mobster. He slaps her and warns her off the Thayer case. She kicks Smeissen in the groin and is beaten, including in the face. Feeling bad, she gets a cab home: the first passes by; the second driver is concerned for her.

V.I. has a bath and a scotch and, an hour late, in pain, has dinner with Ralph. She tells him about Smeissen. Ralph reports that unions don't buy disability from his company. She suspects Masters is in corrupt life insurance, but Ralph disagrees. They go to her place, as she feels a need for comfort, and she goes straight to sleep.

The next morning, seeing her bruises, Ralph remarks that he has never met a woman who fights. He invites her out for the day (a Saturday), but she insists on working on the case and is suspicious about his lack of interest. V.I. goes to her friend Lotty Herschel, a doctor, who gives her painkillers. Then V.I. gets a cab to her car and drives to the Thayer house. Thayer believes McGraw has hired her to blackmail him. He writes her a check for $5,000 to lay off. He says the police have arrested a drug-addict burglar for shooting Peter. She says that is nonsense and meets Thayer's daughter Jill, who fears her father shot Peter in a temper. V.I. gives Jill her card and leaves, goes to buy a gun and has shooting practice. She feels weak, checks into a motel and sleeps for twelve hours.

When V.I. gets home Mallory's assistant is outside her flat: it is ransacked, but he has not noticed. Mallory arrives and says the Thayer arrest was made by a probably crooked senior cop, Vespucci: the case is now closed. V.I. goes to Lotty's and returns McGraw's call; he wants to stop her looking for Anita. He knows Smeissen. She loads the gun, imagines shooting the people who ransacked her apartment, and finds her office ransacked. Thayer's apartment is also. She searches it and finally finds a single-sheet workers' compensation document about "indemnity" (152).

V.I. and Lotty eat out, and V.I. arranges her flat to be fixed. That night she dreams of her Italian mother. The next morning Jill Thayer rings at 7:30 a.m. and asks V.I. to come over: Thayer has been shot leaving for work. She gets Jill to hire her for $1 to look into the new murder. The family squabble and are hostile to her. Jill leaves with V.I. to stay at Lotty's—she assures Jill that whatever her father has done, she can control her own life.

V.I. asks Jill whom her father has spoken to: Masters is among them, and Thayer also had a row on the phone. Jill sleeps: "Something about her pierced my heart, made me long for the child I'd never had" (186). Ralph calls and she asks him to check Masters-McGraw phone calls. She rings Murray Ryerson, a journalist, for pictures of them. At lunch Murray gives her the pictures and confirms the Vespucci/Smeissen connection. She assumes McGraw and Masters operated together and checks bars to see if they met. It's not Peter Wimsey, she thinks (198). She has no luck. At Lotty's, Jill is fine, helping with children. V.I. goes to sleep and is again late for dinner with Ralph. He says McGraw never called Masters and asks about her marriage. She says she was too independent and work got in the way. Ralph says the insurance claim draft is at maximal level and he will return it to the office. She is pleased she has a copy. They go to his place.

In the morning she wonders if he is checking on her or just attracted. At Lotty's they are still fine. When she goes for a run, police stop her—a witness says Thayer's killer had a Z scar on his face. Smeissen has such a man and, worried about Jill, V.I. arranges protection from Paul, brother of Lotty's Puerto Rican nurse. V.I. checks bars again, finally finding out where the two men met. Jill will search her father's office in the morning.

V.I. goes to a University Women's Union meeting at night. After a discussion of feminist issues, one woman challenges V.I.'s presence and she defends herself as seeking Anita. No one offers any information, and V.I. leaves, feeling Peter Wimsey would have charmed them. She is followed in a car and assumes they are looking for Anita. She parks and takes a bus to the airport, then a cab to Lotty's. Jill and Paul are happy together. V.I.'s flat is fixed. She rings Ralph: he has not found the file on the claimant, but money has been paid regularly. A man rings to see if V.I. is there—and rings off. At 3.30 a.m. a woman from the university meeting rings: she knows where Anita is.

15. Indemnity Only

A Smeissen man is out front but asleep. V.I. drives 140 miles to Hartford, Wisconsin, and talks with Anita. She confirms Peter found out about the disability scams—all the board and her father were involved. She wants to get back to Chicago, so V.I. has Murray arrange a hotel room in secret. Jill has found documentation of the account Thayer opened. Lotty says her house has been broken into. V.I. collects her belongings: Lotty says V.I. is Nemesis and feels she is the "daughter of my spirit" (292).

Her flat is beautiful. She calls Ralph: he still trusts Masters, who is visiting Ralph that evening. She hurries there, with the gun. Masters arrives just after her, with Smeissen and Tony, and has picked Jill up in the street. V.I. faces them down. When Tony's attention wavers, Jill hides behind a chair, as V.I. has instructed her, and she attacks Masters. Ralph gets shot, but she takes control and calls Mallory.

The next morning Ralph, bandaged up, says she doesn't need him: "It just wouldn't work out" (313). She calls Murray; he knows about the arrests. She fetches Anita and they go to see her father—on the way they discuss V.I.'s father. Anita tells her father he betrayed them and the union. He regrets it and refers to King Midas, whose daughter turned to gold. V.I. says Midas repented and had his daughter back. McGraw looks pleading. Murray is waiting for the story. V.I. does not say good-bye.

In this briskly ended story Paretsky asserts central features of the feminist private-eye form. Of major interest to early commentators was the insistence on a name that was not evidently gendered—Maureen Reddy's first and lengthy point in her 1988 commentary. V.I. is also physically involved in action, able to track, break in, search and, when attacked, fight: she is also willing, if reluctantly, to use a gun. She regularly receives minor injuries, particularly bruises and abrasions that link her to the victimized experience of many of the characters, especially women—male private eyes when attacked tend to lapse into peaceful unconsciousness, without wounds to show for it later.

Like her male Californian predecessors, she is highly mobile around the city, though V.I. changes vehicles more than they do, sometimes because her car is unreliable, she has been abducted or simply for convenience or even concealment. More sociable than the tough guys, she uses contacts from her past life in her inquiries and they can recur through the novels. In each early story she meets a man of some interest and with some caution engages with them, sexually rather than emotionally—though later in the series she has recurrent though often offstage partners like the African American police detective Conrad Rawlings or the internationally located journalist Morrell.

Also unlike the male model is V.I.'s constant awareness of family. Her father was a kindly police sergeant whose Polish ethnicity probably held him back from higher promotion; his colleague Bobby Mallory and other characters regularly refer to his values. Her Italian mother, who died when she was fairly young, was a major force on her for order and self-improvement, as well as singing. *Deadlock* is about her cousin's murder, while different aunts are central to *Burn Marks* and *Killing Orders.*

V.I. also has a strong capacity for friendship: Kathleen Klein says V.I. "forms strong emotional bonds, makes friends, worries about people toward whom she has no professional obligations" (215). Not all her male friendships are sexual: after the first novels, she shares with Grafton's Kinsey Millhone and Cody's Anna Lee the feature of having as neighbor a friendly and generally supportive but physically weak and asexual man, here Mr. Contreras.

From the beginning, Lotty Herschel is V.I.'s close woman friend. A kindly and professional Jewish doctor who had escaped from Germany as a child, she is very fond of V.I., though her direct aggressiveness to others can be unsettling and they are almost estranged in *Killing Orders* (1985). They return to a sense of shared value: *Total Recall* (2001) looks into ethnic issues linked to Lotty's history and she is one, but by no means the only, character through whom Paretsky develops a strong sense of the multiethnic issues in America. Horsley notes that one of V.I.'s "leading traits is her tolerant multiculturalism" (265).

Another major departure from the "tough-guy" pattern is opening the plot with some personal encounter and then developing links with major crime and social corruption, moving in the reverse of Chandler's use of gangsters and corruption as a distraction from the personal—and usually female—betrayals at the core of the plot. In this process both Paretsky and V.I. exhibit a strong understanding of the detailed processes of business and city politics—*Indemnity Only* turns on the insurance world in which Paretsky worked for some years, *Deadlock* (1984) deals with the substantial complexities of maritime business on the Great Lakes, while *Bitter Medicine* (1987) is an exposé of vicious business practices at the heart of the health industry.

Those who suffer are usually innocent small-scale victims. Paretsky has summed up the situation in the statement (quoted by Priscilla Walton and Manina Jones, 211) that murder/mayhem is committed "by the hired hands of the wealthy elite." It has been noted by several commentators that V.I. is concerned not only with finding the causes of such violent disruption but also in trying, often with Lotty's help, to provide assistance to the damaged survivors of social mayhem. Walton and Jones see V.I. in this way as a "practical feminist" (37) and stress her role in helping reestablish the innocent who have suffered, as well as in catching the criminal

There have been several feminist voices critical of Paretsky's version of activism, the most negative being the British feminist Sally Munt, who in an extended argument (41–48) sees V.I.'s actions as a form of tokenism complicit with patriarchy. Munt asserts that by imitating male modes of behavior the novels implicitly support them, and V.I.'s independence is seen as both "fervent individualism" (45) and "a bourgeois fantasy of empowerment" (47). V.I.'s interests in clothes and men make her seem "a glamorous spectacle" (47) and so for heterosexual women "aspirational" in a sexist way. Munt concludes that although the novels have some "sympathetically feminist aspects" (42), V.I. basically exhibits a "fantasy of femininity" (48). Gill Plain, another British commentator, though less dismissive than Munt, has an ultimately negative view, seeing Paretsky's work as "a feminist fairy tale" (154), with V.I. tending towards "frenzied hyperactivity," especially in her iconic red shoes (149). Plain finds V.I.'s position grows increasingly strained through the novels and sums up that she is "threatening to implode under the contradictions" (164).

Both critics find more politically acceptable the consciously separatist figure of the lesbian detective, which appeared early and with some strength in M.F. Beal's *Angel Dance* (1977) and Eve Zaremba's *A Reason to Kill* (1978) and became well-known through Katherine V. Forrest's Los Angeles–based Inspector Kate Delafield novels, starting with *Amateur City* (1984). Lesbian crime fiction, with its capacity to ironize macho male detection, has been a varied field. Barbara Wilson began with a searching examination of crime and social dissent in *Murder in the Collective* (1984) and followed with the issue-based *Sisters of the Road* (1986) and *The Dog-Collar Murders* (1989), after which she transferred her considerable power into the postmodern thriller with *Gaudi Afternoon* (1990). Also notable have been the witty contributions of Mary Wings from *She Came Too Late* (1986), and Claire McNab's series beginning with *Lessons in Murder* (1988), where Inspector Carol Ashton is as glamorous as her Sydney harbor setting.

Another criticism of Paretsky finds her work primarily personal rather than political. First voiced by Walton and Jones, the issue is that though she does attend to "issues of law, society, and justice" and "'Who done it?' often turns out to be a societal entity" (273), the effect of her plotting and the heroic achievements of V.I. are essentially only to deploy individual agency to ameliorate individual people's situations. Though that makes a good dramatic story, it leaves the forces of corruption largely in place and does not amount to a program for radical social change, including gender liberation. Munt takes this view firmly, and Plain argues that the larger hostile forces still exist at the end of the story—only personal rescue has occurred, not social change. Paretsky rebutted this somewhat idealistic radical view when she said in an interview (quoted by Klein, 215) "you do not change or affect entrenched powerful institutions and my books make this clear."

A view of Paretsky that is more subtle and inherently supportive is taken by Lee Horsley. She comments that the uses of the term "female dick" for figures like V.I. is sometimes deliberately challenging and sometimes just "a burlesquing of Freudian penis envy" (265) and tends to take a complex view like this of the whole situation. She sees V.I. as essentially representing communal solidarity, primarily through her friends, constructing with them a "non-patriarchal surrogate family" (266). Horsley does not accept that V.I.'s fondness for clothes and interest in men are disabling features but sees Paretsky as having "a manifest aversion to female passivity" (265), as in the fatalistic mother in *Bitter Medicine,* and overall Horsley, like Paretsky herself, feels the way the novels expose the power of corruption and inhumane social forces, especially towards woman, is of considerable importance in political terms.

Other commentators see Paretsky as a positive feminist. The criticism of Paretsky for V.I.'s sense of style and occasional swagger might seem a little hard on the author, since she has consistently taken a well-thought-out and personally active role in forms of feminist activity.

Walton and Jones quote her on "the symptom of fears about women's social power" (96), which she identified as the force behind the increasing anti-female sadism of 1980s crime fiction, principally the growing use of and emphasis on detailed violence by men. Johnson argues that Paretsky presents V.I. as both realizing the value and experiencing the risk of emotionality, saying she "strengthens V.I. to face a system that will exploit a woman's emotions and use them to discredit her if it can" (105).

She was a major force in establishing in 1986 Sisters in Crime, an organization devoted to supporting and publicizing women's crime fiction, and she has spoken and written widely and often on the subject of gendered issues in crime fiction—that the argument still needs to be made is suggested by the residual hostility to the feminist position expressed as recently as 2005 by Charles Rzepka, who feels "the villainy of .Warshawksi's male foes can approach the flat monstrosity of melodrama" (240–41).

There are clear developments through the novels. The early ones move through a series of institutions that abuse their power, including the Catholic church in *Killing Orders* (1985). Reddy argues that Paretsky's work became through the 1980s "increasingly feminist and more subversive" (11), and the political range of her themes have become even wider in later work: the 2003 *Blacklist* deals with both modern terrorism and the McCarthy period and through her international journalist lover Morrell V.I. is able to reflect on the mission that America has post 9–11 undertaken in intervening in Middle Eastern national politics.

While V.I. and comparable characters have had a large following in terms of sales and readership around the world, there has been a notable failure to convert this literary enthusiasm to film and television in spite of the floods of visual material in the crime genre. In 1991 the film *V. I. Warshawski* was planned as the start of a series starring Kathleen Turner, at that time a major star—though both Jane Fonda and Bette Midler had been considered for the role. The script was based on *Deadlock,* which deals with the murder of V.I.'s ice-hockey-playing cousin Boom-Boom, but there were major changes. Boom-Boom becomes V.I.'s boyfriend, not cousin, and he is given a thirteen-year-old daughter who ends up in V.I.'s care, a figure based on Jill Thayer in *Indemnity Only* and made younger to press V.I. into the role of surrogate mother. As well as wisecracking and city tourism—including a boat chase—a substantial amount of sexist gaze is provided, as Walton and Jones have outlined (234–43): they see the film moving Paretsky's broad-based feminism into the domain of the anti-feminist force that Susan Faludi identified as the 1980s "backlash," seen in films like *Fatal Attraction.* V.I. is presented as a femme fatale (high-heeled shoes and stockings are stressed) and yet combines that threatening role with a form of surrogate maternity. The film was a box-office failure, though Turner's role was praised: she was the only feature of the film the author felt able to approve.

Paretsky observed a pause between 1994 and 1999, but since then seven more V.I. novels have been published, most recently *Critical Mass* (2014) and she has produced two non-detective titles, one about miracles in the modern USA, *Ghost Country* (1998), one a widely admired novel of rural history, *Bleeding Kansas* (2008). The form to which she has given such energy has thrived and found many authors and versions. Striking variants have been the somewhat traditionalist Alaskan Inuit women inquirer Kate Shugak in the series by Dana Stabenow and, in the series starting with *Blanche on the Lam* (1992), the more confrontational Blanche White, an African American woman oscillating between servant and detective, created by BarbaraNeely (the lack of space between her own names is—like the main character's name—one of her many challenges to white convention).

The unpartnered, active, decisive, feminist detective has become central in crime fiction, in substantial part through the well-focused and energetic novels of Paretsky, as well as through her continuing responses to changing politics on America and its world. The failure of this vivid writer and the very dynamic genre she leads to conquer the still heavily gendered world of film and television suggests there is still a real need for the presence of figures like V.I. in a popular fiction that realizes the forces of social culture.

References

Horsley, Lee. *Twentieth-Century Crime Fiction*. Oxford: Oxford University Press, 2005.

Johnson, Patricia E. "Sex and Betrayal in the Detective Fiction of Sue Grafton and Sara Paretsky." *Journal of Popular Culture* 27.4 (1994): 97–106.

Klein, Kathleen. *The Woman Detective: Gender and Genre*. Second edition. Chicago: University of Illinois Press, 1995.

Munt, Sally. *Murder by the Book? Feminism and the Crime Novel*. London: Routledge, 1994.

Plain, Gill. *Twentieth-Century Crime Fiction: Gender, Sexuality and the Body*. Edinburgh: Edinburgh University Press, 2001.

Reddy, Maureen. *Sisters in Crime: Feminism and the Crime Novel*. New York: Continuum, 1988.

Reynolds, Moira Davison. *Women Authors of Detective Series: Twenty-One American and British Writers, 1900–2000*. Jefferson, NC: McFarland, 2001.

Rzepka, Charles. *Detective Fiction*. Cambridge: Polity Press, 2005.

Walton, Priscilla, and Manina Jones. *Detective Agency: Women Rewriting the Hardboiled Tradition*. Berkeley: University of California Press, 1999.

16

The Name of the Rose, Umberto Eco

Umberto Eco, born in 1932, avoided studying law as his father would have preferred and undertook a classic Italian arts education, ending with a doctorate on Saint Thomas Aquinas and medieval aesthetics. Eco also paid close attention to the most modern areas and soon became a major international figure in the field of semiotics. Analyzing the variety and volatility of meaning in language, Eco, like Roland Barthes, also studied cultural phenomena widely, producing in 1966 an edited book on the James Bond phenomenon.

Fiction also attracted Eco: on the back of the original edition of *The Name of the Rose* (1980, in English 1983) he said "those things we cannot theorize about, we must narrate" (Caesar, 151), and in 1978 he developed the idea of writing a mystery about the murder of a monk (Lodge, ix). At first it was to be a modern story, but his range of interests dominated and he produced a medieval mystery novel including a major debate about the interrelation of language, reality and authority. He intended to call it *The Abbey of Murder*, but the publisher's dissent led to a much further-reaching title (Rollin, 164).

The Name of the Rose is a large, complex novel, full of references and untranslated quotations—*The Key to the Name of the Rose* by Adele J. Haft, Jane G. White and Robert J. White is very useful. Eco rejected advice to cut down the first hundred pages (Lodge, xiv), yet in spite of its weightiness, it is a recognizable and enjoyable mystery. Major intellectual, historical and political themes develop, and they also must have influenced the novel's huge sales, which surprised publishers: many American and English firms had rejected it (Lodge, viii). *The Name of the Rose* has also been a highly influential force in two major extensions of modern crime fiction, the historical crime story and the postmodern mystery.

The story begins in November 1327. At an unnamed abbey in the mountainous north of Italy, people are gathering for a meeting preliminary to a major—and historical—one with the Pope in Avignon. The Emperor's delegate is William of Baskerville, a tall, fair-haired Franciscan, apparently from Ireland. He was a church inquisitor into heresy, showing both "perspicacity" and "humility" (29), but resigned, finding the work brutal. His assistant is a young Benedictine monk, Adso of Melk (in southern Austria), who recounts this story, which has been discovered in a nineteenth-century manuscript of dubious authority.

As they approach the abbey along a snowy road, agitated men appear. William says the fine dark horse Brunellus has gone to the right: he will be at the dung heap. They catch the horse and are astonished when William says he never saw him, just hoofprints in the snow and horsehair on a branch; he assumed it was valuable, to cause such a pursuit and because the learned usually name a favorite brown horse Brunellus. Apart from this amazing demonstration, William already has a reputation for solving mysteries and the abbot tells him they have one—a young monk has been found dead on the rocks.

William is keen to explore the abbey's famous library and meet after eighteen years Ubertino, a great scholar and (factually) the leader of the Franciscans who oppose Christ's ideal of poverty against the church's modern power and authority. William discusses herbs with Severinus the herbalist and in the scriptorium they meet Malachi the librarian, see the dead monk Adelmo's beautiful work, and meet the old, blind Jorge of Burgos, who argues with another monk, Venantius, over laughter, including the lost second book of Aristotle's *Poetics*, on comedy: Jorge thinks it an evil subject. William believes Adelmo killed himself, because of where and how he fell.

Early on the second day a body is found head-down in a vat of pig's blood. It is Venantius, whom they met in the library. His face is swollen, so he did not drown: William thinks he has been poisoned. William finds a magnetic stone and explains it to the others. The young monks Benno and Berengar are nervous: Berengar admits he was the last to see Adelmo alive and says he looked haunted. In the library, William feels Venantius' desk is of interest but is distracted from it and has a lengthy debate with Jorge, who repeats that laughter is a sin and Christ never laughed.

Benno tells William that Berengar loved Adelmo and he saw them suspiciously together: Adelmo killed himself afterwards. The abbot is nervous about William entering the library—only the librarian and assistant go there, but an old monk reveals another access to it. After supper they enter the library, but someone is there, who throws a book and steals William's glasses. They look at a book Venantius was reading, and when Adso brings the lamp close letters appear, in code. William works out that it starts: "The secret is the end of Africa." They find the library and its many rooms very confusing. When they return to the church the abbot tells them Berengar is missing—William assumes it was him in the library.

Early on the third day Adso thinks about the beauty of books—and how people lick their fingers to turn the pages. The kitchen hand Salvatore tells his story of being with the radical Franciscans who became roaming criminals; then William discusses "the new science" he learned at Roger Bacon's Oxford. William has deciphered the message they found. The abbot discusses the coming negotiations: William, who has new glasses from the abbey smith, gets Adso to draw a plan of the library: they will use the magnet as a compass to find their way around it. Ubertino gives Adso a lengthy account of Fra Dolcino, the leader of the Franciscan radical rebels, and his fellow leader, the beautiful Margherita; Adso thinks of an execution he has seen. He then looks at the manuscripts and is excited by thoughts of Margherita, mixed with the Virgin Mary. He sees a light in the kitchen and as he enters a man leaves; a woman remains, whom Adso thinks young and beautiful: they soon make love. He confesses his sin to William, who says it was not great. The very old Alinardo likens the deaths to the seven trumpets of the Apocalypse: a storm with the first, blood with the second, the third will involve water and the fourth the sun. At William's suggestion they find Berengar in the bathhouse, drowned.

Berengar's tongue is black and so are his fingertips—like Venantius'—when they check. Severinus, who runs the infirmary, discusses poison: his phial of it has disappeared. William gets Salvatore and also Remigio to talk about their past with Fra Dolcino. Severinus finds William's glasses inside Berengar's clothing. Adso agonizes about his sin with the girl. The Franciscan delegation led by (the real) Michael of Cesena arrives and discuss the schemes of the Pope against them; then the Pope's delegation arrives led by the inquisitor Bernard de Gui, also historical.

Alinardo talks more about the Apocalyptic links of the deaths so far. William discusses his reasoning method with Adso and says he has many hypotheses but cannot yet choose one, unlike in the Brunellus case. Salvatore tells Adso about a spell to procure a woman's love using a basilisk. That night they enter the library again and make a map of it (reproduced in the text) but cannot understand the instructions to enter the last room, "the end of Africa." Adso has more memories and anxieties about his sin. Salvatore is caught by Bernard's men with a woman: it is Adso's girl and she is arrested as a witch.

The fifth day sees a lengthy debate between the Papal and Franciscan delegations about the poverty of Christ, which becomes very bad tempered. Severinus calls William out to say he has found a strange book in the infirmary. William says he will come later. Jorge hears this and goes off; the cellarer follows Severinus. William speaks at length on behalf of the imperial party, arguing the limits of the church's power: all are silenced, but William says he will not go to Avignon because of (feigned) illness.

Severinus is found dead in the infirmary, his head smashed by a gold sphere (somewhat like the sun of the fourth trumpet); the book has disappeared. Remigio the cellarer has been caught searching the infirmary and arrested but insists Severinus was dead when he arrived. William examines Severinus' fingers: he is wearing gloves. Remigio speaks to Malachi the librarian—who, Benno tells William, has been in the infirmary previously. Bernard conducts a lengthy inquiry in which Remigio eventually, fearing torture, confesses to being a rebel Franciscan and also, improbably, to the abbey murders: he was in the infirmary seeking two letters from Dolcino he had previously hidden in the library. Salvatore gives evidence against him and they will try him in Avignon. This case has destroyed the negotiations and Bernard and the Pope's party have won. Ubertino, advised by William, flees in fear; Michael agrees to go to Avignon, against William's advice. Adso, speaking from the present, says Ubertino was murdered two years afterwards and later on reports that Michael failed at Avignon and sought the Emperor's protection. Jorge gives a lengthy sermon about the coming of the Antichrist. Adso laments that the girl, his "only earthly love" (407), is to be burnt as a witch.

Early on the sixth day Malachi dies in the church, speaking of "the power of a thousand scorpions" (414): his fingers are black. Benno becomes assistant librarian and the new cellarer, Nicholas, shows William and Adso the abbey treasures, which he previously cared for. William asks about Jorge and the succeeding librarians—they have not been Italians. William is skeptical about holy relics like wood from the true cross. Adso falls asleep in church and has a long, elaborate dream that William says is like the carnivalesque *Coena Cypriani,* "Cyprian's Feast," from about the year 400.

William finds a reference to the missing volume—which includes both a version of the *Coena Cypriani* by "Alfricobas" and also what William calls *"the book"* (442), *Aristotle on Comedy*. The abbot wants no more inquiries into the library. Jorge is missing during dinner, and after it they enter the library and now the last room. Adso made a joke that made William realize that "the first and seventh of four" refers to two letters in the word for "four," *quattuor.* As the seventh day starts they press the *q* and *o*, the room opens—and Jorge is waiting for them.

The abbot, he says, is dead, suffocated in a passage below, being too short to reach the letters to enter, but he knew everything, from William. William says Jorge has controlled the librarianship, even the abbot's position, and hating its theme, he has hidden the Aristotle book and poisoned its pages with the phial he took from Severinus. Malachi loved Adelmo and gave Berengar the book, which had already killed Venantius, in revenge. Then Jorge turned Malachi against Severinus, so he killed him, then read the book and died. Jorge shows him the book of Aristotle, which is on very rare paper, not vellum, and some pages are stuck together, but William is wearing gloves. William says he himself is "a fool" because he believed the idea about the sequence of deaths following the seven Apocalyptic trumpets—and he realizes Jorge got Malachi to kill Severinus and told him about the poison being like scorpions to fulfill the fifth pattern. But it was Jorge's obsession with the Apocalypse that made William suspect him—and it was when watching the stables for the sixth death context that Adso's joke gave him the key. Jorge says it was "a confused echo" (471) of the trumpets. They argue about laughter: Jorge is still fiercely against it. Then he starts to eat the book, quoting the seventh Apocalypse sequence—"to your lips it will be as sweet as honey" (481). He runs, they chase him, and he knocks down the lamp. The books catch fire, then the whole library. The sparks set fire to the church; horses and mules catch fire and spread the blaze.

William says Jorge was Antichrist "deformed by hatred of philosophy" (491). Adso says William defeated him by exposing his plot but "'There was no plot,' William said, 'and I discovered it by mistake'" (491). On "The Last Page" Adso remembers that the abbey burned for three days and many died. Afterwards, the conflict between Pope and Emperor worsened and William, with Adso, traveled for safety to Munich, where they separated. Adso heard William died in the plague some twenty years afterwards. Much later, Adso returned to the abbey and found a bookcase with a few scattered pages: he collected two sacks of them and so has "a lesser library" (500), but he is uncertain of their meaning. His final words are "stat rosa pristina nomine, nomina nuda tenemus" (502)—"the rose stands ancient in name—we hold bare names": Tani unpacks this further as "the ancient exists (only) in relation to its name, we hold (only) bare names" (71–72), a statement that justifies the semiotic multiplicities that Eco admires.

From the start the novel proclaims itself a detective story. The name Baskerville is from Conan Doyle (some commentators feel "Adso" sounds close to "Watson"), and William is, like Holmes, tall, lean, intense—and even uses drugs, in this case herbs. William's probable Irish origin seems to honor Conan Doyle, though Eco also links it to the major role of Irish learning in the Dark Ages. While the horse-detecting opening seems Holmesian, it is actually very close to Voltaire's story of Zadig (see Richter, 261), a favorite archetype for French crime writers and learned English-language ones like Dorothy Sayers.

As is traditional, the story recounts mysterious events and the detective makes inquiries, and the wealth of scholarship in the library, shared by William and other monks, seems to offer a learned mystery, as by Sayers or Dickson Carr. While this seems headed for a clever resolution, that is not where the book arrives. As Zamora outlines, the seven deaths and seven days do not fit each other. Adelmo has died before the first day; nobody dies on the fourth day; it seems likely that, depending just when around midnight the abbot suffocated, he and Jorge both die on the last day. In addition to this random effect, the deaths are announced almost casually, suggesting there is much more than just murder going on in this novel. In the end we discover that Jorge knew William was thinking about the Apocalyptic pattern and had himself planted the idea of scorpions in Malachi's mind to confirm it. In fact, the weather was trivial to the first death, the pig's blood was connected, the golden weapon not really like the sun, and Berengar liked baths anyway. Coincidence ruled, and as William finally says in bitter self-criticism: "There was no plot.... and I discovered it by mistake" (491).

William is right: Jorge was not plotting anything in a malevolent series: he used the poison as the ultimate protection for the manuscript he most hated but was too fine a scholar to destroy until he used it to destroy himself as well. If anything is to blame for all the deaths and the eventual destruction of the abbey and the library it is certainty—being certain about Christian correctness and the value of authority, and behaving according to unquestioned principles. The ultimate rejection of detective certainty and analytic confidence that the novel finally provides is recognizable as part of the anti-detective novel, a feature of modern crime fiction, as the Italian critic Stefano Tani describes it, "into which the detective novel is turned by postmodernism" (xiii) to become "a high-parodic form that stimulates and tantalizes its readers by disappointing common detective-novel expectations" (xv).

The Name of the Rose is at the heart of what is called the postmodern crime novel. Postmodernity in general questioned what Lyotard in *The Post-Modern Condition* (1979) called "the grand narratives" of literature and thought—he criticized the centrality of the individual subject, the novel's construction of a shapely and rational program of understanding of events, and argued that humanist liberal self-confidence is a flawed and coercive model. It is a view at once deeply skeptical and, for many, excitingly interrogative.

The initiating name in postmodernist crime fiction is the Argentinean Jorge Luis Borges, who was both blind and the national librarian, so an evident source for the character Jorge of Burgos. The character's intrinsic destructiveness might, as *The Key* suggests, seem linked to Eco's ultimate disapproval of Borges' deeply conservative positions—Eco calls him a "tragic pessimist" but himself "tragically optimistic" (Haft, White, and White, 27–28). Nevertheless, Borges' ideas about the library as a labyrinth figuring the complexities of the world, found in the short story "The Library of Babel," are clearly of great importance in Eco's thought. A closer model to the plot is Borges' short story "Death and the Compass," where a detective works out a scheme for four murders but fails to grasp that he will be victim of the last. In the proto-humanist values of William, Eco somewhat moderates the austerity of Borges' thought, and in his *Reflections on the Name of the Rose* he speaks of a more ultimately positive postmodern model, the American novelist John Barth (see Parker, 58–61).

Through the massive popularity of his novel Eco evidently stimulated further work of this kind. Tani published in 1984 *The Doomed Detective,* a book about the possibilities of a postcertainties crime fiction, and in 1985 Paul Auster's *City of Glass* started his influential New York Trilogy, usually taken as the classic work of postmodernist crime fiction. As part of this mode, Eco includes scholarly jokes: there is a monk called Umberto of Romans—French readers might know him as Umberto of the Novels—and the name Alcofribas attached to the carnivalesque *Coena Cypriani* is Rabelais's own anagrammatic pseudonym (Richter, 263); when in his final conversation with Adso William quotes medieval German, it is in fact Eco's backdating of a statement by the modern Wittgenstein.

Part of the power of Eco's postmodernism is that it links to doubts expressed over centuries about central features of Christian faith: as Theresa Coletti comments, the novel "aligns the philosophical element of medieval semiotics with its modern concerns" (31). Eco's understanding of medieval versions of the modern is, as Lodge notes (xi–xii), a major reason why he set his novel in the fourteenth century and not the, to him, much more familiar time of Saint Thomas Aquinas a century before. By locating William in the Oxford of Roger Bacon, the very early scientist, especially in optics (William's glasses are a meaningful sign), Eco opposes the conservative Christian view that all true reality, of objects and words, is in the creative hands of God— known as Realism—with Nominalism. The new counterargument led by William's friend and namesake William of Ockham asserted that names are merely words (or signs as the twentieth century would call them) and people and periods understand and contextualize them quite differently: out of the latter position rises what Tani calls William's "post-modern awareness" (72).

The early fourteenth century also saw another conflict that the novel describes in some detail, between the Pope and the Emperor over the Franciscan friars—Judy Ann Ford provides an account of the context. Saint Francis stood for austere holiness and a direct engagement with ordinary people, not worshiping God behind abbey walls like the Benedictines. Some Franciscans insisted that true poverty, in the name of Christ himself, involved serious hostility to rich institutions, including the church. By the fourteenth century members of a Franciscan wing called Fraticelli, "little brothers [of Christ]," were effectively revolutionaries. Pope John XXII wanted to crush them, with the support of the Franciscan order, but the Emperor saw the Franciscans as a card to play against the power of the church, and this conflict, with some of the real players, is a central part of the novel.

The interest in, even fascination with, this medieval material is a major part of the novel's success, and in itself that function is innovative. The historical novel had been created by Scott as a basis for understanding the origins of both nations and modern morality, and his approach is referenced in the opening doubts about Adso's manuscript—which are also linked with postmodern skepticism about sources. Popular historical novels had developed in the mid-twentieth century when writers, led by Georgette Heyer, projected romance back to the Regency period of its major progenitor, Jane Austen, but while crime writers often set their stories about a generation back, like Dickens and most classic novelists, this was primarily just to control events, and locating a crime story in the medieval past was quite unknown.

Medievalism itself, the use of the premodern period as a basis for literature and art, is, scholars have established, a response to anxiety about the nature of the present. Romantic writers like Keats and Coleridge turned to the past in distress at modern urban, industrialized and militarized society; later nineteenth-century artists, notably the Pre-Raphaelite movement, escaped to the past as both art and attitudes became enmeshed in the world of mechanical and automatized responses. Medievalism rose again when in the 1970s the long postwar boom ended with rising oil prices and confidence in steadily growing human improvement was disrupted both by the arms race and by growing social and political conflict within Western Europe. Barbara Tuchman's very influential book published in August 1978 called the medieval period "a Distant Mirror": Eco would discuss the recently developed overlaps between the Middle Ages and the present in an essay, "Living in the New Middle Ages," published in 1985 and reprinted, slightly revised, in his collection *Travels in Hyperreality* (1986).

Some historical crime fiction had begun to appear—Peter Lovesey's late nineteenth-century Sergeant Cribb series began in 1970, and 1977 saw the series by Edith Pargeter (as "Ellis Peters") begin, featuring the Welsh monk Brother Cadfael, not dissimilar to William of Baskerville, set around Shrewsbury during the twelfth-century English civil war. After the impetus added by Eco, the historical mystery became a major sub-genre of the form, with settings ranging from the classical world with Lindsey Davies to the 1890s New York mysteries of Caleb Carr.

Within this medievalism, most of the writers were merely nostalgic, but

Eco, characteristically, used the setting to speak as powerfully about modern politics as he did about philosophy and semiotics. The 1970s saw the rise of new para-criminal radical forces, called in Italy the Red Brigades, extreme left-wing groups acting against what they saw as the oppressive capitalist state: in his popular columns in the newspaper *Espresso* Eco wrote about these events (Kellner, 15). The senior politician Aldo Moro was held hostage for fifty-five days; a return of prisoners was demanded, but when it failed he was executed. This occurred in 1978, the year Eco conceived his story of murder, and the extremist Franciscans are similar in policy and activity to the Red Brigades, even with overlaps in their leaders—Brother Dolcino and Renato Curcio both became radical in Trento, and both married a woman named Margherita, who supported them, to death.

The Name of the Rose operates at a number of levels, not all dignified. Veeser reports that in Greece it sold very well as an anti–Catholic book (105), and the *New York Times* claimed many did not finish "one of the great unread sellers of recent years" (Rollin, 159). In a high-level blurb written for original publication (quoted by David Lodge, xiv, and Michael Caesar, 151), Eco identifies three groups of readers—those who read it for the plot, the mystery people; then those who like "the debate of ideas" and seek "connection with the present," the political/historical group; and the third category, who will see it as "a book built of books," understanding the post-modern, relativist skepticism of the project not as leading to anarchic individualism but as a network. Eco foresees the multifocal anti-authoritarian "rhizomatic" thinking that Deleuze and Guattari have described (de Lauretis, 248, and Parker, 55). This rich mix of reading approaches responds to the way Eco himself is simultaneously creative wit, historian, and powerful critical thinker—and the mix is in some subtle way supervised by the spirit of insightful laughter, as defined by William of Baskerville and, in theory at least, described and valued by Aristotle (Coletti in her chapter 4 outlines the context and major elements of this important medieval debate). In what seems the central thematic moment of the novel, responding to Adso's dream of the *Coena* (discussed in detail by Coletti, 134–39), William will, as Caesar describes (138), synoptically reconstruct this lost book in the spirit of the modern master of both carnival and popular democracy, Bakhtin (see Lodge, xxi–ii).

Eco has gone on to write searching novels that combine conceptual power and an anxious awareness of the present, along with forms of popular culture—*Foucault's Pendulum* (1989) is a fantasy that becomes all too true, and *The Prague Cemetery* (2011) is rich with nineteenth-century criminal and political conspiracies. His work remains both exciting and demanding and finds a wide audience among those, often young, who desire testing and mind-expanding reading—not many of them admired the 1986 film of *The Name of the Rose,* which was inevitably restricted to the mystery and the medieval setting.

Eco has expanded the crime fiction form in several major directions, historical, political, and conceptual prominent among them—and yet he always finally teases us with the possibility that we only read signs and we may be all wrong. Even the sixth and seventh deaths could be fitted into the Apocalyptic scheme, and the novel's final statement suggests—William might well think it "the condemnation of our pride" (493)—that all we possess of knowledge is ultimately only names, signs, to reshape and understand as well as we can. Yet not all Eco implies is neutral. Recognizing the tragic, he is also optimistic, and even though misguided, the pertinacious and inquisitive detective did find the villain. As Michael Cohen comments, Eco, as a man of wide inquiries and many faiths, appears to believe "that authoritarianism threatens rational inquiry and faith" (75).

The summary given in *The Key*—"monks, metaphysics, murder"—conveys both the range and also the intensity of *The Name of the Rose.* Searching, informative, entertaining, demanding, it is one of the modern high-water marks of crime fiction, a clear sign, if Eco would countenance such a thing, of the increasing power and range of the genre in the modern period.

References

Caesar, Michael. *Umberto Eco: Philosophy, Semiotics and the Work of Fiction.* London: Polity, 1999.

Cohen, Michael. "The Hounding of Baskerville: Allusion and Apocalypse in *The Name of the Rose*," in *Naming the Rose: Essays on Eco's The Name of the Rose.* Ed. M. Thomas Inge. Jackson: University of Missouri Press, 1988, 65–76.

Coletti, Theresa. *Naming the Rose: Eco, Medieval Signs and Modern Theory.* Ithaca: Cornell University Press, 1988.

de Lauretis, Teresa. "Gaudy Rose: Eco and Narcissism," in *Reading Eco: An Anthology.* Ed. Rocco Capozzi. Bloomington: Indiana University Press, 1997, 239–55.

Ford, Judy Ann. "Umberto Eco: *The Name of the Rose,*" in *The Detective as Historian: History and Art in Historical Crime Fiction.* Ed. Ray B. Browne and Lawrence A. Kreiser, Jr. Bowling Green, OH: Popular Press, 2000, 95–110.

Haft, Adele J., Jane G. White and Robert J. White. *The Key to the Name of the Rose.* Harrington Park, NJ: Ampersand, 1987.

Kellner, Hans. "'To Make Truth Laugh': Eco's *The Name of the Rose,*" in *Naming the Rose: Essays on Eco's The Name of the Rose.* Ed. M. Thomas Inge. Jackson: University of Missouri Press, 1988, 3–30.

Lodge, David. "Introduction," to Umberto Eco, *The Name of the Rose.* London: Everyman, 2006, vii–xxiv.

Parker, Mark. "*The Name of the Rose* as a Postmodern Novel," in *Naming the Rose: Essays on Eco's The Name of the Rose*. Ed. M. Thomas Inge. Jackson: University of Missouri Press, 1988, 48–61.

Richter, David. "The Mirrored World: Form and Ideology in Umberto Eco's *The Name of the Rose*," in *Reading Eco: An Anthology*. Ed. Rocco Capozzi. Bloomington: Indiana University Press, 1997, 256–75.

Rollin, Roger. "Postscript: *The Name of the Rose* as Popular Culture," in *Naming the Rose: Essays on Eco's the Name of the Rose*. Ed. M. Thomas Inge. Jackson: University of Missouri Press, 1988, 157–72.

Tani, Stefano, *The Doomed Detective: The Contribution of the Detective Novel to Postmodern American and Italian Fiction*. Carbondale: Southern Illinois University Press, 1984.

Zamora, Lois Parkinson. "Apocalyptic Visions and Visionaries in *The Name of the Rose*," in *Naming the Rose: Essays on Eco's The Name of the Rose*. Ed. M. Thomas Inge. Jackson: University of Missouri Press, 1988, 31–47.

17

Southern Seas,
Manuel Vázquez Montalbán

Manuel Vázquez Montalbán was born in 1939 in Barcelona, just after the civil war ended in Spain with victory for Franco: his father, a communist laborer, was jailed like many supporters of the previous government. Very unusually for a poor child, Vázquez Montalbán went to the University of Barcelona, gaining first-class honors in philosophy and literature. He followed his father's politics but found work as a journalist on a Franco-supporting paper—there were few non-governmental opportunities. He was active in political resistance and in 1962 was jailed for six years: he served eighteen months and was tortured. When freed, he was black-listed from journalism and worked mostly as a researcher.

He began to publish as a poet in 1967 and then, as Spain slowly became a more open society, wrote sharp, witty essays critical of the establishment in the new magazine *Triumfo* (Triumph—an ironic title). By the 1970s Franco's rule, as William J. Nichols argues (39–48), was being weakened by international influences, and Vázquez Montalbán was among the opposition.

Working in prose and following the contemporary trend towards antiauthoritarian postmodern satire, he produced *Yo maté a Kennedy* (I killed Kennedy) in 1972, an espionage-style fantasy including a CIA agent named Pepe Carvalho. Vázquez Montalbán developed the character as a Barcelona private eye in *Tatuaje* (1975, Tattoo); this was followed by what Vázquez Montalbán calls his "chronicle novels" (40), well described in Susana Bayo Berlinguer's survey. *La soledad del manager* (The angst-ridden executive, 1977) dealt with the new Spain's engagement with the world, especially American business—and corruption—and then Vázquez Montalbán both mastered the form and dealt fully with the context of Barcelona in *Los mares del sur* (1977, Southern Seas), which in 1978 won the prestigious Spanish Planeta Prize—

not just for crime fiction—and a French prize for international crime fiction in 1981.

Both before and during the Franco years, Spain had almost no crime-fiction tradition. There had been some imitators of Poe and Conan Doyle and of marginal impact were the Kafkaesque *El Innocente* (1953) by Mario Lacruz and the 1960s novels by Francisco Garcia Pavón about a rustic police chief named Plinio (see Hart, chaps. 2 and 3). Closer to Vázquez Montalbán are the self-consciously Catalan Manuel Pedrolo, producing private-detective novels from the 1950s, and Jaume Fuster, with two novels from 1971 and 1976 that mix detection and social comment.

José F. Colmeira has argued that crime fiction on the American private-eye model helped fill "the void produced by the exhausted resource of social realism and the elitist experimentation of the post–Civil War Spanish novel," the form offering "a high degree of self-reflexivity as well as great potential for social criticism" (152). Vázquez Montalbán's first fiction tended towards postmodern experimentalism, what he later called "subnormal writing" (Berlinguer, 21), and then, though he was never particularly pro–American he, like French writers in the 1940s and 1950s, was attracted to a form that, not trusting either police or amateurs, was not discredited by recent European conservatism and chaos. He took the sub-genre seriously: in *Southern Seas* a seminar on the private-eye novel praises Chester Himes and sees the form as rising in the depression and having some neo–Romanticism but also, Carvalho concludes, being rich in "moral ambiguity" (51–2).

Known in Spain as the *novela negra,* the form was well placed to expose corruption in government, police and business and had no interest in the English amateurs or the trusty police of the new American procedurals. It was through the private-eye mode that Vázquez Montalbán and others expressed what they felt was wrong about their world. The situation was not very different from that in France, where post–1968 writers of the *néo-polar* like Didier Daeninckx used the private-eye form to put the French state and its politico-social culture under close scrutiny, and this is likely to have been a significant influence.

Vázquez Montalbán's objections were not only to the world of Franco but even more to the slow, incomplete nature of the changes to the system. Events seemed rapid: King Juan Carlos, charged with the succession by Franco, supervised the lead-up to free elections in 1977 and a new liberal constitution in 1978. Many called this the *Transicio,* "Transition," and the real *Cambio,* or "Change," occurred in 1982 when a socialist government was elected. But commentators like Vázquez Montalbán felt that though no longer all-powerful, the army and the church were still very important and the world of business, which had developed from the 1960s in place of the rural and internalized economy that Franco had favored, had not been challenged by any new state or radical institutions.

The other force that was destabilizing for people, as they thought what it meant to be a Spaniard in the post–Franco world, was regionalism. Where Spain had under Franco been a tight, hierarchical and traditional unit, powerfully focused on Madrid and Castilian Spanish, now regionalism was to a degree encouraged and the Catalan and Galician regions were resurgent in self-confidence—though the Basque struggle for freedom led by ETA remained, as it still does, a step too far for the Spanish authorities. But as Stewart King notes (268), Pepe Carvalho was born in Galicia, lives in Barcelona, and "does not identify easily with either community," describing himself in *Murder in the Central Committee* to a former CIA colleague as a "mestizo," a person of mixed blood.

Vázquez Montalbán established a new voice for his time and place: a challenging, even rude and aggressive voice—but a major one in both world literature and crime fiction. He sought to reverse the constraints of the Franco years when, as he said in a 1991 essay, "they kidnapped the conscience of a society" (Nichols, 134). In approaching this goal, his novels vary considerably in location and theme, but *Summer Seas* is his first confident work and offers a major account of how he sees both Spain and Barcelona in the light of his personal, social, historical, and even gastronomical opinions.

The story starts, and moves, rapidly. In Barcelona a youth steals a Jaguar, gives his friends a joyride, and loses control; he runs from the police into a half-built house and finds a dead man.

Pepe Carvalho, private detective, is shopping at a delicatessen near the central Ramblas, then buys a German shepherd puppy. At home his friend, cook and general assistant Biscuter gives him a message, and he goes to see the lawyer Viladecans. Stuart Pedrell, a rich businessman, was found dead in January—two months ago—after he disappeared for a year after saying he was going to the South Pacific. Pedrell's wife arrives, a slim beauty starting to age. The police have failed to discover anything: all Pedrell had on him was a line of Italian poetry: "There is no longer anyone to carry me to the south" (14).

A policeman tells Pepe they have dropped the inquiry, as the family wished. He takes his girlfriend the prostitute Charo and Biscuter out to dinner. Pepe and Charo go home to the new dog, Bleda ("Softy" in Catalan); Pepe lights a fire with a copy of Forster's *Maurice,* and after some squabbling he and Charo make love.

The next day Pepe examines Pedrell's office, with many books and a diary containing poetry: the line "I read, much of the night, and go south in the

17. Southern Seas

winter," then a longer quote in Italian, and then the line he had on him. Pedrell's secretary says he booked a trip to Tahiti before he left. There are modern paintings, including by Artimbau, whom Pepe knows. At Artimbau's studio Pepe sees "a book of drawings on the death agonies of General Franco" (29): Artimbau says Pedrell made money in the 1950s by cornering casein imports. His partners were Planas and the Marquess of Munt. After becoming rich Pedrell went back to the university to study philosophy. He had girlfriends and became interested in Gauguin in the South Seas; he often quoted the line found on him.

At Pedrell's grand house, Pepe meets his blond daughter Yesica (known, not unironically, as Yes), smelling of marijuana. She has four brothers, the oldest in Bali. He finds her attractive, and she finally embraces him in her distress; he gives her his number in case she remembers something.

He meets Panas, a brisk businessman, obsessed with health. He says Pedrell was wealthy, Munt very wealthy, and he, Panas, did all the work. Pepe visits a seminar on the *roman noir*. Did Dostoevsky write them? Did they start with the Great Depression? One speaker mentions Chandler, Hammett and Ross Macdonald and another adds Chester Himes as a match for Balzac. Someone says the writers are close to fascism; another links them to neo–Romanticism. Pepe thinks about moral ambiguity.

He worries about his drinking and rings his accountant friend Fuster to find a literary expert on the poetry. He goes to see the Marquess: they have fine pâté with Chablis. The Marquess was with Franco's *nacionales* in the civil war. He suggests Pedrell enrolled at a foreign university.

Yesica, at Pepe's house, says he admired her father and her mother is "a brute" (67). They make love and she takes cocaine. The next day Pepe finds out from Teresa, a shop-owner friend, that Pedrell had an affair with the rich "Lila" Vilardel, so he sees her. She says Pedrell did not contact her while he was missing and previously he was "picking up infants" (79).

Yesica leaves Pepe's house, saying, "I'll kill myself." He says, "I don't prevent suicides. I only investigate them" (82). He searches for her among the beggars, prostitutes and poor shops near the Ramblas; then he has a meal of chorizo and potatoes cooked by Biscuter. Pepe follows up on an art student the shop owner linked to Pedrell. She speaks well of him, but refused to go with him to the South. Pepe admires her blond friend and leaves for dinner with Fuster at the house of Beser, the literary expert. They eat paella and drink a lot. Beser identifies the first line as from Eliot's *Waste Land*; the second passage is from *The South Seas* by Pavese; he finally finds the third in Quasimodo's *Lamento per il sud* (Lament for the South).

The next day Pepe has a hangover and thinks about the South as being an opposite. He looks at a map: opposite where Pedrell's body was found is San Magin, a new, largely immigrant suburb where his firm erected buildings. Pepe thinks how under Franco bad satellite towns spread "to complete the punishment of the vanquished" (103). He travels to San Magin on the underground, seeing "the fresh marks of personal defeat on people's faces" (104). He shows Pedrell's photo around; a few have seen him. A church caretaker says he came to their political club; he was called Antonio but known as "The Accountant"; he knew a radical girl, Ana Briongos, but he disappeared. The caretaker was a radical police officer in the civil war, who was jailed until 1946. He has recently received a good police pension and wonders about "the principle" (117).

The man who found Antonio work says he did it for his employer, Pedrell; he provided a flat as well. In the flat Pepe finds maps and books. He goes out and calls Biscuter and tells him to give the dog the hake in cider he has cooked for dinner. He thinks about Pedrell: "He had lived out the novel he could not write" (128).

Pepe goes early to meet Ana: she weeps to hear Antonio has been stabbed, and will meet Pepe after work. He takes the metro into the city, where poverty is older than in San Magin. Biscuter says Caro and Yesica have called and Pepe is invited by Senora Pedrell to celebrate Planas' election to lead a business association. Pepe borrows Biscuter's only tie, smelling of mothballs. A baker visits to ask Pepe to find his wife who has gone off with a Basque pelota player. He will do it in a few days. At the party Planas makes a speech about the value of entrepreneurs and the Marquess is ironic. Pedrell's wife wants results quickly. He leaves to meet Yesica in a Chinese restaurant. She wants to live with him. She says Planas and the Marquess surrounded her father "with mediocrity ... He was dying of disgust, just like me" (148). Pepe says she can come to his house late that night.

Pepe visits Charo—she is ironical, then cries. He reminisces about her, then promises a trip over the weekend. When he leaves he nearly drives to see the dog but goes to meet Ana. She and Pedrell met over discussing the Moncloa Accords in 1977; she was amazed when she heard he was Pedrell. She is pregnant. She says his death was probably due to a robbery. Pedrell's employee in San Magin tells Pepe that Ana has a half brother who has had trouble with the law. Her father tells Pepe the brother, Pedro, is troublesome.

Pepe asks Bromide the shoeblack about knife gangs. Planas rings to complain Pepe has been stirring things up in San Magin. Yesica has climbed the garden gate and brought cheese and a book to burn (by Carson McCullers). They make love and she takes cocaine. The next day the policeman tells Pepe they were checking the knife gangs, but the family made them draw back. He says the KGB have agents everywhere and he likes the South, "where the individual still has room to fight" (180). At lunch Planas and the Marquess warn Pepe off San Magin. Planas will pay Pepe as much as Pedrell's wife to produce something "plausible" (184).

The elections are on—Pepe thinks "nothing would stop the irreversible march towards democracy. Everybody said so" (186). He also thinks "none of the election programmes said anything about tearing down what the Franco regime had built" (186–87). He sees Charo, then goes to meet Pedro, with knife, gun and knuckle-duster. Ana meets Pepe and asks him not to go. He does, and Pedro has two friends. They fight: Pepe breaks one's arm, knocks out the big friend, wounds Pedro and takes him to his sister's. Pedro admits they attacked Pedrell because of the sister: they didn't mean to kill him. They left him in San Magin.

Pepe goes home, plays with the dog, and at 3:00 a.m. rings Lila Vilardel. Viladecans answers the phone. Pepe says he will see them in the morning. When he does, he suggests Pedrell rang them badly wounded, they brought him to the flat and he died, so they dumped him to avoid scandal, then they hired Pepe to find out where Pedrell had been. Viladecans fails to buy Pepe's silence. Lila, descended from the last Catalan to be a slave trader, says an abandoned mistress can feel "more humiliated than a wife" (207).

Pepe writes his report drunk and posts a farewell letter to Yesica, giving her Beser's address to help her find a clever boyfriend at the university. He remembers the baker's wife and finds her with the Basque pelota player. Pepe says he is from ETA and that the player has been pretending to be a terrorist. ETA are angry, Pepe says, and he must leave, showing his gun. The man hurries off and Pepe tells her to return to her husband; she does. When he gives Pedrell's wife the report, she cries. Pepe says: "When rich people suffer, it costs them less" (213). He asks for 300,000 pesetas; she gives him a 50,000-peseta bonus. He says he won't see her daughter again. She asks if he will go to the South Seas with her (the trip Pedrell had booked). Pepe says, "I'm too old to be a gigolo" (213) and that he has obligations, a dog and two people.

He leaves and goes home. The dog is not there. He finds her in the garden, with her throat cut. He buries the dog, shouts, "You dirty, filthy bastards!" and drinks ice-cold *orujo*, strong Galician brandy.

The central story of *Southern Seas* is geographically and symbolically strongly connected to Barcelona—Vázquez Montalbán called it his "urban novel" (Nichols, 110). It outlines what Colmeira calls the post–Franco "disillusionment of the political transition" (155), focusing on a history and a fable about Stuart Pedrell. He represents the entrepreneurs who began to make their way by the 1960s, leading what Nichols calls "the infiltration and birth of consumer capitalism in Spain" (76); Pedrell's role as an international importer links to the country's turn towards the outer world. But his supporters are less innovative: the Marquess is of the old school, who entered Barcelona with the *nacionales,* Franco's men, and has remained a symbol of the link between business and the old elite. The hardworking, body-obsessed Planas represents the managerial class, keen to keep things quiet, to organize matters on behalf of profit.

Against these two highly focused and aggressive men, Pedrell seems indecisive—or a figure of where Spain now stands. He is culturally aware, in both literature and art; he went back to the university to study philosophy; he is easily distracted both into charity and with young women. The idea of the South Seas, especially through the medium of Gauguin's career, fascinates him as a better path. Vásquez Montalbán sees this as "the deception perpetrated by utopian concepts" (Nichols, 86) and Pedrell's dream of escape is ironically transmuted as he hides himself on a brutal new estate that he himself created. Though things can get worse: what Nichols calls this "uninnocent victim of his own class guilt and sentimental miseducation" (116) is later remembered, in *Offside* (in English 1996), as "an immature and imbecile adolescent" (186), compared to the profiteers of the 1990s. As Antonio the Accountant, he is actually involved in discussion of the way Spain is reconstructing itself—the Moncloa accords that he and Ana discussed were a worker-restraining basis for the compromise between reformism and the past that led in 1977–78 to the new constitution and elections.

Through Ana, Pedrell is moved towards both ordinary people and the left—but this opportunity, which he appears to be welcoming, is tragically disrupted by the continuing disaffection and violence of other ordinary people, Ana's half brother and his friends, who attack him apparently for getting Ana pregnant. Yet this low-level malice is not the whole story: Pedrell, badly wounded, rings his old mistress who is with his lawyer, and they, through their selfish defensiveness, fail to prevent his death and then merely dump his body—even bungling that, as it is found the next day.

Where Chandler made Rusty Regan merely a victim of the emotions and malpractices of the rich Sternwood family, Vázquez Montalbán makes his lost urban soul Pedrell a figure of the society in which he and all the other characters disorientedly move. They are both damaged by and contributors to the sense of *desencantando,* "disenchantment," that Vázquez Montalbán finds already by the late 1970s "as global as the economy" (46), while the sense of possible change is dissipating. The upper-class men, other than Pedrell, are manipulators and the women are adrift: Pedrell's wife, his discarded mistress, and the shop owner only seek status and uncertain pleasures. Yesica, cultured and volatile like her father, is vulnerable to both men and drugs, and Carvalho's final plan for her physical and spiritual satisfaction in the academic world seems less than fully credible—she will return to his affections in *El hombre di mi vida* (The man of my life, 2000).

The novel is also rich with people at a lower social level who have suffered both financially and physically during the Franco years and also, unlike the rich, retain clear memories of an alternative world. Biscuter served in jail with Carvalho for political crimes as well as car theft; the church caretaker in San Magin was an anti-fascist police officer in the 1930s and was jailed till 1946 but now, with some surprise and concern, is receiving a police pension. There are reverse lower-class pasts—Bromide the bootblack ("Bromura" in Spanish, with the same meaning) was a civil war fascist who volunteered to fight with the Spanish "Blue Division" on the Russian front and gained little from his commitment. Whatever its origin, the misery of the people is both present and past as Carvalho sees on the long underground ride to the dreary new suburb of San Magin.

Between the settled, vicious rich and the distressed, displaced poor, Carvalho himself is a volatile figure. He is highly cultured, with many books in his home—but uses them to light fires. He selects E. M. Forster's *Maurice,* which appears to reject the sensitive modernist novel and also the gay theme that caused the book to be long unpublished. Carvalho's own personal loyalties are strong but notably to the dispossessed and alienated such as Biscuter and Charo rather than to any church or political party—he is a highly sociable person, especially at mealtimes, yet also capable of seriously industrious detecting as with Pedrell's photo in San Magin and, like his private-eye forebears, when there is call for it he can burst into sudden and successful violence.

The meals are a central feature, and Vázquez Montalbán has produced several separate books in this area. The food signifies authenticity, to a region, even a town or village, and the values of strongly natural—and often less than health-giving—ingredients. Carvalho likens it to Holmes' violin playing in *Murder in the Central Committee* (233), but this obsession also asserts Carvalho's authentic social and physical life, which often extends to sexual encounters.

Carvalho is unlike Chandler's detective both in what Vázquez Montalbán called "Marlowe's lack of culture" (in an interview with Micheal Eaude) and also in his warmly busy domestic life, which here extends to the puppy Bleda, bought when he is food-shopping and rapidly becoming part of the benign domestic ambience—and finally brutally killed because Carvalho generates, in a very violent scene, the treacherous hostility of Pedro's friends and the dog, the most innocent figure in the novel, dies for this. As Nichols notes (115), Carvalho at the very end seems to direct his grief and rage at "the illuminated city" (217), modernity operating in full malignity through its own deformed peasantry.

Later novels move beyond the city itself as an emblem of the forces of modern Spain: *Murder in the Central Committee* (1981) is a sharp account of a locked-room murder that also exposes the weakened Communist Party of the transition phase. In his later period, Vázquez Montalbán was interested in the social critic Jürgen Habermas, who sought the establishment of new, radical and inclusive forms of political community, depending on a tolerant comprehension of diversity, and not only resisting nationalisms but also, as King comments, "contesting homogeneous notions of regional identities" (273). Vázquez Montalbán was also specific in his critique of global capitalism. Both *El laberinto griego* (The Greek labyrinth, 1991) and *Sabotaja olympico* (Olympic sabotage, 1993) deal with the impact on Barcelona and the region of the 1992 Olympics, with its profiteering and high-handed social engineering: later work goes further as Vázquez Montalbán's critique extends to Argentina in *The Buenos Aires Quintet* (1997), and in the two-volume posthumously published novel *Milenio I* and *Milenio II* (2004) Carvalho and Biscuter travel around what Vázquez Montalbán called "a world which wages holy war and creates economic and military hegemonies in the name of God" (Berlinguer, 35). Vázquez Montalbán's fiction, fame and activity all became worldwide as his reputation grew, across Europe and then the world, and in 2003 at the early age of sixty-four he was to die at Bangkok airport on an international speaking tour.

In what seems his most characteristic novel, *Summer Seas,* Vázquez Montalbán shaped a story that both realizes and symbolizes the social and the psychic chaos of the post–Franco years. By relocating the tough and interrogative voice and viewpoint of the early Hammett stories, he has probed the values and structures of the Spanish present, where words like "reformism," "transition," "change" and "disenchantment" are not just about individual human feelings but are also forces summarizing the massive social and emotional structures of a major country undergoing substantial—though for some like Vázquez Montalbán not enough—change.

While he has been extremely popular, in Spain and abroad, his work was not at first favorably received: Berlinguer reports in some detail how *Summer Seas* "was at first savaged by the literary establishment" (28) and Caragh Wells describes critics, both conservatives and purist radicals, who objected to what they saw as Vázquez Montalbán's sentimentality: she asserts this was "an antidote to the wider culture of historical amnesia which the author believed to be one of the main deficiencies of the post–Franco period" (190).

Though he has been a dramatic and charismatic leader, Vázquez Montalbán has not been alone. Other Spanish crime writers have participated in what David K. Herzberger calls this "post-totalitarian discourse" (155), such as Eduard Mendoza and Juan Madrid, and a range of women writers are discussed by Shelley Godsland, notably Maria-Antonia Oliver and Alicia Giménez-Bartlett. The connections have been international: as Nichols has shown, Vázquez Montalbán offers a striking parallel to his acknowledged colleague Paco Ignacio Taibo II in Mexico. More generally, in what Berlinguer calls Vázquez Montalbán's "unfolding of a sustained polemic" (19) he can be seen, like other internationally prominent authors of the very modern period, as a writer who has found in crime fiction not a mere set of puzzles or a way of validating social confidences as has been usual in the past, but a mode of writing to tackle some of the largest, and for much fiction unmanageable, issues of the present.

References

Berlinguer, Susana Bayo. "The Carvalho Series of Manuel Vázquez Montalbán: A Passing in Review." In *Hispanic and Luso-Brazilian Detective Fiction: Essays on the Genero Negro Tradition*. Ed. Renee W. Craig-Odders, Jacky Collins and Glen S. Close. Jefferson, NC: McFarland, 2006, 19–45.

Colmeira, José F. "The Spanish Connection: Detective Fiction After Franco." *Journal of Popular Culture* 28 (1994): 151–61.

Eaude, Micheal. "Notes from Barcelona's Dark Side." *The Guardian*, June 18, 2002.

Godsland, Shelley. *Killing Carmens: Women's Crime Fiction from Spain*. Cardiff: University of Wales Press, 2008.

Hart, Patricia. *The Spanish Sleuth: The Detective in Spanish Fiction*. Rutherford, NJ: Fairleigh Dickinson University Press, 1987.

Herzberger, David K. *Narrating the Past: Fiction and Historiography in Postwar Spain*. Durham: Duke University Press, 1995.

King, Stewart. "Peripheral Detectives and Detectives on the Periphery: Crime Fiction in the *Nacionalidades Históricas*," in *Beyond the Periphery: Narratives of Identity in the Basque Country, Catalonia and Galicia*. Ed. Stewart King. Special Issue of *Antípodas: Journal of Hispanic and Galician Studies* 18 (2007): 265–85.

Nichols, William J. *Transatlantic Mysteries: Crime, Culture, and Capital in the "Noir Novels" of Paco Ignacio Taibo II and Manuel Vázquez Montalbán*. Lewisburg, PA: Bucknell University Press, 2011.

Vázquez Montalbán, Manuel. "On the Non-Existence of the Detective Novel." *Antipodás: Journal of Hispanic and Galician Studies* 18 (2007): 35–46.

Wells, Caragh. "The Case for Nostalgia and Sentimentality in Manuel Vázquez Montalbán's 'Serie Carvalho.'" *Hispanic Review* 17 (2008): 281–97.

18

The Naming of the Dead, Ian Rankin

Ian Rankin was born in 1960 in Fife, southeastern Scotland: like Conan Doyle, Chandler and Chandra he memorably characterized a city to which he was not native. He went to the University of Edinburgh and was writing a PhD on Muriel Spark, another Scottish writer of high impact and interrogative spirit, but, as Gill Plain relates (*Ian Rankin's Black and Blue*, 16–17) he moved towards fiction and in 1987 published *Knots and Crosses,* a crime novel that, though not highly successful, was recognized as having an interesting new voice.

British crime fiction, like the novel in general, had long been routinely set in London, unless it was provincial and usually rural, but the late twentieth century saw more non–London urban writing, most strongly in Scotland, where Rankin initiated "Tartan Noir." Also involved were Christopher Brookmyre, with Edinburgh stories close to postmodern experiment, and the tougher realism of Denis Mina, with women investigators operating in Glasgow, but Rankin was a decade ahead of them.

John Rebus is a police detective who likes rock music, enjoys a drink, knows Edinburgh intimately, and tends to persevere with an inquiry he thinks is important when his superiors disagree. His personal life is a mess, even a vacuum: at the start, a divorce is under way, his daughter and wife are disappearing, and he has few friends, male or female, but is not going to give in.

Rebus will always do, and enjoy, detailed work on the street or in the office: the novels mix the lonely dissident hero of the private-eye tradition with the police procedural. The latter is usually seen as a formation of the years after the Second World War, when on television with *Dragnet* (starting in 1949) and in the novel with the 87th Precinct stories of Evan Hunter, as "Ed McBain," from 1956 on, American police on the street were closely observed and their routine practices presented as both realistic and successful.

There was some history to the sub-genre. Stories from the mid-nineteenth century at times present police detectives who watch people, bribe informers, and use elementary procedures to gain success: the "Waters" stories by the still-unidentified "William Russell" started in 1849 and by the mid-century police detectives were common, with some women among them (Knight, 30–36). But this pattern did not move into the emergent crime novel, and under the influence of Stevenson, Conan Doyle and Chesterton even short stories became a good deal more exotic.

Later there were some hyper-procedural novels like Freeman Wills Crofts' arias of analysis by Inspector French, often focused on the railway timetable, but the idea that a normal police person could operate to resolve public anxieties only became widely credible after, and probably relating to, the success of those other public operators, the armed forces personnel of the Second World War, beginning with Lawrence Treat's *V as in Victim* (1945). The new police had relatively forceful heroes, like McBain's Steve Carella and John Creasey's Inspector Gideon of the Yard, but in general they seemed surprisingly unauthoritative figures. They could focus resistance as in the African American and lesbian sub-genres, but in Britain they were usually quiet provincial operators. Rebus, however, is always at the core of dramatic events in a major capital, increasingly with complex international connections, and he is also always a sensitive, brave but also public-spirited hero—he is both public and private eye.

Rankin gained good opinions and reasonable sales as he moved on—after the first, the next six Rebus novels were written in France (Plain *Ian Rankin's Black and Blue*, 17). Rodney Marshall sorts Rankin's novels into the first three as "early Rebus" and then from *Strip Jack* (1992) on eight novels seen as being "classic Rebus," where he operates in the largely male world of the variously criminal city and begins to extend out into the country as a whole. Central to this process is the eighth Rebus novel, *Black and Blue* (1997), much more ambitious and described by London's *The Guardian* as "a book with epic reach" (Plain *Ian Rankin's Black and Blue*, 68): this lifted Rankin's work to a higher level, in terms of both sales and recognition. The earlier novels sold about thirty thousand in six months, but it approached half a million in the same period. A long book, with a rich "psychologically gothic atmosphere" (MacDonald, 68), it looks back to the past more than its predecessors but also has a wider geographic and thematic reach. Set in Glasgow and Aberdeen as well as Edinburgh and reaching up to the Shetlands, it engages directly with criminal traditions as well as the ultra-modern oil industry, is more assertively involved with rock music and, perhaps crucially, is a serial-killer story about the mysterious recent "Bible John." It won a British Crime Writers' Association award: Gill Plain, who calls it "a state of the nation novel" (2013, 19), has devoted a study to it (2002), and in this novel Rankin moved from being a successful crime writer to a major figure in the genre.

He started from uncertainty: the plan was to kill Rebus at the end of the first novel, and Rankin named him jokingly—"rebus" is a Latin word for "an enigmatic puzzle." The character was also deep in self-doubt, but he has survived many painful cases. Rankin has added a major character: Siobhan Clarke, first appearing in *The Black Book* (1993), increasingly works beside Rebus, sometimes a little against him. English and a dedicated detective, she is not easily thrown off course, nor yet attracted into a relationship with Rebus, though she clearly respects his policing instincts and tolerates his unimpressive personal habits. As well as doubling the viewpoint in this way, Rankin has moved on in the conscious range of his work. Marshall sees a "late Rebus" sequence as beginning with *The Falls* (2001), in which Rebus' approaching retirement casts a shadow over both his engagement and the attitudes of other police to him. *Fleshmarket Close* (2004) begins to take on international rather than merely national issues, and it is *The Naming of the Dead* (2006) that makes a major statement about national politics and their interrelation with the everyday here and now: Peter Messent reports that Rankin summarized its theme to him as "geopolitics" (182).

The story is multiple. During the holding in Edinburgh in 2005 of the major international meeting of the G8—the most powerful countries—Rebus plods away at a serial-killing case, which turns out to be deeply involved with political events; Siobhan would like to be a protestor; much is drunk; the authorities are challenged; Edinburgh and the expanses of southern Scotland are traversed in inquiry; the forces of distortion and disruption, both local and distant, are comprehended.

This interwoven set of plots is in keeping with the popular music Rebus seems to feel is a world beyond corruption. The novel is divided into four sections, called Sides, and given ominous names: "The Task of Blood"; "Dance with the Devil"; "No Gods, No Masters"; "The Final Push." All are from popular and political culture: the first begins a 2009 graphic comic about gangsters, *Slaughterman's Creed;* the second is a song from a 2001 Immortal Technique album; the third is an anarchist slogan stemming from Louis Blanqui in 1880; the last is the actual name of the final concert of the 2005 Live 8 series, occurring alongside the G8 conference. The other dividers of the action are the nine days of the novel, Friday, July 1, to Saturday, July 9, those of the G8 meeting, including the day of the London bombings, July 6, 2005.

The story begins at the funeral of Rebus's brother Michael, dead of a stroke (he served time for drug dealing previously). At a well near the G8 base, a place where people put clothes in memory of family and friends, a patch has

18. The Naming of the Dead

been found cut from the jacket of the murdered Cyril Colliar, stand-over man for "Big Ger" Gerald Cafferty, local gangster and long-term Rebus enemy—and also quasi-friend. Rebus and Siobhan (always named in this uneven last/first name way) visit the well and are bullied by Steelforth, visiting English head of G8 security.

Siobhan knows Rebus will not give up his inquiries, as Steelforth wants, but she has other concerns. Her parents are up from London for the demonstrations and are camping next to a strong-willed hippy, Santal. Local roughs harass the campers, but Councillor Tench helps them. Rebus is called late to Edinburgh Castle, where Ben Webster, London MP, has fallen to his death. Rebus visits his hotel, for which the mysterious Pennen Industries was paying. Steelforth arrives and again warns him off.

Rebus meets the MP's sister, a London police detective, Stacey. Their mother was murdered not long ago in Scotland, and their father died soon after. Siobhan goes to the demonstration, where Santal is filming. Cafferty calls menacingly on Rebus, wanting to join the case. In more campsite trouble Siobhan, threatened by the thugs' leader, is rescued by Tench. Rebus suspects two other men, Trevor Guest and Edward Isley, might have been killed as well as Colliar.

In the next section the three men, all sex offenders, are found on Beastwatch, a name-and-shame Web site run by the parents of a raped woman. A vengeful serial killer seems likely. Rebus discuses Pennen with Steelforth, who defends him. Later that night Rebus is taken by three self-proclaimed police and locked in an empty jail; when he is released in the morning by the normal police, he assumes it was Steelforth's doing, and he involves Mairie Henderson, a journalist. Once an old friend, she wrote a book on Cafferty, but they are patching up their distance and she interviews Pennen. Eric Bain, a police expert, helps with the Web site; he has a new, glamorous girlfriend.

When answering Siobhan's phone, Rebus recognizes the voice of Ellen Wylie, a policewoman, and finds that she wrote on the Web site because of her sister Denise's abusive partner. Rebus brings Ellen into the case, but the Chief Constable says the inquiry is shelved during the G8 crisis. Siobhan's mother has been hurt in a riot: Siobhan cannot get film of the attack from Santal but notices she films demonstrators, not police. Rebus feeds more material to Mairie. Cafferty takes him to hear Tench speaking and pretends he and Rebus are close—Cafferty feels threatened by Tench's activities. The English police investigator of the Guest case is in Edinburgh and takes Rebus to a strip club where a Kenyan diplomat is arguing with a stripper: Rebus talks to him about Pennen and (we later discover) recognizes her as Eric Bain's girl.

Section 3 starts with the leaders arriving and riots developing. Mairie interviews the Kenyan, and Siobhan, having realized Santal is in fact Stacey Webster undercover, goes with Rebus to the G8 base. Steelforth is furious they broke Stacey's cover and denies the CCTV revealed anything on Webster's death. They watch George Bush famously fall off his bicycle and are told to stop inquiries by the Chief Constable. He suspends Rebus, so the case is moved to his flat: Ellen reveals that Tench, who knows her sister, was a Beastwatch writer. Stacey sees Rebus, gives him a disc of photos of Siobhan's mother being hit; they discuss their dead brothers, but she vanishes mysteriously from the pub.

The next morning Tench meets Rebus and says he used the Web site to fight against criminals. The London bombs have exploded, and Siobhan's parents leave. She has seen her mother was attacked by the campsite thug, whom Tench supported at court. Rebus sees a Scottish MP and Trade Minister to ask more about Webster and Pennen, and this causes more trouble. Rebus visits Tench and finds the thug's name is Carberry. Ellen tells him Tench was friendly with her sister. Cafferty finds Siobhan and they discuss getting to Tench through Carberry; Mairie is closing in on Pennen.

The last section begins with treatment of the London bombings and police beginning to return there. Siobhan plays snooker with Carberry; Cafferty appears and uses Siobhan as co-interrogator to turn Carberry against Tench. Rebus talks more to Mairie, then finds that Tench introduced Guest, the later-murdered criminal, as a volunteer at a care center. Rebus rings Mairie, who tells him Pennen Industries provided mercenary security in Iraq. He then visits Tench, who says Cafferty is the enemy. Rebus and Siobhan see Dr. Gilreagh, a university psychologist: she thinks the mix of clothes at the well is inauthentic. Ellen has found Guest knew, and fought, a man called Barclay from Coldstream. Mairie interviews Pennen at a golf range and is chased off by three suntanned men like those who captured Rebus. She goes home and is "writing Richard Pennen's destruction" (411).

Tench has been stabbed dead with a kitchen knife. They assume it is Carberry. Rebus visits Cafferty's house to threaten him not to draw in Siobhan. He then goes to the strip club and tells Eric's girlfriend he knows she is giving Cafferty Eric's information and she should leave him. The English policeman rings to say Guest once lived in Coldstream, and Rebus says to himself, "Clickety-click" (439). He sees Bain and tells him he has been passing police data to Cafferty via his girlfriend, then goes to Coldstream and finds where Barclay lives. He meets a coach driver and admires his simple, honest way of life. Siobhan visits Ellen, finds Denise upset—and notices a kitchen knife is missing.

Barclay, a rural craft worker, takes Rebus to the house where the Websters' mother was murdered by Trevor Guest, when he robbed it. Guest's was the most savaged of the three bodies. Eric tries to commit suicide with pills, but Siobhan arrives in time. On his return to Edinburgh, Rebus works out that Stacey killed Guest in revenge for her mother, then two more men, as serial-killer-style cover. She must have told her brother this when they met at the Castle. Rebus later talks to Steelforth, who says the CCTV showed the two arguing and then the brother falling after a wrestle. Steelforth denies he is hiding Stacey, saying she has disappeared, taking advantage of the bombing chaos in London after her train arrived. He also says Pennen's arms and mercenary business is failing through corruption charges and he is not taking the job Pennen has offered him. Rebus and Siobhan go drinking: he quotes a Steely Dan album title, *Two Against Nature*.

In the epilogue Siobhan is aggressive to Cafferty, who says she enjoyed working with him; Rebus tells Steelforth he will consult him over his final report; he takes the train to London (concealing this from Siobhan), goes to an address Steelforth has just given him and beats up the leader of the three fake cops, on behalf of himself and Mairie. He puts up posters inquiring for Stacey/Santal, as lost after the bombings. The long story ends: "No way Rebus would be giving up on this one. Not for a good while yet" (515).

As in previous novels, the story is rooted in the detail of a city that Rebus really knows: he recognizes people's voices on the phone, spots their faces in unusual contexts; Siobhan is also good at making intimate connections. They enjoy policing: Rebus feels happy showing people photos in Coldstream; Siobhan immediately notices the missing knife in Ellen's kitchen.

The huge world is also visible to them: they are standing there when President Bush, as really happened, fell off his bicycle; the complexities and criminalities of the arms trade, international policing and the even more arcane area of third-world funding are all penetrated, partly by Mairie Henderson, but she is stimulated by Rebus, starting from the strange interaction of Ben Webster and Pennen. The plot asserts the interrelation of the public and the private. Tench is for some time set up as the agent of Edinburgh corruption, but in fact he dies for the most banal of personal reasons; Ben Webster's fall from the Castle seems linked to major international events but is in fact the almost casual offshoot of his mother's meaningless murder and his sister's secret vengeance.

The mix of the public and the private can be fuller, more political. The novel's title refers to a formal ceremony held to read aloud a thousand names of those who have died in Iraq. Rebus himself makes his own naming of the dead, especially in his thoughts about his brother Michael, and Siobhan, listening to the dead-naming ceremony, feels this was what she did, her whole working life. She named the dead. She recorded their last details, and tried to find out who they'd been, why they'd died. She gave a voice to the forgotten and the missing. A world filled with victims, waiting for her and other detectives like her [135].

This is what Rebus insists on doing for the three deeply flawed, but not therefore negligible, dead men. One of the first things Rebus notices odd about Stacey is that she, unlike him, has not attended her brother's funeral. She avenges, not just names, her dead, and a parallel fury leads Denise to murder her faithless lover Tench.

The themes of the city and the nation are here seen as a basis for a broader international understanding, a fuller exploration by Rankin of what P. M. Newton calls "charting his homeland Scotland, as it devolves from England and rediscovers its identity" (28). The long history of invasions from outside is recalled as the G8 gathers, and both the demonstrators and especially the police come from all over the country—the English voices that have invaded and have no idea of where they are in Scotland have a particularly sharp historic edge. But other invasions are also in mind: Pennen Industries is involved in, as well as fake international charities, supplying materials and security men to Iraq: the brutal fake police have been there—they are all suntanned—and Rebus' seizure very clearly invokes the practice of "extraordinary rendition," as Newton notes (33). The huge number and the ferocity of the demonstrators against G8 is strongly linked to the 2003 invasion of Iraq, and the fact, at once real and massively symbolic, that the G8 conference was itself disrupted by the London bombings is the ultimate way in which, as Newton comments, the events in the novel "resound with the politics of the post 9/11 world" (33).

Part of the power of the book is that the massive importance of international politics is itself seen as a possible distraction from the importance of continuing mundane issues. As Plain notes, the novel poses the question "does one death matter in the face of seismic world-political events" ("The Map That Engenders the Territory?" 22). Rebus is recurrently blocked in working on the apparent serial killings because it increasingly seems to many that a few dead sex offenders no longer matter.

The determined policewoman Stacey Webster, so capable as undercover hippy Santal, is the central actual criminal, avenging personally her parents' deaths and concealing it as serial killing. Ellen's sister Denise is a more casual revenge killer, and even Siobhan is motivated to seek personal settlement for her mother's injury. Though Rebus has stood up for the value of inquiring into the murdered men, at the very end he takes personal vengeance on the leader of the fake police: even Rebus is drawn into the personalized destructiveness. But the novel ends with him putting up posters in quest of Stacey: he is still a policeman, still seeking the rule of law. And the novel is not entirely without what Marshall calls "a chink of hope" (241): on his trip to the borders Rebus meets an everyday coach driver he admires for living simply his working life, and it is from a rural craftsman, a link with ancient Scotland, that Rebus gains his key piece of information. Between rigorous critique and possible hope, a Rebus story tends to end on an open, doubting note: Rankin says in his book *Rebus's Scotland* "the books always feel like a debate, sometimes with a concrete answer at the end, oftentimes not" (quoted in Marshall, 7).

More can be implied in the novels. There is a reserved area within Rebus that is ultimately religious. *Hide and Seek* mentions the "small, dark personal God of his" (82), and Brian Diemert draws attention to the "spiritual themes and motifs" (164) that lie behind a good deal of the novels' titles—though some are from rock albums. There is also a good deal of literary reference, especially in the early novels, tending to be replaced later by music. A recurrent theme is that of the double, both the possible redemption found in Dostoeovsky (a favorite of both Rankin and Rebus) and the darker Scottish theme of the schizophrenic Jekyll and Hyde tradition, which the Edinburgh writer Robert Louis Stevenson set in London: Plain sees a connection back to Scott as well as Stevenson (*Ian Rankin's Black and Blue*, 13). As Diemert discusses (166–70), the Gothic element is strong, with Rebus from the start haunted by his experiences in the British army's very tough Special Air Services; the criminal of the first novel is an old military colleague, almost a Mr. Hyde double for Rebus and his police sergeant respectability, already filling the role that the serious local criminal Cafferty will increasingly play in the later novels.

Cafferty haunts Rebus and begins to possess Siobhan in some way. Discussed in detail by Sara Martin Alegre, Cafferty both is Rebus' dark double, whose life the detective saves at the end of *Exit Music* (2007), where Rebus retires, and can also, in the absence of politicians or police who can be trusted, even seem to be the voice of the author, as when he says, of the councilor he hates, "Sometimes I think that's how half the globe operates. It's not the underworld you should be watching—it's the *over*world" (253). As Messent notes (189), Cafferty the criminal and Tench the local politician are, with telling impact, local versions of the international manipulators of the G8 and their business associates like Pennen. Messent also comments that "the reader is expected to question the ways in which official authority systems work" (183).

Between Rebus' inner sense of order and his chaotic outer and policing life lies a great distance. He has no personal life beyond his memories and music—people, as Ellen tells her, think Siobhan must be or at least have been his lover, but they are merely mostly respectful co-workers. There was at the start an on-off police lover, Detective-Inspector Gill Templer, but she moved on after *The Falls:* Rebus has a few other professional-class lady friends, but not in the later books. His dedication to reordering criminal misdoings is his drive, and his approaching retirement and the lack of support and interest of his colleagues beyond Siobhan are making that harder to enact.

After *Exit Music* Rankin started a new series about Inspector Malcolm Fox, a new-style managerial policeman, not as fascinating to the public as Rebus and not selling nearly as well. The old sleuth, glass of malt in hand, has not been easily eluded by his author, and in *Saints of the Shadow Bible* (2013—another music-based title) he has returned, now a civilian—not that he ever really fully joined the police in any limiting sense—but still at work in a cold-case unit, annoying his bosses, pestering positively the promoted Siobhan (Laura Severin traces her growing, even feminist, strength), and finding patterns of explanation and retribution in his slowly developed understanding of a set of old cases across Scotland, and also, like much in the series, exploring the interface of authority and corruption.

In *The Naming of the Dead,* as Marshall notes (232), the policing of politics became powerfully a central issue, but Rankin and Rebus, and the series, as in the best of crime fiction, remain constantly and centrally faithful to a relentless debate about the politics of policing. Messent sums up, "It is the complex and ambiguous nature of the contemporary world Rankin represents that makes his police novels so powerful and so troubling" (185).

References

Alegre, Sara Martin. "Aging in F(r)iendship: 'Big Ger' Cafferty and John Rebus." *Clues* 29 (2011): 73–82.

Diemert, Brian. "Ian Rankin and the God of the Scots," in *Race and Religion in the Postcolonial British Detective Story: Ten Essays.* Ed. Julie H. Kim. Jefferson, NC: McFarland, 164–88.

Knight, Stephen. *Crime Fiction Since 1800: Detection, Death, Diversity.* Second edition. London: Palgrave Macmillan, 2010.

MacDonald, Erin E. "Ghosts and Skeletons: Metaphors of Guilty History in Ian Rankin's Rebus Series." *Clues* 30 (2012): 67–75.

Marshall, Rodney. *Blurred Boundaries: An Exploration of Ian Rankin's Rebus Novels (1987–2012).* San Bernardino, CA: Amazon, 2012.

Messent, Peter. "The Police Novel," in *A Companion to Crime Fiction.* Ed. Charles J. Rzepka and Lee Horsley. New York: Wiley-Blackwell, 2010, 175–86.

Newton, P. M. "Crime Fiction and the Politics of Place: The Post–9/11 Sense of Place in Sara Paretsky and Ian Rankin," in *The Millennial Detective: Essays on Trends in Crime Fiction, Film and Television, 1990–2010.* Ed. Malcah Effron. Jefferson, NC: McFarland, 2011, 21–35.

Plain, Gill. *Ian Rankin's Black and Blue: A Reader's Guide.* New York: Continuum, 2002.

_____. "'The Map That Engenders the Territory?' Rethinking Ian Rankin's Edinburgh," in *Capital Crimes: Crime Fiction in the City*. Ed. Lucy Andrew and Catherine Phelps. Cardiff: University of Wales Press, 2013, 16–28.

Severin, Laura. "'Out from the Mentor's Shadow': Siobhan Clarke and the Feminism of *Exit Music* (2007)." *Clues* 28 (2010): 87–94.

19

Postmortem,
Patricia Cornwell

Patricia Cornwell was born in Miami in 1956, but the family moved to North Carolina after her father, a lawyer, left in 1961. She became friendly with Ruth Bell Graham, wife to the famous evangelist Billy Graham, went to Davidson College, North Carolina, and in 1979 married her college English professor, seventeen years her senior. They separated after ten years, by which time he had become a preacher. She settled to work as a reporter on the *Charlotte Observer,* especially interested in crime, though she also published a biography of Ruth Graham in 1983. In the following year Cornwell became a technical writer in the Virginia Chief Medical Examiner's office, where she was also, very early, a computer analyst and even worked as a volunteer with the Richmond police.

That sounds as if her forensic fiction was predetermined, but she wrote three conventional mysteries that were rejected. Advised by a publisher to drop the male inquirer and stress the realism, she developed on the basis of the real Dr. Marcella Fierro, Deputy Chief Medical Examiner in Virginia (Thomas, 394), her specialist inquirer, Dr. Kay Scarpetta, and so, as Sabine Vanacker comments, "inserted her woman detective into the police procedural" (63). *Postmortem* appeared in 1990, and though Cornwell reports it was rejected seven times (Reynolds, 151), it sold very successfully and is the only mystery to have won four major prizes in a year, taking in 1991, all for a first novel, the Edgar (Mystery Writers of America), the John Creasey Award (British Crime Writers), the Anthony (Bouchercon), and the Macavity (Mystery Readers International); in 1992 it won the French Prix du Roman d'Aventure.

Postmortem has a dense, mobile plot. Dr. Kay Scarpetta, Chief Medical Examiner at Richmond, Virginia, has her ten-year-old niece, Lucy, staying with her. In heavy rain at 2:33 a.m. Scarpetta is called by Detective Sergeant

19. Postmortem

Pete Marino to the fourth of a series of murders. Lori Petersen, a beautiful thirty-year-old doctor, has been strangled after being bound and beaten; her fingers are broken. Her husband found her when returning very late the seventy miles from Charlottesville, where he is studying for a PhD in English literature; he is also an actor.

Under special light in the lab there appear strange marks on the body. Marino thinks it is greasepaint and suspects the husband. When Scarpetta gets home, Lucy has been tidying Kay's computer and is upset by the lurid press coverage led by reporter Abby Turnbull. Scarpetta receives a hang-up call that night. The next day, they find the greasepaint prints on the body are the husband's, but there are also different glitter traces on a knife belonging to the husband, bearing his prints and found in a drawer: it matches the cuts on Lori's body. Marino is more sure of the husband's guilt when he reads his PhD work on violence in Tennessee Williams. He interviews Petersen at length: he says he could smell maple syrup in the house; Marino's suspicions remain.

Scarpetta remembers the stress of being one of few women at medical school, and thinks of her Italian family. She and Marino visit police profiler Benton Wesley. The killer is a "non-secreter" like 20 percent of men, including the husband. Benton says the serial killer will be quite young, fascinated by police work, a loner, and has developed from pornography to murder: the cases are getting closer together, with more violence and torture. Marino has learnt the husband had a sexual assault charge—but later establishes it was abandoned, and probably made up by the woman. At her office Scarpetta is told someone has been trying to enter the computer system.

The police commissioner calls her in: he is angry, blaming on her department the press leaks, especially the material by Abby Turnbull. Scarpetta tells him about the attempt to hack into their computer, and he insists on everything going through his office. At the meeting is the district attorney, Bill Boltz, whom Scarpetta has been seeing: he is fairly distant. The authorities are sensitive because before she died Lori Petersen called the police but did not speak and they allotted it a low priority. At the office they work on the evidence and Scarpetta speculates on the case, with little outcome. She thinks of her predecessor, the authoritarian male Cagney. She finds the case records include a false statement about the belt one victim was wearing.

That night Bill Boltz visits Scarpetta. His wife killed herself a while ago: he and Scarpetta are not lovers, though Scarpetta is attracted to him and he did once try to force her. He says Abby Turnbull tried to seduce him. The next day Scarpetta drives with Marino all round the well-separated crime scenes. The women had no contacts between them, were all professional, and one was black. Scarpetta realizes Marino is shrewd, not stupid, but still finds him off-putting. At Scarpetta's home, Lucy has been difficult but cannot be sent home because her mother is off to Nevada to get married again. At work, Marino is irritated by Wingo, Scarpetta's gay assistant. A mysterious sample in the lab fridge appears to be from the Petersen case and should have been sent for examination. Scarpetta worries that she has made a mistake through exhaustion. Boltz comes to the house and is cross when she keeps thinking about work. She wonders why his wife killed herself. When Scarpetta is in bed, alone, there is another hang-up call.

They discover the shining material, other than the greasepaint fingerprints, is borax, found everywhere in liquid soap. Suddenly Scarpetta is called to another murder. The woman is Abby Turnbull's sister and lives with her. Abby has been tailed and warned her sister to call the police if she saw anyone near the house. Marino tells Abby he knows that she gave Bill Boltz a big spread after sleeping with him: Scarpetta is shocked that Boltz lied to her.

After the autopsy, Marino takes her to Abby's house; on the way Scarpetta listens to police talk on the radio. There is a Beware of the Dog sign at the house: Marino suggests the murderer knew there was no dog. Marino thinks Boltz did it, planning to kill Abby, not knowing her sister lived there. Scarpetta insists the murders were all by one killer, but is disturbed. Wingo asks her if the commissioner is a smoker and she says no. She goes to see a major forensic psychiatrist. He used to think the murderer was a mentally ill local man but now thinks he has been at it for years, is purposeful, and probably was after Abby for her reporting. He tells Scarpetta to get the person she trusts most to find the computer hacker. She and Wesley see Abby: she will publish that they have identified the man's DNA-linked smell, which Scarpetta says is Maple Syrup Urine Disease, a rare condition. They think this will panic him into trying to crack the computer and leave traces. Marino has discovered from a contact a bloodstained jumpsuit from the last murder, and they suggest in the story this carries his DNA.

Scarpetta, looking for connections between the women, starts with the unusual one and rings the black woman's sister. She thinks she has the wrong number as the voice sounds white. But it is her, and her sister spoke the same way. Scarpetta suspects the link is they all had very attractive voices. At home she tells Lucy she trusts her most and Lucy (now eleven) takes Scarpetta through the process of hacking in. They realize the person typed in the incorrect detail about the belt, from Abby's mistaken report, to make the office report look erroneous. With Marino, Scarpetta wonders who listens to many voices—he suggests pizza take-out places, but she goes for hours through police call records and finds the dead women all rang 911 for help. She plays a tape to Marino.

That night she wakes and smells maple syrup: the murderer has a knife at her throat. She is slowly reaching for her gun when Marino shoots him. Marino had recognized the voice of a police operator he knew and followed him. She had forgotten to load her gun in any case. At work the next day Wingo tells her the commissioner brought something in one day: as he was smoking secretly he took a butt and it showed a rare blood type, also found on the slides that seemed her error. They realize the commissioner has been planting material to discredit her and the office, including inserting the error in the computer records. Abby is after him now. Bill Blotz rings Scarpetta and says they do not suit each other—she agrees strongly. Finally, she and Lucy go away on vacation together.

Cornwell and this novel are acknowledged as being the start of the forensic mystery. There had been scientific facts in crime fiction from the non-human hair in the Rue Morgue, and a full-blown scientist detective was created in R. Austin Freeman's Dr. Thorndyke, starting in 1908. The police procedural included forensics, but it was still only technical support. The very successful *Coma* (1977) by Robin Cook made medical themes central but did not prove influential. A more general theme in the 1980s was a rise of both sex and brutality in crime fiction, and a new sub-genre that previsioned the new forensic mood was the serial killer story. Thomas Harris' *Red Dragon* (1981) introduces brutal death scenes presented with cool interest, and through Hannibal Lecter he also moved into the psychic end of human horrors. In fiction as in news and soon in film, the serial-killer would seem a potent element of the randomized nature of both modern society and modern anxiety; forensic elements were vivid but merely supportive, not central as in Cornwell.

The other notable force of the period to which Cornwell was attentive was feminist crime fiction, with Muller, Grafton and Paretsky all well established by the mid–1980s and Sisters in Crime a thriving force to disseminate the new message that not all who are tough are guys. It was Cornwell's special vision to condense the female detective and the forensic realism into one figure. Where the female detective acts as an emblem of embattled feminism, the professional nature of Scarpetta's activity links her directly with the very large number of well-qualified women who operate as equals to men in the modern world and yet feel by no means fully accepted. By being a forensic specialist the feminist perceptions are both more muted and also by their nature more irresistibly professional, but at the same time, as Vanacker comments, it is not a traditional female role:

> Rather than being culturally associated (as female) with life and life giving, this woman hero is a dealer in death who aggressively "manhandles" the corpses of victims and gruesomely thrives off decaying and decomposing bodies [66].

Both professionally qualified and also somehow outside traditional femininity, Scarpetta is still a challenging figure, if not as directly as V.I. Warshawski.

The nature of Scarpetta's skills also has another powerful effect. It is perfectly natural for the text to deal in the most extreme of brutalities—and indeed she must pursue in the service of science further dismemberment and dissection. Yet because the text is written in the first person, Scarpetta is always transmitting hideous effects to the reader, but "the graphic content is merely implied by Scarpetta and not specified" (Head, 38): she shows substantial empathy for the victims, as is discussed by Carmel Farré-Vidal (55–56). The effect of this is to contain in an immediate way any elements of sadomasochistic pleasure that might be available in the text: as Horsley says, Scarpetta "gives voice to what would otherwise simply be 'unspeakable'" (151). She frequently thinks of working for the victims, of being as able as a scientist to make the dead bodies speak and demand justice.

A Scarpetta novel often opens with a particularly hideous scene—and, as with the second, *Body of Evidence* (1991), or *The Body Farm* (1994), physicality can be stressed in the title. It might seem that the Cornwell model both empathizes over the bodies and also leaves evidence for anyone who might want to relish them sadistically: the later novels grow more graphic and sensational. There is, however, another area of Scarpetta's experience that links with both her gender, her professionalism and also her sensitivity: she is frequently alarmed by threats of various kinds and it is common for her to be attacked in her own home by the murderer or sometimes his, or even her, agent.

This results from the fact that Cornwell takes her detective out of the laboratory, as Dr. Thorndyke never went, to become an active, even challenging investigator. In part Scarpetta visits crime scenes as a medical examiner might, but she does a lot more examining and detecting than any forensic specialist ever would; often she is with one of her male supporters, usually the rough but hugely reliable Pete Marino, who at times seems more like an unusually skillful police dog than a partner, or sometimes with her recurrent adviser and soon enough admirer, the suave Benton Wesley. By giving Scarpetta legal qualifications, Cornwell has laid a basis for her wide range of action. Part of the force of the text is, as Peter Messent notes (12), to exploit the powers of modernity like DNA testing and FBI databases, but many of the cases and related dramas also turn on some elements of practice and procedure in law or, as often, local politics and management.

One of the striking features of the female, as well as feminist, detectives is that they tend to connect strongly with family and friends, where the male detective operates in a social cocoon with other people either firmly offstage or just reduced to a token engagement—like Watson's very limited activities with Holmes or Maigret's domestically restricted wife. By contrast, friends and neighbors, even animals, cluster around the feminist detectives, and although she is a very busy office-bound, late-hours working professional, Scarpetta routinely has elements of her family on hand, normally her niece Lucy—here starting at ten, but growing up in the following books more quickly than Scarpetta ages. Not only is she a fond aunt: her sister is a very absent mother concerned with male friends and—surely an ironic touch—writing children's books rather than fostering the brilliant, if wayward, child.

Lucy will develop through the novels into a computer expert working for the FBI, and also someone whose personal life is made complex by her emergent lesbianism. There is more than one professional woman in the family, and while the effect may well be to bring in more readers—the people who admire Lisbeth Salander could have been reading Lucy Farinelli for years—its origin may well be the author's own wide-ranging experience: she was herself a young computer expert and in later life has opted for marriage to another woman. Scarpetta and Lucy seem another of those novel-enriching authorial doubles, like Conan Doyle being in fact both Holmes and Watson and Christie having Poirot's brain but Hastings' English attitudes.

Scarpetta's grace under pressure on the home front, added to success in the laboratory, dedication in inquiries—it takes hours to find the police phoneline link in *Postmortem*—and ultimate courage when threatened do not exhaust the demands on her. Threats come from inside the system: as Messent comments, "the line between a criminal underclass and public officialdom is not as firm as might initially be supposed" (13). As with Warshawski, there is a resistance to and sometimes straight sabotage of Scarpetta's status and operations from senior male figures in the structure of government and management. Vanacker notes that Scarpetta's "professional status is questioned in almost every novel" (77) and this process exposes "the loneliness and vulnerability of the successful woman in the male hierarchy" (76). In *Postmortem* Commissioner Amburgey himself is hostile to her and goes beyond misinterpretation into actually planting evidence of inefficiency in her office and computer system. If there are criminals out there in society whom Scarpetta needs to be at full strength and well supported to defeat, there are also structural menaces to her inside the social mechanisms she inhabits. This recurs from novel to novel: the state attorney general prosecutes Scarpetta in *Cruel and Unusual* (1993), the state governor is inherently hostile to her in the same novel, and in *The Last Precinct* (2000) a different governor supports the master-criminal Chandonne in his machinations against her.

Where Paretsky sees this kind of challenge in a basically liberal-feminist way as an old male world needing to change, Cornwell appears to trace the oppression more to masculine imbalance and personal weakness: they are certainly hostile to her as a woman, but it is an insurgent woman disrupting their comfortable and basically incompetent world. Her opponents react maliciously and irrationally, not with the distant repressive confidence of the powerful gender enemies Warshawski faces—indeed, by *Unnatural Exposure* (1997) the professional hostility comes from a woman pathologist and in *Predator* (2005) another, rather more demented, female threat appears, tellingly named Dr. Self. In *Postmortem*, both Amburgey, in his sneaky behavior, and Bill Boltz, with his capacity for sudden violence, are at base faulty people rather than gender oppressors, and it seems unsurprising that this personalized reading of what might seem like gender oppression merges in later novels with the increasingly melodramatic and apolitically irrational events.

Cornwell has had major areas of impact since the busy years of establishing herself as a major novelist with a new form of crime fiction in the 1990s. One of these has been as a figure of much interest to the media. Evidently a strong personality and not given to concealing disputes, she has figured—usually successfully—in some that have had little or no connection with her work as a crime fiction author. The Graham family objected to aspects of her biography and there was said to have been a six-year dispute, but it appears to have ended with Cornwell publishing a new biography of Ruth Graham in 1997. Cornwell then was charged by Leslie Sachs with plagiarism over *The Last Precinct* and she was fiercely pursued: in the end the courts found entirely in her favor. That was also the case when she had to sue her financial manager and was awarded some $50 million—suggesting her earnings were over $10 million a year. Her elaborate lifestyle, with around-the-world houses and security men, has evidently excited journalists, and more was made of the revelation that she had in 2005 married a Harvard woman academic, Dr. Staci Gruber, though photographs of the pair with Martina Navratilova and Billie-Jean King could also be taken as a doubly benign ending both in terms of gender choice and because in her youth Cornwell hoped to become a tournament-standard tennis player. Linda Mizejewski feels there was a parallel gender-liberating development in the novels "[a]s heroine Kay outlived wooden male suitors, and as Kay's niece Lucy grew more interesting" (7).

With some possible relation to the fiction has been Cornwell's lengthy, expensive and dedicated attempt to solve the question of who was Jack the Ripper. She became convinced that the English painter Walter Sickert was the culprit, bought many of his paintings and published a book in 2002 with the firm title *Portrait of a Killer: Jack the Ripper—Case Closed*. This, too, was unusually controversial, as some journalists managed to persuade themselves she had destroyed a Sickert painting in her quest for proof. That case remains, for most people, still open, though her argument has by no means been dismissed.

Cornwell's massive sales soon attracted others to the form: the most successful has been Kathy Reichs, a Canadian, who offers stories starting in Quebec with *Déjà Dead* (1997) but makes her heroine Temperance Brennan have experience in the United States—like both Reichs and Cornwell, in Charlotte, North Carolina. More procedural than Cornwell, these have been very successful, and other writers have followed the same path, such as Jeffery Deaver, starting with quadriplegic inquirer Lincoln Rhymes in *The Bone Collector* (1997), and Tess Gerritsen, whose stories about Rizzoli and Isles began with Rizzoli alone in *The Surgeon* (2001). The impact has not only been in books. Though a Scarpetta film is only being planned in 2014, the forensic detective series *Silent Witness* was made in Britain in 1996, with Amanda Burton as a calm, purposeful inquirer, and in the United States the very successful *CSI* (Crime Scene Investigation) was launched in 2000 by the major producer Jerry Bruckheimer. Originally set in Las Vegas, this has since spun off into versions in New York and Miami. Another forensic series called *Bones* has been established since 2005 using Reich's own Temperance Brennan but set firmly in the United States, and the Gerritsen-derived series *Rizzoli and Isles* began in 2010.

Just as the police procedural has, in a somewhat melodramatized and usually romanticized form, made its home on TV screens, so the forensic mystery has lent itself very easily to a mix of grim revelations and extreme close-ups, including though the microscope. Compared to Cornwell, they contain much less grim detail and also far less hostility against the routinely very attractive female inquirers, whether from the criminals or from the male colleagues, and Cornwell's reach into the darkness of modern local politics never seems to be of interest. But the magic of science has been fully realized, where Poe and Conan Doyle could only fabricate it through ideas: it is possible to see these films, and these novels, as modern mechanistic society adapting its mere tools into forms of optimistic belief.

Rose Lucas asks after a long and close analysis of the patterns of Cornwell's beliefs and anxieties whether "we can salvage some vestige of meaning and comprehensibility from the very maws of mortality, as they are most graphically depicted in these narratives of violation and assault" (218–19). The enormous success of Cornwell's new form of forensic detection suggests that the audience would like to answer positively, and that is indeed Lucas' own conclusion: "Cornwell's texts are not only about a forensic pathologist, a reader of corporeality, its limitations and misadventures, but they implicitly offer forensics as a mode of reading, and as an epistemology of hopeful rationality" (218).

There remain questions. Some have been uneasy that Cornwell's personal politics tend towards the right, with substantial donations to the Republican Party, though to its more liberal wing, with figures like John Warner and Orrin Hatch. She is also reported to have been much more supportive of George Bush Senior than Junior, and she has backed some Democrats, including Hillary Clinton, and a range of politics-free charities, mostly educational. The novels themselves raise some issues. It is noticeable that as the series goes on it tends to sideline the quite complex pattern of gender and politics in the early stories, and like many before her Cornwell moves towards serial and macabre master criminals to simplify plotting and motivation with figures like Temple Gault from *Cruel and Unusual* (1993) and the Chandonne brothers from *Point of Origin* (1998). Messent sees this as part of the inherent conservatism of the stories, feeling they tend "both to endorse the status quo and, in addition, consign crime to the realms of the morally 'monstrous,'" though he acknowledges that they operate in the ultra-modern context of "the collapse of that web of domestic and community relationships that had conventionally located the subject" (16).

From *The Last Precinct* (2000) on, the novels have changed their style from the past into the present tense, that modern mode of instantaneousness of action and emotion, and they just as tellingly altered their narration into the third person with *Blow Fly* (2003), permitting the grisly detail to be much more disturbing as not being transmitted through Scarpetta's empathetic eyes, so that "the narrative becomes dominated by a violent, masculine voyeurism" (Head, 39)—though the narration has reverted to first person with *Port Mortuary* (2010). With and after *Predator* (2005) the novels make in terms of action and context a generally increasing move towards melodrama or, as Horsley puts it, "into the more ambiguous territory of the gothic" (151).

In another striking change Scarpetta has left the government service and now, like so many other modern professionals, provides her services to various bodies by contract. She was always an ultra-modern figure, when that only meant being a forensic specialist, and a woman, and facing serial killers. In her latest manifestations she seems still responding to the patterns of the present, though not it would seem in an interrogative way—but perhaps still in, as Lucas would hope, a mode of "hopeful rationality." It seems doubtful that Cornwell has radically new and illuminating patterns to offer and her recent police novels with a senior woman and a junior man are not remarkable, but she will retain the credit of having undertaken one of the most original and influential re-formations of crime fiction.

References

Farré-Vidal, Carmel. "Dissection of Patricia Cornwell's Feminist Woman Detective Kay Scarpetta." *Journal of English Studies* 10 (2012): 51–64.
Head, Beth. "A Normal Pathology? Patricia Cornwell's Third Person Novels," in *The Millennial Detective: Essays on Trends in Crime Fiction, Film and Television, 1990–2010*. Ed. Malcah Effron. Jefferson, NC: McFarland, 2011, 36–49.
Horsley, Lee. *Twentieth-Century Crime Fiction*. Oxford: Oxford University Press, 2005.
Lucas, Rose. "Anxiety and Its Antidotes: Patricia Cornwell and the Forensic Body." *Literature, Interpretation, Theory* 15 (2010): 207–22.
Messent, Peter, "Introduction: From Private Eye to Police Procedural—the Logic of Contemporary Crime Fiction," in *Criminal Proceedings: The Contemporary American Crime Novel*. Ed. Peter Messent. London: Pluto, 1997, 1–21.
Mizejewski, Linda. "Illusive Evidence: Patricia Cornwell and the Body Double." *South Central Review* 18 (2001): 6–20.
Reynolds, Moira Davison. "Patricia Cornwell," in *Women Authors of Detective Series: Twenty-One American and British Writers, 1900–2000*. Jefferson, NC: McFarland, 2001, 149–54.
Thomas, Margaret Caldwell. "Patricia Cornwell: Dangerous Dissection," in *Women of Mystery: The Lives and Works of Notable Women Crime Novelists*. Ed. Martha Hailey DuBose. New York: Dunne, 2000, 393–99.
Vanacker, Sabine. "V. I. Warshawski, Kinsey Millhone and Kay Scarpetta: Creating a Feminist Detective Hero," in *Criminal Proceedings: The Contemporary Crime Novel*. Ed. Peter Messent. London: Pluto, 1997, 62–86.

20

The Girl with the Dragon Tattoo, Stieg Larsson

The Girl with the Dragon Tattoo is, even among outstanding crime novels, extremely unusual. It has become the flagship of the remarkable success of Nordic Noir, the modern crime fiction from the Scandinavian countries whose worldwide success has been described by David Geherin. It is the first of a trilogy of novels all over five hundred pages long and is strongly radical and also, though written by a man, forcefully feminist. It has created a startlingly popular central figure, Lisbeth Salander, a small, tattooed and pierced Goth punk, who is both a computer genius and on the edge of autism. Against these notable innovations, the author died at age fifty-one before the first of the three novels appeared. This and a battle for his royalties and reputation add a grim side to the extraordinary phenomenon of a worldwide best seller: the three novels are rapidly approaching a hundred million sales, and each has been filmed in both Sweden and America. Larsson is, as Kurdo Baksi says, "the author of one of the biggest, least-expected, publishing successes of modern times" (7).

Larsson was born in 1954 and brought up in the Swedish north and soon moved into left-wing journalism and politics in the tradition of his communist grandfather, interned in the war for being an anti–Nazi threat to neutral Sweden: the theme of past mistreatment of good-hearted ordinary people will recur in the novels. Larsson was also, from his early experience of seeing a gang rape, concerned about brutality to women. In the 1980s and 1990s he traveled widely but also worked hard as a journalist, exposing the rise of the right that accompanied the worldwide move towards neo-liberalism, notably in formerly left-liberal Sweden (Pettersson, 102–84). Larsson worked with the British radical journal *Searchlight,* co-wrote a large book titled *The Extreme Right* (1991), and early in 1995 set up Sweden's *Expo* magazine and foundation to develop resistant positions.

Such wide and deep political commitment in journalism is an unusual context for a crime writer, but Larsson had apparently always wanted to create stories and by 2002, in spite of his many activities, was at work on what became the *Millennium* trilogy—named for the title he gave the magazine that stands in for *Expo* in the novels. He had long written stories—Baksi suggests Larsson started on the first volume as early as 1997 (111), and Eva Gabrielsson recalls he had written then about an old man receiving a flower each year, as in the prologue to *The Girl with the Dragon Tattoo* (62). But none were published and he apparently thought of the trilogy as a whole and worked on it in an overlapping way (Baksi, 117), then in 2004 delivered the full three-volume novel to his chosen publisher, to receive a rejection apparently without its being read. The second choice, Norstedts, was immediately enthusiastic—and has been rewarded. The book sold well in Sweden, and was a success across Europe before appearing in English. The English translation was in fact done quickly for the Swedish film company Yellow Bird (Forshaw, 43), all three long books in less than a year by Steven Murray, under the pseudonym "Reg Keeland": a good deal of editing followed for the English version.

Although Henning Mankell was already well-known, Larsson's huge success has led to international fame for many Scandinavian crime writers. But as Yvonne Leffler has shown, there were crime writers in the country as far back as 1840, and in the twentieth century a steady flow of fairly traditional crime writing, usually in police mode and almost all by male authors, paralleled the Anglo-American output, briefly discussed by Andrew Nestingen and Paula Arvas in their introduction to *Scandinavian Crime Fiction*. A major departure was the deliberately planned series of ten left-wing mysteries by Maj Sjöwall and Per Wahlöö, starting in 1965 with *Roseanna* (see Pettersson, 219–30). The first of their political kind, as well as highly effective stories, these were widely admired, including by the Larsson family (Forshaw, 18). Their mix of detailed inquiry, exposure of corruption, and defense of ordinary morality is clearly part of Larsson's pattern, and he also uses some thoughtful police characters, with lives as well as cases.

There is a more surprising Swedish literary source. Early on Lisbeth Salander name-checks Pippi Longstocking, the nine-year-old at the core of Astrid Lindgren's very well-known series. Pippi is amazingly strong as well as the enemy of mistreatment and pomposity, and while Lisbeth dismisses crossly any likeness to herself, she is evidently a modernized, even mythicized, version of the girl hero. Another area of origin for Larsson's work has been overlooked. Commentators often remark on the length of the novels and how slowly the first gets going, with some hundred pages of preliminaries about financial reporting, possible corruption, the circumstances of magazines, the problems that face crusading journalists. Dan Waddell, one of the writers Barry Forshaw interviewed for his book, felt no English publisher would ever have taken it on the basis of the opening one hundred pages (263–64). But Larsson is a major part of, and is also writing for, the information generation, people accustomed to accessing major amounts of data in print or electronically and used to television programs and newspaper features that emphasize factual information as the basis of their judgments—Gabrielsson spends some time detailing the real settings and real people involved in the trilogy (85–103). Larsson's massive texts gain much of their weight from connecting with the data of the real world, material that the novels are always marshaling towards strong liberal arguments about mismanagement and manipulation on both political and personal levels. Joan Smith, the British reviewer and crime novelist, is one of the few commentators to grasp this ultra-modern element of Larsson's work (Forshaw, 234).

The Girl with a Dragon Tattoo starts steadily, develops in surprising ways, and also, especially in the middle, intercuts its narrative strands with dramatic confidence. A prologue reports the sending each birthday of a flower in a frame: the recipient is eighty-two, and this is the forty-fourth. They are always beautiful and usually rare: this year, an Australian native. There are never any fingerprints on the frames, and they are posted from various parts of the world.

In December 2002, Mikael Blomkvist, journalist, publisher and part-owner of the Swedish radical political magazine *Millennium,* loses a libel case involving allegations about billionaire industrialist Hans-Erik Wennerström. Blomkvist became known for identifying a gang of bank robbers and he was called "Kalle" Blomkvist after the young detective in other Astrid Lindgren children's books. He was unable to support allegations that Wennerström misappropriated state funds and is sentenced to three months in prison and substantial damages and costs.

Blomkvist is invited to meet Henrik Vanger, retired head of the Vanger Corporation, who has checked his personal and professional history through Armansky, a Croatian immigrant running a security firm. On that job he employed Lisbeth Salander, a brilliant researcher and computer-hacker with antisocial attitudes. About five feet tall, slender and young looking, in her report on Blomkvist she praised his work, noted his connection with Erika Berger, co-editor of the journal, and suggested he was set up for the recent trial.

Blomkvist tells Berger that for his sake and *Millennium*'s he should take leave for a while; he finds some Elizabeth George novels to read. On Christmas Eve Vanger's lawyer asks him to come north to Hedestad—when a small child Blomkvist had been at the house. Vanger persuades him to investigate, while officially writing a family history, what happened to his grandniece Harriet (once Blomkvist's babysitter), who disappeared in 1966 while the island was temporarily isolated by a traffic accident on the bridge. Vanger will pay him well, with evidence against Wennerström as a final bonus. Blomkvist moves to the island and begins researching.

Salander spends Christmas Eve visiting her mother in a nursing home, reads Blomkvist's exposé of slack and corrupt Swedish financial journalists, and (briefly dressed in normal clothes) begins investigations into Wennerström, involving her super-hacker friend Plague. She also breaks into Armansky's office, checking the confidential paperwork. Blomkvist assembles data, including the fascist past of Vanger's brother Richard. He meets Henrik's niece Cecilia, with whom he will have a short and fairly casual affair. Erika Berger visits the island, and Vanger suggests he should invest in *Millennium,* which is in financial trouble. Blomkvist finds some puzzling numbers Harriet left against a list of names.

During this long sequence, Salander visits her new guardian. She was ruled legally incompetent as a child, having attempted to kill by arson her father when he beat her mother. Lisbeth was placed in a psychiatric clinic until fifteen, then had a legal guardian (who recommended her to the security firm), but he recently suffered a stroke and when she asks the new guardian, Nils Bjurman, for an expensive new computer, he forces her to have oral sex first. She does not report him, being "not like any normal person" (203), and "she always got revenge" (205). Blomkvist's investigations and contacts with Cecelia are intercut in increasingly brief sequences with Salander's plans for Bjurman. She visits him; he attacks and rapes her but does not know she has filmed him. When she visits again, she Tasers him, ties him to the bed, shows him the tape, and demands both control of her money and favorable monthly and annual reports. She tattoos on his stomach, painfully, "I AM A SADISTIC PIG, A PERVERT, AND A RAPIST" (235).

Blomkvist has to serve his jail time: he has an iBook and works on the Vanger family chronicle, then moves back north and starts to investigate photographs of the day Harriet disappeared: in one, she looks distracted by something. His daughter visits: she is interested in religion and comments that the numbers against women's names are biblical references: he finds they are from Leviticus, about women being murdered as a form of justice.

Henrik Vanger has a heart attack. Blomkvist tells Vanger's lawyer he needs a research assistant to see if Harriet was investigating a serial killer. The lawyer says he knows a good one, who investigated Blomkvist. He demands to see Salander's report. It is very detailed, including using his wording of the press statement he had drafted but not yet published: he realizes she is a hacker. He goes to visit her in Stockholm: she is in bed with her girlfriend Mimmi and, though fairly aggressive, agrees to work for him.

Blomkvist goes back to the island. Cecilia is now annoyed by his insistent inquiries. He reads Val McDermid's *The Mermaids Singing*. Salander begins to research past brutal murders of women to try to match them to the Leviticus references. Blomkvist obtains more photographs of the day Harriet vanished. Salander drives up to Hedestad on her small motorcycle and in the morning he finds her reading his encrypted files. They work together for a week, and she feels he treats her like a human being. He is reading a novel by Sara Paretsky in bed when, after some thought, Salander enters his room, and they spend the night together.

Soon, Blomkvist has found the person who startled Harriet in the photo — her brother Martin, not known to be in town early that day. Someone kills the cat who has adopted Blomkvist; then someone shoots at Blomkvist. Salander sets up cameras and defenses around Blomkvist's cottage: he discovers she has a photographic memory. She searches the local newspaper archive on the murders of women and finds Martin Vanger's father was in the area for most of them and, after he died, Martin was. While she is researching, Blomkvist, on the basis of the photo of Martin, goes to his house and is taken prisoner. When Salander returns, she notices Martin's photo on the desk, checks the cameras and sees he has visited the house.

Blomkvist is in Martin's cellar, strapped up, nearly asphyxiated by a plastic bag, when Salander breaks in, fells Martin with a golf club and frees Blomkvist. Martin runs to his car, and she follows him on her motorcycle. He crashes into a truck and dies as the car burns. She goes back and frees Blomkvist, then investigates Martin's records: he has killed many women, continuing his father's practices, and photographs suggest he assaulted his sister Harriet.

Blomkvist and Salander go to London; he tries to interview Anita Vanger, but she tells him to leave. Salander's hacker contacts have bugged her phone and she immediately calls Australia. Salander's mother has died, so Blomkvist goes alone to Australia, where, as a widow called Anita, Harriet now runs a Queensland property. She says she is glad Martin is dead: when she saw him that day she realized she would never be safe. Harriet had drowned her father after he raped her when drunk; then her brother started. She knew they had both murdered women. Anita (whom she resembled) smuggled her off the island and she took Anita's passport and name.

Back in Sweden, Blomkvist takes Salander to her mother's funeral. He explains the whole story to Vanger, and Harriet comes back to see her granduncle and will stay. She joins the *Millennium* board. Salander and Blomkvist spend time together. Vanger asks Blomkvist to keep Harriet's story secret, for her sake, and eventually he agrees. Salander insists on substantial compensation for the victims' families and women's services. Henrik gives him data on Wennerström, but it is not very strong. However, Salander now has proof of Wennerström's criminal activities. Blomkvist writes it up, and Berger agrees to print it in *Millennium:* she finally meets Salander, and the two women respect each other.

Salander works out where Wennerström's money is hidden and goes in disguise to several places and diverts all $260 million into her own account. *Millennium* publishes on Wennerström, and Blomkvist's book about Wennerström, *The Mafia Banker,* comes out. Blomkvist is celebrated in the media and *Millennium* becomes famous. Wennerström disappears. Six months later he is found dead in Spain. Four days previously, Salander had reported his whereabouts to a Miami lawyer she knew was pursuing him.

After Christmas Blomkvist visits the frail Vanger, who tells him Harriet is taking over the family company and thanks him: "You are a person with morals, Mikael" (531). Salander buys him an Elvis Presley sign but when taking it to his flat sees him come out with Erika Berger, hugging and kissing. She says, "What a pathetic fool you are, Salander" (533), throws away the present, and the novel ends.

The titles and the book jackets, as well as the film publicity and presentation, make it clear that the central figure in the overwhelming success of the Larsson trilogy has been Lisbeth Salander. Yet she does not appear until well into the first novel and, more surprisingly, the original Swedish title meant "Men who hate women." Eva Gabrielsson implies that the publishers dissented against this title, but Larsson insisted (72). Salander grows as the first novel develops. She has two progressive sequences, the first rising from a minor figure to heroism as she sorts out Burman, and then a second and more assertive transformation in relation to Blomkvist's concerns. This reshaping of Salander from a minor into a major character is crucial to the massive success of the trilogy. In the later novels she will dominate from the start and then be sidelined for a lengthy series of action as other issues and characters are dealt with—the same pattern Conan Doyle deployed with Sherlock Holmes when he reappeared in *The Hound of the Baskervilles.* But if Salander did gain Larsson's attention in the process of writing, as this pattern might suggest, she was always central to his concern with women's rights, especially those mistreated by male brutality and the bureaucratic system. This is the area touched on by all of Larsson's epigraphs, from the opening comment that 18 percent of Swedish women have been threatened by a man to the later statements that tend to remember and celebrate instances of real Amazons in history.

The pattern of story and character that Salander cuts across and, with worldwide response, redirects is a more familiar one. Mikael Blomkvist is evidently a close parallel to Stieg Larsson himself, as a crusading journalist exposing right-wing corruption and the new 1990s racism in Sweden and especially as the founder and continuing operator of a journal committed to those values. Also, he is a recognizable figure in crime fiction, an investigator committed to human values and opposed to criminal corruption, a man with dogged persistence and deep fidelity.

When he is called to the elderly rich client there are clear reminiscences of Philip Marlowe at the Sternwood home, and then as the mystery of Harriet Vanger develops, the patterns of the enclosed mystery—here a locked island rather than a room or house—emerge and are acknowledged in the novel. Blomkvist is a more modern investigator than Marlowe or his successors: like James Bond he tends to fall into bed with attractive suspects and assistants (a link confirmed in casting Daniel Craig to play him in the Anglophone films).

Dual operatives with essentially separate audience appeal are nothing particularly new—in some ways Blomkvist is Watson to Salander's close-to-the-postmodern-edge Holmes, and the older/wiser and younger/bolder mixed-gender double was in the 1960s TV *Avengers* with Steed and Mrs. Peel. But Larsson's special effect is to show both operating alone with difficulty and also deciding to co-operate at certain periods—but never for long being together in anything like full emotional status, though at the very end of the third volume, they do seem to call a truce on the difficulties they have felt between themselves since a brief passage of positivity near the end of the first novel.

The question must arise why Salander is so iconic a figure. Baksi suggests (114) that she is, with her technical skills and loner aggression, and perhaps also her smoking habits, a reversed representation of Larsson himself—the initials might be a coded key to that, though Larsson's father has suggested the author's niece Theresa, with both anorexia and a tattoo, as a model (Forshaw, 21). But Salander also represents youthful alienation, much as Julian Assange did with his unusual looks, antagonism to authority and absolutely up-to-date mastery of the electronic media through which the young trace their communications and even identities. As a worldwide figure on which are projected both the fury and fantasy of the disempowered young, Assange was a version of the Salander effect until the forces of law and media found ways of diminishing his status—Salander has never suffered the impact of real-world conservative power. At the same time it can be argued, as Nestingen essentially does (180–81), that she represents a response to international neoliberal forces, which is in a way less than politically challenging because it is in itself entirely privatized and asocial, and could even be read as fantasy. Sheng-mei Ma sees the figure as essentially a "veiled alien," linking through her "counterculture punk rock outfit" (130) with a modern international myth of youth resistance.

Larsson apparently planned ten volumes—presumably on the model of the Sjöwall and Wahlöö series. The three books of the *Millennium* trilogy made a varied start in terms of theme and form. *The Girl with the Dragon Tattoo* interweaves financial corruption from the recent past with an underlying masculine hatred for women, expressed personally and through institutional formations and itself linked with the fascist aftermath of the war that remains a debatable element of Sweden's past—and that of most European nations: Karsten Wind Meyhoff discusses this "Rewriting History" in Larsson and also Jo Nesbø.

The second book, *The Girl Who Played with Fire*, opens with a long sequence about both Salander and Grenada, an island in which Larsson had a close political interest (Pettersson, 47–61). Back in Sweden the political nature of the narrative is intensified when Blomkvist's two co-researchers into conservatism are murdered—and this is itself linked to the past of Salander's own father, a Russian agent who defected and became involved in the self-protection of the Swedish secret state and also the exploitation of young women from the East in prostitution. This dramatic plot moves up from the dual murder into a major final crisis with Salander herself trying to kill her father, meeting her giant and deeply criminal half brother, and developing her heroism towards cartoon superhero levels by surviving being buried and also taking a bullet in the head.

The excitable politics of the second volume are in the third, *The Girl Who Kicked the Hornet's Nest,* projected into the pain of the present and also memorialized from the past, as honest police struggle with a rogue section of the secret service and some other police, while Salander slowly, and with secret computer activity, recovers from her bullet in the brain. The longest of the books, with major slabs of data and explanation, this also has new directions, introducing Blomkvist's sister as a capable liberal lawyer who defends Salander successfully in court and giving Blomkvist a calm affair with a tall gymnasium-toned policewoman. Emphasis falls finally on the long legal sequences where Salander is acquitted for minor crimes, and the aging anti-state spies are themselves disposed of with somewhat improbable speed.

A knowledgeable publisher's reader commented that the three volumes have different formal structures (Baksi, 123): the first is like a classic mystery with its enclosed element and detailed inquiries, the second more like a police procedural as the legal authorities battle against real crimes and their own destabilization, and the third moves into the realm of espionage thriller, exposing the state's internal corruption with some political detail—the murder of the Swedish leader Olof Palme in 1986 is a recurrent reference point in Larsson's work. Larsson accepted this analysis, and it relates in part to his very considerable knowledge of the genre but also to his capacity to maintain mobility of form as well as content and vary the tone as his action moves along with skilled variation—working, as David Geherin puts it, like "a seasoned film editor" (23).

What might someone have produced over time who could offer three books like these as his first efforts in crime fiction? The ten volumes of the *Millennium* project must remain a myth in writing and reading. There was when Larsson died apparently some of a fourth volume on his computer; in this, Gabrielsson has said, Salander "gradually breaks free of all her ghosts and enemies" (206). That book has now been commissioned from another author as Larsson's material has become immersed in the argument about ownership of his rights, financial and literary, between his brother and father and his longtime partner, Eva Gabrielsson. In what seems a strong irony, they never married and secured her position, because he felt that being so readily identifiable would have exposed her, and him, to possible right-wing violence. The fourth volume is out there somewhere: Blomkvist would surely have talked someone into publishing it, but Salander would have electronically stolen the whole thing.

Somehow, and tragically, the open ending both fits and emphasizes the power of Larsson's comet path across the skies of crime fiction. His personal courage, his deeply impressive narrative skills, and his remarkable ability to connect with the real forces of modernity—political, personal and technical—will remain a gold standard for the form and its possibilities.

References

Baksi, Kurdo. *Stieg Larsson: Our Days in Stockholm: A Memoir of Friendship*. Trans. Laurie Thompson. New York: Pegasus, 2010.
Forshaw, Barry. *The Man Who Left Too Soon: The Biography of Stieg Larsson*. London: Blake, 2010.
_____, ed. *Death in a Cold Climate: A Guide to Scandinavian Crime Fiction*. London: Palgrave Macmillan, 2012.
Gabrielsson, Eva, with Marie-Françoise Colombani. *"There Are Things I Want You to Know" About Stieg Larsson and Me*. New York: Seven Stories, 2011.
Geherin, David. *The Dragon Tattoo and Its Long Tail: The New Wave of European Crime Fiction in America*. Jefferson, NC: McFarland, 2012.
Leffler, Yvonne. "Early Crime Fiction in Scandinavian Literature," in *Crime and the Sublime*. Ed. Maurizio Ascari and Stephen Knight. Special issue of *La questione reoantica* 2 (2010), 71-81; reprinted in *From the Sublime to Crime*. Ed. Maurizio Ascari and Stephen Knight. Monaco: Libero, 2014, 213-42; E-publication.

Ma, Sheng-Mei. "Zen Leytsch: Mystery Handyman, with Dragon Tattoos," in *Detecting Detection: International Perspectives on the Uses of a Plot*. Ed. Peter Baker and Deborah Shaller. London: Continuum, 2012, 115–38.

Meyhoff, Karsten Wind. "Digging into the Secrets of the Past: Rewriting History in the Modern Scandinavian Police Procedural," in Andrew Nestingen and Paula Arvas, eds., *Scandinavian Crime Fiction*. Cardiff: University of Wales Press, 2011, 62–73.

Nestingen, Andrew. "Unnecessary Officers: Realism, Melodrama and Scandinavian Crime Fiction in Transition," in *Scandinavian Crime Fiction*. Ed. Andrew Nestingen and Paula Arvas. Cardiff: University of Wales Press, 2011, 171–83.

Nestingen, Andrew, and Paula Arvas, eds. *Scandinavian Crime Fiction*. Cardiff: University of Wales Press, 2011.

Pettersson, Jan-Erik. *Stieg Larsson: The Real Story of the Man Who Played with Fire*. Trans. Tom Geddes. New York: Sterling, 2011.

21

Sacred Games, Vikram Chandra

Sacred Games (2006) is the largest crime classic, at some nine hundred pages, and in its range of characters, variation and interrelation of incidents, and its extension of themes into the challenges of the modern world, both Indian and international, it is by any account a major crime-based novel.

Vikram Chandra was born in 1961 in New Delhi: the family moved when he was sixteen to what was then called Bombay—making him another writer who, like Conan Doyle and Chandler, made iconic the life of a city he knew as a stranger. The family was talent rich: his mother wrote plays and films, his sisters are well-known in India as a film writer/director and film critic. He headed to America's Kenyon College—in an interview with Louisa Ermelino he said he was attracted by the prestigious *Kenyon Review*—and after also studying in California started postgraduate work in film studies at Columbia University, then moved on to write his first novel. Though he returns regularly to Mumbai, Chandra has settled in the USA, married to the writer and editor Melanie Abrams; they both teach creative writing at Berkeley.

Red Earth and Pouring Rain (1995), based on the life of James Skinner, a nineteenth-century Anglo-Indian soldier, was extremely successful, and Chandra followed with the five stories in *Love and Longing in Bombay* (1997), the longest of which, "Kama," shows the Sikh Inspector Sartaj investigating a family murder in Bombay and also working through his own concerns. Christopher Rollason discusses ways in which this looks towards the major "urban epic" to come (75) and Cielo Fiestino, noting that the probable criminal (unprovable as such by Sartaj) is the extreme Hinduist son of the murdered couple, sees the story as Chandra's call for "an anti-fundamentalist Bombay" (113), a theme that will reverberate through *Sacred Games*. Chandra returned to Sartaj as the focal figure of the novel he worked on for seven years. A massive account of a huge city, *Sacred Games* both substantially sophisticates the existing range of Indian crime fiction—and world crime fiction—and also looks back, as Chandra evidently knows, to the mid-nineteenth-century tradition of the massive urban novel.

For a long time, Indians read classic mysteries in English rather than producing them and for many in the West the only example of Indian crime fiction would be H. R. F. Keating's Inspector Ghote stories, starting with *The Perfect Murder* (1964). The external English gaze is evident in both the neat solvability of the crimes displayed and the affectionate interest in India—itself a form of patronization. Local forms of the genre did develop: Sharadindu Bandyopadhyay's Bengali-language Byomkesh Bakshi stories, starting in 1932, with a Holmesian Calcutta-based detective, were very successful and the well-known film director Satyajit Ray produced from 1965 a series of stories also in Bengali about the youthful private eye Feluda (who also owes something to Holmes). Pulp fiction has appeared in native languages like the many novels produced by Blaft Publishing and the more than a hundred Urdu best sellers by "Ibn-e Safi" (Asrar Ahmad) about Captain Hameed and Colonel Faridi starting in 1952. English-language crime fiction also developed, and parallel to Chandra's interest in the genre are two impressive and inventive crime-based novels by major authors, *The Calcutta Chromosome* (1995) by Amitav Ghosh, a widely admired futuristic and postmodern thriller, and the very successful *Anil's Ghost* (2000) by the Canada-based Michael Ondaatje, bringing forensic detection to investigate political strains in modern Sri Lanka.

But while Chandra might have been prompted by the fresh and revisionist tone of major writers enriching the popular mode of crime fiction, he is also very well-read in English and American literature, as well as traditional Indian culture. The image of Dickens' *Bleak House* can be seen behind *Sacred Games,* with its range of classes and conflicts between past and contemporary culture, while both give a central role to a genial, less than certain, but ultimately enduring and revealing police inspector. Whether or not Chandra is aware of the riches of the mid-century "Mysteries of the Cities" novels that lie behind *Bleak House,* huge, rambling, yet morally focused stories from writers such as Eugène Sue in Paris, George Reynolds in London and Poe's friend George Lippard in Philadelphia, that is in effect the genre in which his encyclopedic epic of Mumbai operates.

The opening events suggest the range of action. Sartaj Singh, Mumbai police inspector, past forty, divorced, is called to a domestic dispute: a husband has thrown his wife's dog out of a fifth-floor window and she is, with a large knife, attacking the door of the bathroom where he is hiding. Soon afterwards, the local Flying Squad shoots dead two men working for the gangster chief

Ganesh Gaitonde. Between these extremes, Sartaj's world extends—he disciplines a boy at his parents' request but refuses a tip from them; then he is the bagman carrying a huge bribe to a superior officer's banker; in evidently related action, he arranges a fake raid on a nightclub.

From the intense detail emerges a double structure. One focuses on the gangster chief. Sartaj receives a tip-off that Gaitonde is hiding in a new secure house; he and the police turn up; there is a long debate between criminal and policeman. Sartaj finally brings in a bulldozer to break in; Gaitonde shoots himself and the girl in the house. Immediately afterwards, the narrative adopts Gaitonde's own voice and tells of the start of his life, moving from a poor rural childhood through increasing his criminal status by shooting his own gang leader, taking his money and setting up criminal activities with a sizeable and, importantly for the story, a multinational and multireligion gang. His great rival will be the Moslem gangster Suleiman Isa and in ten often lengthy sequences Gaitonde tells his own story of becoming a major criminal force, a *bhai*, who for both operations and security moves to Singapore and travels the world. He extends into filmmaking when he gains a beautiful (surgically enhanced) Miss India as his mistress and makes, starring her, a very expensive unsuccessful film—one very negative reviewer has his legs broken.

We also experience Sartaj's varied detecting in the city, across classes, castes and nationalities. Early on a boy has been murdered, apparently by two others, in a large slum area. Sartaj intermittently investigates a crime that most feel very minor, but it steadily escalates, involving him in the world of illegal Bangladeshi immigrants, encountering upwardly mobile local social workers and semi-politicians, and ends in a raid where his own assistant and friend, Katekar, is killed with a hatchet. Very different is a case where the woman whose dog was killed comes to Sartaj privately as she is being blackmailed over an affair with a handsome airline pilot. Sartaj investigates; her lover is behind it all, a man obsessed with modern foreign cars and toys and short of money as well as feeling. Sartaj's worldly wise new assistant, Kumble, wants just to take the man's money, but Sartaj's sense of social outrage leads him to assault the blackmailer seriously.

As well as long-running cases, Sartaj has a busy, often gloomy social life across the city and its peoples. He occasionally has dinner with his colleague Majid and his pleasant wife but also interacts with variously corrupt colleagues: as Sartaj's wealthy wife has left him, he has to take minor bribes himself to survive. At times he sees his mother and remembers his noble policeman father, and after Katekar's death Sartaj visits the troubled family.

Sartaj has recurrent and limited relations with women: he speculates about the over-dressed, over-anxious blackmail victim, even seems slightly interested in Anjali Mathur, an austere government security official, but slowly grows closer to Mary, sister of the woman found dead with Gaitonde. Sartaj both personally and professionally is, for all his size, smartness of dress and menacing manner when in police mode, a rather reticent and humble man. The ending to the novel is his own intense pleasure in resuming what he sees as ordinary life as he rides his motorcycle to the police station through the terrible Mumbai traffic and its multicultural hordes of people: "Sartaj drank it all in, incredulous that he had missed all this while he had been away, and that he was glad to be back" (899).

The Sartaj-Gaitonde alternation comprises the basic structure of *Sacred Games,* as if Chandra has deliberately intercalated a police procedural narrative with a confessional crime novel of gangster life. That in itself would be a substantial and innovative achievement, especially in the light of the dense Mumbai city experience and the exotic colloquial language that enriches the vigorous English narration. But Chandra takes these strands of his massive novel to another level of subtlety and challenge when he moves on to consider and realize the issues of the modern world's increasingly conflicting faiths and nationalisms and the dangerous international situation that is the result of the heightened tension of the last decades.

The variation of the name from Bombay to Mumbai—registered in the novel—is more than just asserting the local version. It is also an assertion of Hinduism, and the story of Ganesh Gaitonde develops towards religious politics. Gaitonde is recruited, when in jail, to use his contacts and capacities in the service of the Indian secret service. Very sensitive to threats from Pakistan in particular, and Islamic forces in general, they are aware of a Pakistani plan to forge huge quantities of Indian currency, with criminal assistance, and so Gaitonde's natural hostilities to his Moslem gangster rival Suleiman Isa and his potential service to the Indian state can be condensed. Such politicization is unusual for Gaitonde: his gang is, while seriously criminal and casually murderous, notably multicultural in political and religious terms.

This change of position for Gaitonde towards state service is matched by another that shares a benign appearance and malign outcome. He becomes more religious in his attitudes and anxieties and comes under the power of a wheelchair-bound guru, whose rarely referenced name is Shidhar Shukla. Slowly Chandra builds the story that this guru intends to assemble and explode in Mumbai an atomic device: extreme Hinduist thought holds that modern corruptions, from secular imperialist capitalism to hostile Islam, must be wiped out of India and a simple true Hindu life reestablished. The explosion, however, will be blamed on a fake Islamic body that the guru has invented to gain money from Pakistan—sometimes in forged Indian notes. The guru's extreme

Hinduism is not devout but part of his financial interests that can have criminal outlets and practices.

As Sartaj, at first, arrived at Gaitonde's nuclear bunker in Mumbai, where he planned to survive the nuclear explosion, so at the conclusion the Inspector uses all his policing skills and dubious contacts to find out just where the guru is in the sprawling city and leads a police attack with security specialists and radiation experts. In a neat reminder of low-level everyday policing, Sartaj's worldly assistant, Kumble, makes sure they all know who identified the address.

Sartaj has himself, like Gaitonde, been involved in the raising of the thematic stakes in the novel from crime in the city to international religious politics. After the siege of Gaitonde's house, Sartaj is contacted by the secret service, wanting to know why Gaitonde has moved back to Mumbai and who the dead girl was. This leads Sartaj to investigate her and meet her sister; equally, by interviewing the film star he finds out about the guru and that Gaitonde had ideas about Pralay, the Hindu end-of-the-world scenario.

But Sartaj does not get far with these investigations. The guru story unfolds principally through Gaitonde's own posthumous autobiography. Sartaj's main role in the religious and nationalist themes of the novel is to represent an Indian minority. He is the only Sikh police inspector in Mumbai and, with some fidelity to his ethnic origin, has the image of the Sikh wise man Guru Gobid Singh in his office as a "somewhat twisted assertion of secularism" (5) against the religious pictures belonging to other police. His multicultural position is both a reason for being a good detective and also a prime value in the text, as Caroline Herbert argues (962–65). Ultimately the two plotlines about Gaitonde and Sartaj are contrasted as different paths for a modern Indian, and Chandra does not miss the opportunity to give this relationship a symbolic moment. Gaitonde himself refers back to a time when they met, when Sartaj half-recognized him, and at the same time Gaitonde passed into the power of the guru corrupt in both criminal and religious terms as "a reluctant Hindu nationalist" (Herbert, 956).

This theme is stressed by the author when Sartaj's last action before plunging with pleasure back into the teeming multicultural city is to accompany his mother to the Golden Temple at Amritsar, the center of Sikhdom. It is possible, the novel finally asserts, to possess your own personal identity, including its fully religious form, and also be a citizen of the most modern world. In this climax Chandra is taking crime fiction to a substantial level of important contemporary statement and also meshing it with recent Indian commentary. The last two decades have seen increasing religious nationalism, notably in Mumbai, and parallel violence from outside as in the 1993 and the 2008 terrorist attacks in the city. Both Hindus and Moslems, not only extremists among them, have felt that modern secularism is a turn towards the capitalist West, and as a result commentators like Aamir Mufti have argued for what they call "critical secularism," which will see and reject the follies and degradations of Western consumerism but still value the moral principles of democracy and liberalism, rather than slide into the paths to extremism that can follow from backward-looking nationalism and religionism (see Caroline Herbert's essay on this material). Chandra's *Sacred Games* equates such religio-nationalist extremist attitudes with organized crime.

Remarkable as it seems, the two massive, linked structural sequences focused on Sartaj and Gaitonde, and their sublimation in higher topics, do not exhaust the book. Chandra has added three sequences of "insets" before pages 300, 700 and nearly 900. The first is "The Great Game"—Kipling's name for imperial espionage is reused for India's own modern and independent supra-regional defenses. At some length—nearly fifty pages—it focuses on the aging and ill K. D. Yadav, the Indian spymaster, and the young and intense Anjali Mathur, who has already contacted Sartaj. It tells Yadav's story and also develops Gaitonde's links to this particular "game."

The second inset is "Five Fragments, Scattered in Time," in part synopsizing elements of the political plot: a man called Trivedi (also known as Sharma) operates as the link between Gaitonde and the guru. Here we find that the guru has invented an Islamic group in order to relieve the Pakistanis of money: it remains unclear if he knows it is forged. In another fragment we hear how Shahid Khan, a Sikh Pakistani, nearly got hold of the actual Indian currency plates and did at least commandeer some real paper. A short sequence recounts border activity including military action between Pakistan and India, and another tells of the death of K. D. Yadav. Seemingly a random part of the huge range of ordinary-person action is a fragment about two women, Ram Pari and Navneet—the latter being Sartaj's mother's beautiful long-lost sister.

Even this last apparently loose end becomes part of Chandra's extraordinarily interconnected structure when in the final inset we read two stories, the shorter being about an old Sikh woman dying in America, with granddaughters firmly localized there. In her delirium she says, "Nikki, take me home" (885)—that was Sartaj's mother's nickname, so this is the lost Navneet: she ended up there through her son, the Shahid Khan of the currency business. As Chandra said in an interview, he is creating "a huge web of agendas and politics and ideologies" (quoted by Dora Sales Salvador, 138).

If the short final inset involves ordinary people in the elaborate interactions of the very complex plot, the longer final one asks deeper questions about progress and its reverse in India. The story is told of Aadil—a very poor rural boy, reminiscent of Gaitonde but apparently with a different future. He is good at and eager about his studies and with great hardship goes to secondary school, university and graduate work. His family has been in part impoverished through the land thefts of a neighbor, N. P. Yadav (conceivably related to the spymaster with the same surname), and though a promising scientist, Aadil cannot afford to get a PhD. He returns to the farm and, angered by both local greed and his memory of the urban rich, turns to political violence as a Marxist activist, ends up in jail, escapes, rejoins the guerrillas but is disgusted by their brutality and flees to Mumbai, to operate as a small-time crook with some slum boys. As such, like Navneet, Aadil had an earlier role in the story: he was the shrewd white-haired leader of the young Bangladeshi thugs who cut the throat of Sartaj's original assistant policeman, Katekar.

It is as if no one can really stand outside the intense complexity of modern India and its forces of chaos, as if everyone in the huge cast of the story operates in interactions that are baffling to comprehend and evaluate. This is evidently the full meaning of the title *Sacred Games:* Chandra has said it took a long time to emerge (interview with Antonia Navarro-Tejero, 238). It refers to what Hindus call *leela*, the game played by the gods in the sacred texts (Leela is also the name of Chandra's daughter). As Geetha Ganapathy-Doré notes (116), the text at recurrent times references the notions of humans as toys, and this idea is referred to in the text, no doubt ironically, by the most troubled and religious of all the characters. Early on, when speaking to Sartaj, "'It is only a game, my friend,' Gaitonde says. 'It is only a game, it is leela'" (40); later he will tell Jojo, "Parmatna has written it already ... we are just actors in his play" (531). Sheobhushan Shukla links this view of the games of fate with Chandra's extensive knowledge of the ancient Indian epics that move easily between the divine and human world (184–86).

Chandra himself has called *Sacred Games* an "anti-thriller" (in an interview with Salvador, 138), in terms of its strategy to extend crime fiction beyond local and personalized alarms and excitements to wider themes that include a supratemporal sense of structure linking with past literature, West and East, and also the broad consideration of contemporary social and international threats. But Chandra has nevertheless paid faithful attention to the modes of both the police procedural and the crime novel and even assigns to Sartaj the sudden insightful breakthrough of the great detectives. He half-consciously identifies the link between the elaborate wheelchair used by Gaitonde's adviser Bunty and the similarly rare model he has seen with an important guru and suddenly realizes who the man is behind Gaitonde whom the security forces are so urgently seeking.

Sacred Games is a most ambitious novel, its complex themes in keeping with its physical size. In this respect its only parallel appears to be Stieg Larsson's *Millennium* trilogy, which, remarkably, appeared at almost the same time, and also projects its treatment of crime through the complex politics of one modern country to international concerns of current importance and great gravity. Yet the overall tone of Chandra's novel can be positive. As Sartaj visits a brand-new bank to deposit some dividend checks in his mother's account, he speaks to an old acquaintance, an ex-army security guard in a smart new uniform. He shows Sartaj five Tibetan sadhus, holy men, who are outside in the street, making from colored sand a large and beautiful mandala. In both Hinduism and Buddhism, this is the symbol of the cosmos. Later in the day Sartaj goes back that way and sees how the mandala "was inhabited now by a host of creatures, large and small, and a swirl of divine beings enveloped the entirety of this new world" (228). The guard had told Sartaj that when once the mandala was finished they would sweep it all away. This world that is very ancient, and always recurring, is set among an apparently drastically modern creation of banks and dividends and security guards. In the context of both worlds, simultaneously impermanent and lasting, Chandra seems to speak of writing this novel: "Sartaj did not understand any of it, but it was beautiful to see it come into life, so he watched for a long time" (228).

Chandra's work, like that of other international Indian English-language writers, has not gone uncriticized by other Indians, involved in what he has called, as he titled an essay about this criticism, "The Cult of Authenticity." His international success may well have been a factor in the hostility, but the specific charge has been that he and others present to an international market a quaint and touristic version of Indianness—he was in particular accused of inauthenticity in giving his *Love and Longing in Bombay* stories titles from Indian religious philosophy like "Dharma," "Shanti" and "Kama." His convincing response asserts first the extent of his local research, including among Mumbai gangsters, and second that rather than betraying his region of origin, he works in a larger world: "My region is a hugely cosmopolitan place" (9).

As well as taking an international evaluative perspective, Chandra offers a localism that is itself powerful, with great attention to detail, notably of the places, peoples and especially languages of Mumbai. Sheobhusan Shaklu suggests the language effect is the reverse of touristic and that Chandra "has made tremendous efforts to Indianize English" (196). As a result of that process and his redeployment of the socially and morally explorative major English novel form to India today, Shaklu offers the conclusion that Chandra has "decolonized what has been the instrument of colonization" (196).

In modern times preoccupied with drastic international challenges, it is somewhat comforting to know that readers have recognized the power of the book and that publishers realized they had here a chance to produce something special. There was a substantial bidding war before *Sacred Games* was bought by HarperCollins—the sum of $1 million has been mentioned. Since then there have been, as after *Life and Longing in Bombay,* rumors about another major work in process. It remains to be discovered whether this will embrace and surpass the traditions of crime fiction as substantially and importantly as *Sacred Games* has done.

References

Chandra, Vikram. "The Cult of Authenticity." *Boston Review*, http://w.w.w.boston review.net/vikram-chandra-the-cult-of-authenticity.

Ermelino, Louisa. "Author Profile: Wiseguys of Mumbai." www.PublishersWeekly.com, October 23, 2006.

Fiestino, Cielo. "A Story from Vikram Chandra's *Love and Longing in Bombay*: 'Kama'— Detecting in Bombay," in *Entwining Narratives: Critical Explorations into Vikram Chandra's Fiction*. Ed. Sheobhusan Shukla, Christopher Rollason, and Anu Shukla. New Delhi: World Association for Studies in Literatures in English, 2010, 105–13.

Ganapathy-Doré, Geetha. "Supermodernity's Meganarratives: A Comparative Study of Vikram Chandra's *Sacred Games,* Gregory David Roberts' *Santaram,* and Suketu Mehta's *Maximum City,*" in *Entwining Narratives: Critical Exploration into Vivram Chandra's Fiction*. Ed. Sheobhusan Shukla, Christopher Rollason, and Anu Shukla. New Delhi: World Association for Studies in Literature in English, 2010, 114–30.

Herbert, Caroline. "Spectrality and Secularism in Bombay Fiction: Salman Rushdie's *The Moor's Last Sigh* and Vikram Chandra's *Sacred Games.*" *Textual Practice* 26 (2012): 945–71.

Navarro-Tejero, Antonia. "A Conversation with Vikram Chandra," in *Entwining Narratives: Critical Exploration into Vivram Chandra's Fiction*. Ed. Sheobhusan Shukla, Christopher Rollason, and Anu Shukla. New Delhi: World Association for Studies in Literature in English, 2010, 212–39.

Rollason, Christopher. "The Tale-Teller and the Text: Storytelling in Vikram Chandra's *Red Earth and Pouring Rain* and 'Love and Longing in Bombay,'" in *Entwining Narratives: Critical Exploration into Vivram Chandra's Fiction*. Ed. Sheobhusan Shukla, Christopher Rollason, and Anu Shukla. New Delhi: World Association for Studies in Literature in English, 2010, 54–78.

Salvador, Dora Sales. "'Only Life Itself': Noir Fiction and Beyond in Vikram Chandra's *Sacred Games,*" in *Entwining Narratives: Critical Exploration into Vivram Chandra's Fiction*. Ed. Sheobhusan Shukla, Christopher Rollason, and Anu Shukla. New Delhi: World Association for Studies in Literature in English, 2010, 131–47.

Shukla, Sheobhusan. "The Other as the Subject in Vikram Chandra's Sacred Games," in *Entwining Narratives: Critical Exploration into Vivram Chandra's Fiction*. Ed. Sheobhusan Shukla, Christopher Rollason, and Anu Shukla. New Delhi: World Association for Studies in Literature in English, 2010, 182–97.

Index

Absent in the Spring (as "Mary Westmacott") 99
The Adventures of Sherlock Holmes 89–93
The Adventures of Susan Hopley 65
Agatha (film) 105
Ahmad, Asrar 221
Alder, Bill 121, 123, 126
Alegre, Sara Martin 197, 198
All the Year Round 44
Allingham, Margery 74
Amateur City 165
And Then There Were None 97, 99
Angel Dance 165
The Angst-Ridden Executive (*La soledad de manager*) 180
Anil's Ghost 221
The Animal Lover's Book of Beastly Murder 145
Aquinas, St. Thomas 171, 175
Aristotle 177
Armadale 44, 51, 52
Arvas, Paula 217, 219
Ascari, Maurizio 20, 22
Ask the Cards a Question 159
Assouline, Pierre 121, 122, 124, 126
Austen, Jane 4, 6, 135, 176; *Pride and Prejudice* 112
Auster, Paul 175
Autobiography 72
The Avengers (TV series) 216

Bacall, Lauren 134
Bacon, Roger 171, 175
Baker, Josephine 117
Baksi, Kurdo 210, 211, 217, 218
Baldwin, James 154
Balzac, Honoré de 55, 61
Bandyopadhyay, Sharadindu 221
Barnard, Robert 103, 106
Barr, Robert 94, 96
Barrie, J. M. 87

Barth, John 175
Barthes, Roland 169
Barton, E. R. 108
Baudelaire, Charles 48
Bayard, Pierre: *Who Killed Roger Ackroyd?* 104, 106
Beal, M. F.: *Angel Dance* 165
Becker, Lucille F. 117, 124, 126
Belsey, Catherine 91, 96
Benezet, Antony 28
Bentley, E. C.: *Trent's Last Case* 112
Berlinguer, Susana Bayo 180, 181, 188, 189
The Big Sleep 123, 129–136
Bismarck, Otto von 61
Bitter Medicine 164, 166
Black and Blue 191
The Black Book 192
Black Mask 128, 129
Black Sheep (also as *Cast the First Stone* and *Yesterday Will Make You Cry*) 149
The Black Sleuth 154
Blacklist 166
Bland, Eleanor Taylor 158
Bleak House 49, 71, 72, 77
Bleeding Kansas 167
Bleiler, E. F. 56, 57, 63
Blind Man with a Pistol 150, 156
Blowfly 206
The Blue Dahlia (film script) 130
The Blunderer 138
The Body Farm 204
Body of Evidence 204
Bogart, Humphrey 134
Bonaparte, Marie 41
Bond, James 216
Bones (TV series) 207
Bonniot, Roger 63
Booth, Martin 88, 96
Borges, Jorge Luis 174–5

Bourke, James Lee 135
Brabazon, James 115
Brackett, Leigh 134
Braddon, Mary: *Lady Audley's Secret* 47, 83
Brett, Jeremy 94
Brockden Brown, Charles 5, 6, 7, 21, 23–32, 34, 35, 39, 40, 49; *Edgar Huntly* 23–32, 49
Brookmyre, Christopher 190
Brophy, Brigid 137, 145
Bruce, John Edward: *The Black Sleuth* 154
Buchan, John 103
Burgess, Anthony 53
Burke, Edmund 20
The Bushranger of Van Diemen's Land 81
Busman's Honeymoon 114
Butler, Marilyn 19, 20, 22

Cade, Jared 105, 106
Caesar, Michael 169, 177, 178
Cain, James M. 7, 130, 133, 139, 142; *The Postman Always Rings Twice* 138
Calanchi, Alessandra 31, 32
The Calcutta Chromosome 221
Caleb Williams 13–21
Cameron, Donald: *The Mysteries of Melbourne* 80
Carlson, Eric W. 36, 39, 40, 42
Carr, Caleb 176
Carr, John Dickson 94, 96, 174
The Case-Book of Sherlock Holmes 93
Caterson, Simon 76, 80, 83, 84
Cavani, Liliana 145
Chamoiseau, Patrick 158
Chandler, Raymond 6, 7, 63, 97, 99, 106, 127–36, 138, 154, 164, 186, 190; *The Big Sleep* 123, 129–136; *The Blue Dahlia* (film script) 130; *Double Indemnity* (film script) 133, 139; *Farewell My Lovely* 129, 132, 133, 134–5 (film), 154; *The High Window* 129, 133, 135 (film); *The Lady in the Lake* 129, 133, 135; *The Long Goodbye* 127, 129, 130, 132, 133, 135; *Playback* 129, 130, 135; *The Poodle Springs Murder* 135; *Strangers on a Train* (film script) 134, 138
Chandra, Vikram 4, 5, 7, 21, 190, 220–8; "The Cult of Authenticity" 227, 228; *Love and Longing in Bombay* 220, 227, 228; *Red Earth and Pouring Rain* 220; *Sacred Games* 220–8
Checkmate 72
Chesterton, G. K. 7, 102, 191
Cheyney, Peter 7
The Chinese Shadow (L'Ombre chinoise) 124, 125
Christie, Agatha 5, 7, 19, 62, 72, 73, 97–106, 107, 108, 117, 123, 124, 128, 159, 205; *Absent in the Spring* (as "Mary Westmacott") 99; *And Then There Were None* 97, 99; *Autobiography* 72; *The Clocks* 72; *Curtain* 99; *Endless Night* 104; *Five Little Pigs* 105; *Hickory Dickory Dock* 105; *The Mousetrap* 105; *The Murder of Roger Ackroyd* 78, 99–105, 108, 123, 128; *The Murder on the Links* 100; *Murder on the Orient Express* 72, 99, 104; *The Mysterious Affair at Styles* 98, 100, 102; *The Pale Horse* 102; *Sad Cypress* 103; *Sleeping Murder* 99; *Third Girl* 105
City of Quartz 132, 136
Clarke, Marcus: *His Natural Life* 81
Cleese, John 94
Clemit, Paula 19, 20, 21, 22
The Clocks 72
Cloudesley 21
Clouds of Witness 107
Cody, Lisa: *Dupe* 160
Cohen, Michael 178
Cohen, Octavius Roy 154
Coleridge, Samuel Taylor 176
Colette, Sidonie-Gabrielle 124
Coletti, Therese 175, 177, 178
Collins, Wilkie 3, 6, 44–54, 71, 73, 80, 108, 111–12; *Armadale* 44, 51, 52; *The Dead Secret* 45; *Hide and Seek* 28, 45; *The Law and the Lady* 52; *The Moonstone* 4, 44–53, 80, 81, 82, 83, 89, 108, 109, 111–12, 115, 142; *The Woman in White* 44, 45, 47, 48, 53, 72
Colmeira, José F. 181, 185, 189
Coma 203
Conan Doyle, Adrian 94
Conan Doyle, Arthur 3, 5, 7, 39, 40, 87–96, 173, 181, 190, 205, 215; *The Adventures of Sherlock Holmes* 89–93; *The Case-Book of Sherlock Holmes* 93; *The Great Shadow* 89; *His Last Bow* 93, 98; *The Hound of the Baskervilles* 93, 215; *The Lost World* 93; *The Memoirs of Sherlock Holmes* 93; *Micah Clarke* 89; *The Parasite* 87; *The Refugees* 89; *The Return of Sherlock Holmes* 93; *Rodney Stone* 89; *The Sign of Four* 52–3, 55, 61, 62, 77, 82–3, 88, 89, 99, 108; *A Study in Scarlet* 70, 87, 88, 93; *The Valley of Fear* 93; *The White Company* 89
Confiant, Raphaël 158
The Conjure Man Dies 154
Cook, Robin: *Coma* 203
Cooper, James Fenimore 31, 60
Cornhill Magazine 88
Cornwell, Patricia 7, 200–9; *Blowfly* 206; *The Body Farm* 204; *Body of Evidence* 204; *Cruel and Unusual* 205, 208; *The Last Precinct* 205, 208; *Point of Origin* 208; *Port Mortuary* 208; *Portrait of a Killer* 206; *Postmortem* 200–7; *Predator* 205, 208; *Unnatural Exposure* 205
Corris, Peter 7
Cotton Comes to Harlem 151–7, 157 (film)
Cournos John 112, 115
Cox, Anthony Berkeley 5, 139
Craig, Daniel 216
Creasey, John 191
Critical Mass 167
Crofts, Freeman Wills 20–21, 191
Crowe, Catherine: *The Adventures of Susan Hopley* 65
Cruel and Unusual 205, 208

"The Cult of Authenticity" 227, 228
Cumberbatch, Benedict 94
Curcio, Renato 177
Curtain 99

Daeninckx, Didier 8, 181
Dannay, Frederic, and Manfred B. Lee (as "Ellery Queen") 4, 7, 21, 73, 97
The Dark House 82
Darwin, Erasmus 29
Davies, Lindsay 176
Davies, Mike: *City of Quartz* 132, 136
Davis, David Brion 31, 32
Davitt, Ellen: *Force and Fraud* 65, 81
The Dead Letter 36, 44, 65, 70, 71
The Dead Secret 45
Deaver, Jeffery 207
de Goncourt, Edmond, and Jules 40
Déja Dead 207
de Lauretis, Teresa 177, 178
Deleuze, Gilles 177
Delon, Alain 145
De Quincey, Thomas 81
Derrida, Jacques 41
Dickens, Charles 44, 48, 49, 53, 71, 76; *All the Year Round* 44; *Bleak House* 49, 71, 72, 77; *Great Expectations* 83; *Household Words* 48, 49; *The Mystery of Edwin Drood* 49, 53; *Our Mutual Friend* 49
Diemert, Brian 197, 198
Disraeli, Benjamin 61
A Distant Mirror 176
Dixon, Robert 80, 84
The Documents in the Case 108–9
The Dog-Collar Murders 165
Dostoevsky, Fyodor 144, 197
Double Indemnity (film script) 133, 139
Douglas, Carole Nelson 95
du Boisgobey, Fortuné: *The Mystery of an Omnibus* 80
Du Bose, Martha 66, 73, 74
Duhamel, Marcel 150, 154, 157
Dumas, Alexandre, Sr.: *Les Mohicans de Paris* 60
Dupe 160
Dupin, C. Auguste 20, 33–42, 61, 88
Durham, Philip 130, 136
The Dynamiter 70, 88

Eaude, M 182, 189
Eberhart, Mignon 7
Eco, Umberto 5, 7, 169–79; *Foucault's Pendulum* 177; *The Name of the Rose* 169–78, 178 (film); *The Prague Cemetery* 177; *Reflections on The Name of the Rose* 175; *Travels in Hyperreality* 176
Edgar Huntly 23–32, 49
Edith's Diary 144
Edwin of the Iron Shoes 159
Elementary (TV series) 94
Eliot, T. S. 4, 48, 53, 108, 114
Ellis, Edward: *Ruth the Betrayer* 65

Endless Night 104
Ermelino, Louisa 220, 228
Eskin, Stanley E. 123, 126
Evanovich, Janet 7
Exit Music 197

Fabre, Michel 149–50, 157, 158
The Falls 192, 197
Faludi, Susan 167
Farewell My Lovely 129, 132, 133, 134–5 (film), 154
Farré-Vidal, Carmel 204, 209
Faulker, William 134
"Felix, Charles": *The Notting Hill Mystery* 44, 64, 79
Fenn, George Manville: *The Dark House* 82
Féval, Paul 55–6
Fiedler, Leslie 31, 32
Fierro, Marella 200
Fiestino, Cielo 220, 228
File 113 (Le Dossier 113) 56, 62, 70
Fisher, Rudolph: *The Conjure Man Dies* 154
Five Little Pigs 105
Five Red Herrings 114
Fleetwood 21
Fleshmarket Close 192
Fonda, Jane 167
For Love of Imabelle 150
Force and Fraud 65, 81
Ford, Judy Ann 175, 178
Forrest, Katherine V.: *Amateur City* 165
"Forrester, Andrew": *Revelations of a Lady Detective* 65
Forshaw, Barry 211, 212, 216, 218
Forster, E. M.: *Maurice* 187
Fortune, Mary (as W.W.) 65, 81
Foucault, Michel 61
Foucault's Pendulum 177
Freeman, R. Austin 7, 203
Fuster, Jaume 181

Gaboriau, Émile 4, 6, 7, 55–64, 70, 76, 77, 79–80; *File 113 (Le Dossier 113)* 56, 62, 70; *The Little Old Man of Batignolles (Le Petit Vieux de Batignolles)* 63; *Monsieur Lecoq* 55–63, 88; *The Orcival Crime (Le Crime d'Orcival)* 56, 62, 70, 83; *The Widow Lerouge (L'Affaire Lerouge)* 56, 88
Gabrielsson, Eva 211, 212, 215, 218
Gallimard 150, 154
Ganapathy-Doré, Geetha 226, 228
Gardner, Erle Stanley 128
Gaspey, Thomas: *George Godfrey* 83
Gaudi Afternoon 165
Gaudy Night 112, 113, 114
Geherin, David 210, 218
George, Elizabeth 212
George Godfrey 83
Gerritsen, Tess 207
Ghosh, Anil: *The Calcutta Chromosome* 221
Ghost Country 167

Gide, André 125, 126
Gielgud, John 94
Gillette, William 89, 94
Gimenez-Bartlett, Alicia 189
The Girl Who Kicked the Hornet's Nest 217
The Girl Who Played with Fire 217
The Girl with the Dragon Tattoo 72, 211–17
Godsland, Shelley 189
Godwin, William 5, 6, 7, 13–22, 23, 24, 25, 32, 35; *Caleb Williams* 13–21; *Cloudesley* 21; *Fleetwood* 21; *Mandeville* 21; *St. Leon* 21
The Golden Slipper 74
Goldwyn, Samuel 157
Gollancz, Victor 108, 115
Grabo, Norman S. 29, 32
Grafton, Sue 160, 203
Graham, Ruth B. 200, 206
Great Expectations 83
The Great Shadow 89
The Greek Labyrinth (El laberinto Griego) 188
Green, Anna Katharine 6, 21, 61, 63, 65–75, 77, 80, 83, 159; *The Golden Slipper* 74; *The Leavenworth Case* 65–73; *That Affair Next Door* 74
Green, Julien 143
Greene, Graham 143, 145
Greene, Helga 135
Greer, Germaine 159
Greimas, A. J. 40–1
Griswold, Rufus 42
Gruber, Staci 206
Guattari, Félix 177

Habermas, Jürgen 188
Haft, Adele J. 174–5
Hagar of the Pawnshop 83–4
Hagar's Daughter 154
Hamilton, Hamish 130
Hammett, Dashiell 21, 123, 128, 129, 130, 132, 133, 136
Harris, Thomas: *Red Dragon* 203
Hart, Patrice 181, 189
Harte, Brett 87
Have His Carcase 111, 114
Hawks, Howard 134
Hawthorne, Nathaniel 31
Hayward, W. S. 65
Hazlitt, William 13
Head, Beth 204, 209
Heilbron, Caroline G. 115, 159
Heller, Tamar 51, 52, 53
Hennessy, Rosemary 90, 96
Herbert, Caroline 224, 225, 228
Herzberger, David K. 189
Heyer, Georgette 103, 176
Hickory Dickory Dock 105
Hide and Seek (Collins) 45, 48
Hide and Seek (Rankin) 197
The High Window 129, 133, 135 (film)
Highsmith, Patricia 6, 137–46; *The Animal Lover's Book of Beastly Murder* 145; *The Blunderer* 138; *Edith's Diary* 144; *Little Tale of Misogyny* 146; *The Price of Salt* (also as *Carol*) 138; *Ripley Under Water* 145; *Ripley Underground* 145; *Ripley's Game* 142; *Small g: A Summer Idyll* 145; *Strangers on a Train* 137–8, 138 (film); *The Talented Mr. Ripley* 138–45, 145 (film)
Hilfer, Thomas 144, 146
Hillerman, Tony 7, 158
Himes, Chester 6, 8, 149–58, 181; *Black Sheep* (also as *Cast the First Stone* and *Yesterday Will Make You Cry*) 149; *Blind Man with a Pistol* 150, 156; *Cotton Comes to Harlem* 151–7, 157 (film); *For Love of Imabelle* 150; *The Lonely Crusade* 149, 150; *Plan B* 150, 156; *Run Man Run* 154
Hiney, Thomas 127, 133, 136
His Last Bow 93, 98
His Natural Life 81
Hitchcock, Alfred 138
Hodgson, John A. 90, 95, 96
Hoffman, E. T. A. 34
Holmes, Sherlock 20, 55, 61, 77, 87–95, 98, 102, 111, 136, 173, 187, 205, 215, 216, 221
Hopkins, Pauline: *Hagar's Daughter* 154
Hopper, Dennis 145
Horsley, Lee 113, 115, 132, 136, 144, 146, 155, 157, 158, 164, 166, 168, 204, 209
The Hound of the Baskervilles 93, 215
Household Words 48, 49
Housman, A. E. 111, 112
Hughes, Langston 149
Hugo, Victor 55
Hume, Fergus 6, 7, 61, 63, 76–84; *Hagar of the Pawnshop* 83–4; *Lady Jim of Curzon Street* 84; *Madame Midas* 83; *Miss Mephistopheles* 83; *The Mystery of a Hansom Cab* 76–84
Humer, W. F.: *The Mystery of a Wheelbarrow* 83
Hunter, Evan (as "Ed McBain") 61, 190, 191
Hutter, Alfred 52, 53

I Killed Kennedy (Yo maté a Kennedy) 180
Inchbald, Elizabeth 20
Indemnity Only 160–7
Irwin, John T. 41, 42–3

James, Henry 139, 140, 144
James, P. D. 7; *The Skull Beneath the Skin* 159; *An Unsuitable Job for a Woman* 159
John XXII, Pope 176
Johnson, Barbara 41
Johnson, Patricia E. 166, 168
Jones, Manina 159, 164, 165, 166, 168
Juan Carlos, King 181
Judson, E. Z. C. 4

Kafer, Peter 28, 32
Kaminsky, Stuart 160
Keating, H. R. F.: *The Perfect Murder* 221
Keats, John 50, 176

Kellner, Hans 177, 178
Kelly, Gary 17, 18, 19, 22
Kemp, Sandra 52, 53
Kenney, Catherine 111, 112, 115
Killing Orders 164, 166
King, Laurie R. 94
King, Martin Luther 157
King, Stuart 182, 189
Klein, Kathleen Gregory 137, 142, 143, 146, 164, 165, 168
Knight, Stephen 20, 33, 80, 81, 84, 96, 103, 106, 191, 198
Knots and Crosses 190
Knox, Ronald 95
Koestler, Arthur 145
Krause, Sydney J. 28, 29, 30, 31, 32
Kropotkin, Peter 21
Lacan, Jacques 144
Lacruz, Mario 181

Lady Audley's Secret 47, 83
The Lady in the Lake 129, 133, 135
Lady Jim of Curzon Street 84
Landrum, Larry 23, 32
Larsson, Stieg 7, 8, 72, 210–18; *The Girl Who Kicked the Hornet's Nest* 217; *The Girl Who Played with Fire* 217; *The Girl with the Dragon Tattoo* 72, 211–17
The Last Precinct 205, 208
The Law and the Lady 52
The Leavenworth Case 65–73
Leaves from the Notebook of a New York Detective 7, 21, 66, 128
Leblanc, Maurice 84
Leckie, Jean 95
Lee, Manfred B. *see* Dannay, Frederic, and Manfred B. Lee
Le Fanu, Sheridan: *Checkmate* 72
Leffler, Yvonne 211, 218
Lemire Elise 41, 43
Leroux, Gaston: *The Mystery of the Yellow Room* 98
Lessons in Murder 165
Lindgren, Astrid 211, 212
Lippard, George 4, 22, 41
The Little Old Man of Batignolles (*Le Petit Vieux de Batignolles*) 63
Little Tale of Misogyny 146
Liu, Lucy 94
Lodge, David 169, 175, 177, 178
The Lonely Crusade 149, 150
The Long Goodbye 127, 129, 130, 132, 133, 135
Longfellow, Henry Wadsworth 40
Longstocking, Pippi 211
Lord Peter Views the Body 108
The Lost World 93
Love and Longing in Bombay 220, 227, 228
Lovesey, Peter 176
Lucas, Rose 207–8, 209
Lyotard, Jean-François: *The Postmodern Condition* 174

Ma, Sheng-Mai 216, 219
MacDonald, Erin E. 191, 198
Macdonald, Ross 135, 160
Madame Midas 83
Madrid, Juan 189
Maida, Patricia D. 68, 70, 71, 72, 74
Maigret, Jules 63, 154, 205
Maigret in Court (*Maigret aux assises*) 125
Maigret in New York (*Maigret á New York*) 125
Maigret's Return (*Maigret*) 125
Makinen, Merja 98, 102, 103, 106
Malory, Sir Thomas 128
The Man of My Life (*El hombre de la mia vida*) 187
Mandeville 21
Mangham, Andrew 49, 52, 53
Mankell, Henning 211
Margolies, Edward 149–50, 157, 158
Marlowe, Christopher 129
Marlowe, Philip 128–35, 161, 187, 216
Marnham, Patrick 117–18, 124, 125, 126
Marsh, Ngaio 74
Marshall, Peter H. 18, 22
Marshall, Rodney 191, 192, 197, 198
Matthews, Brander 40
Matthiesen, F.O. 31
Maurice 187
Maybrick, Florence 112
McCann, Sean 132, 136, 154, 155, 158
McCracken David 18, 22
McDermid, Val 214
McLaren, Paul 158
McNab, Claire: *Lessons in Murder* 165
Meade, L. T. 108
The Memoirs of Sherlock Holmes 93
Mendoza, Eduard 189
Messac, Régis 61, 66, 74
Messent, Peter 192, 197, 198, 204, 205, 209
Meyer, Nicholas: *The Seven-per-Cent Solution* 94
Meyhoff, Karsten Wind 217, 219
Micah Clarke 89
Midler, Bette 167
Millar, Margaret 8, 139
Millennium I (*Milenio Carvalho I*) 188
Millennium II (*Milenio Carvalho II*) 188
Miller, D. A. 61, 63
Miller, Johnny Lee 94
Millett, Kate 159
Milliken, Stephen F. 150, 158
Milne, A. A. 128
Mina, Denise 190
Mingella, Anthony 145
Miskimmin, Esme 108, 114, 116
Miss Mephistopheles 83
Mizejewksi, Linda 206, 209
Mohan, Rajeswari 90, 96
Les Mohicans de Paris 60
Monsieur Lecoq 55–63, 88
Montalbán, Manuel Vásquez 6, 7, 8, 180–9; *The Angst-Ridden Executive* (*La soledad de manager*) 180; *The Greek Labyrinth* (*El*

laberinto Griego) 188; *I Killed Kennedy* (*Yo maté a Kennedy*) 180; *The Man of My Life* (*El hombre de la mia vida*) 187; *Millennium I (Milenio Carvalho I)* 188; *Millennium II (Milenio Carvalho II)* 188; *Murder in the Central Committee (Asesinato en el comité central)* 187, 188; *Olympic Sabotage (Sabotaja olympico)* 188; *Southern Seas (Los mares del Sur)* 180–8; *Tattoo (Tatuaje)* 180
The Moonstone 4, 44–53, 80, 81, 82, 83, 89, 108, 109, 111–12, 115, 142
Morgan, Janet 99, 106
Moro, Aldo 177
Mosley, Walter 154, 157–8
Mountbatten, Lord Louis 100
The Mousetrap 105
Muller, Gilbert H. 149, 156, 158
Muller, John P. 41, 43
Muller, Marcia: *Ask the Cards a Question* 159; *Edwin of the Iron Shoes* 159
Munt, Sally 164–5, 168
Murch, Alma 66, 72, 74
Murder by Decree (film) 94
Murder in the Central Committee (Asesinato en el comité central) 187, 188
Murder in the Collective 165
Murder Must Advertise 114
The Murder of Roger Ackroyd 78, 99–105, 108, 123, 128
The Murder on the Links 100
Murder on the Orient Express 72, 99, 104
The Mysteries of London 83
The Mysteries of Melbourne 80
The Mysteries of Paris (Les Mystères de Paris) 55
The Mysterious Affair at Styles 98, 100, 102
The Mystery of a Hansom Cab 76–84
The Mystery of a Wheelbarrow 83
The Mystery of an Omnibus 80
The Mystery of Edwin Drood 49, 53
The Mystery of the Yellow Room 98
The Name of the Rose 169–78, 178 (film)
The Naming of the Dead 192–7

Narcejac, Thomas 61, 64, 121, 125, 126
The Narrative of Arthur Gordon Pym 34
Navarro-Tejeri, Antonia 226, 228
Neely, B. (as Barbara Neely) 158, 167
Nestingen, Andrew 211, 212, 219
New Arabian Nights 88
The Newgate Calendar 20
Newnes, George 89, 93
Newton, P.M. 196, 198
Nichols, William J. 182, 185, 186, 187, 189
Nicol, Bran 138, 142, 146
The Nine Tailors 114
Nordon, Pierre 96
The Notting Hill Mystery 44, 64, 79

Oates, Joyce Carol 132, 133, 136
Ockham, William of 175
Oliver, Maria-Antonia 189

Olivier-Martin, Yves 56, 64
Olympic Sabotage (Sabotaja olympico) 188
Ondaatje, Michael: *Anil's Ghost* 221
The Orcival Crime (Le Crime d'Orcival) 56, 62, 70, 83
Orford, Margie 8
Our Mutual Friend 49

Packard, Lesley 157
Paget, Sidney 89
Paine, Tom 19
The Pale Horse 102
Palme, Olof 218
Panek, Leroy Lad 71, 74, 129, 133, 136
The Parasite 87
Paretsky, Sara 6, 7, 160–8, 203, 214; *Bitter Medicine* 164, 166; *Blacklist* 166; *Bleeding Kansas* 167; *Critical Mass* 167; *Ghost Country* 167; *Indemnity Only* 160–7; *Killing Orders* 164, 166; *Total Recall* 164; *Viewpoint* 167
Pargeter, Edith (as "Ellis Peters") 176
Parker, Mark 175, 177, 179
Parker, Robert B. 135
Pavón, Francisco Garcia 181
Payn, James 88
Pearsall, Ronald 87, 96
Pedigree 125
Pedrolo, Manuel 181
Pepper, Andrew 151, 155, 158
The Perfect Murder 221
Peter the Lett (Petr le Letton) 118
Peters, Catherine K. 48, 53
"Peters, Ellis" *see* Pargeter, Edith
Peterson, Audrey 70, 74
Pettersson, Jan-Erik 210, 211, 217, 219
Picasso, Pablo 157
The Picture of Dorian Gray 88
Pinkerton, Allan 128
Pittard, Christopher, 80, 83, 89
Plain, Gill 133, 136, 165, 168, 190, 1911, 192, 191, 197, 199
Plan B 150, 156
Playback 129, 130, 135
Poe, Edgar Allan 3, 4, 5, 6, 7, 14, 21, 31, 33–43, 48, 60, 63, 65, 77, 92, 99, 181; *The Narrative of Arthur Gordon Pym* 34; *Tales of the Grotesque and Arabesque* 34
Point of Origin 208
Poirot, Hercule 100–5, 107, 205
The Poodle Springs Murder 135
Port Mortuary 208
Porter, Dennis 17, 121, 124, 125, 126
Portrait of a Killer 206
The Postman Always Rings Twice 138
The Postmodern Condition 174
Postmortem 200–7
The Prague Cemetery 177
Predator 205, 208
The Price of Salt (also as *Carol*) 138
Pride and Prejudice 112
Priestman, Martin 91, 96

Index   235

The Private Life of Sherlock Holmes (film) 94
Proudhon, Pierre-Joseph 21
Pykett, Lyn 49, 50, 53

"Queen, Ellery" *see* Dannay, Frederic, and Manfred B. Lee
Quintus Servinton 81

Rabelais, François 175
Rabinowitz, Peter 132, 136
Rahn, B. J. 113, 116
The Rajah's Diamond 88
Rankin, Ian 6, 7, 8, 190–8; *Black and Blue* 191; *The Black Book* 192; *Exit Music* 197; *The Falls* 192, 197; *Fleshmarket Close* 192; *Hide and Seek* 197; *Knots and Crosses* 190; *The Naming of the Dead* 192–7; *Saints of the Shadow Bible* 198; *Strip Jack* 191
Rathbone, Basil 94
Ray, Satyajit 221
Reade, Charles 53
A Reason to Kill 165
Rebus, John 190–98
Red Dragon 203
Red Earth and Pouring Rain 220
Reddy, Maureen 163, 166, 168
Reflections on The Name of the Rose 175
The Refugees 89
"Regester, Seeley" (Metta Fuller) 6; *The Dead Letter* 36, 44, 65, 70, 71
Reichs, Kathy: *Déja Dead* 207
Rendell, Ruth 8
The Return of Sherlock Holmes 93
Revelations of a Lady Detective 65
Reynolds, Barbara 107, 112, 113, 114, 116
Reynolds, G. W. M. 41, 49, 55, 221; *The Mysteries of London* 83
Reynolds, Moira Davison 138, 146, 160, 168, 200, 209
Richardson, William J. 41, 43
Richter 173, 175, 178
Rinehart, Mary Roberts 73, 98
Ripley Under Water 145
Ripley Underground 145
Ripley's Game 142
Rodney Stone 89
Rohmer, Saxe 103
Rollason, Christopher 220, 228
Rollin, Roger 169, 178
Rousseau, Jean-Jacques 21
Rowcroft, Charles: *The Bushranger of Van Diemen's Land* 81
Rowland, Susan 97, 102, 106
Run Man Run 154
"Russell, William" 60, 191
Ruth the Betrayer 65
Rycroft, Charles 52
Rzepka, Charles 82, 84, 113, 116, 166, 168

Sachs, Leslie 206
Sacred Games 220–8
Sad Cypress 103
St. Leon 21
Saints of the Shadow Bible 198
Salander, Lisbeth 205, 210, 211–15, 216, 217, 218
Sallis, James 149, 157, 158
Salvador, Dora Sales 225, 226, 228
Savery, Henry: *Quintus Servinton* 81
Sayers, Dorothy 7, 39, 48, 53, 73–4, 99, 107–16, 173, 174; *Busman's Honeymoon* 114; *Clouds of Witness* 107; *The Documents in the Case* 108–9; *Five Red Herrings* 114; *Gaudy Night* 112, 113, 114; *Have His Carcase* 111, 114; *Murder Must Advertise* 114; *The Nine Tailors* 114; *Lord Peter Views the Body* 108; *Strong Poison* 109–15; *The Unpleasantness at the Bellona Club* 107; *Whose Body?* 107, 111
Scarpetta, Kay 200–8
Schenkar, Joan 139, 143, 144, 145, 146
Schlegel, Friedrich 34
Sciascia, Leonardo 8
Scott, Clement 77
Scott, Sir Walter 3, 87
Série Noir 150
The Seven-per-Cent Solution 94
Severin, Laura 198, 199
Shakespeare, William 4, 5
Shaw, Joseph 128
Shaw, Philip 17, 19, 20, 22
She Came Too Late 165
Shelley, Mary Wollstonecraft 21
Shelley, Percy Bysshe 21, 31
Shiloh, Ilana 143, 144, 146
Shorley, Christopher 117, 121, 126
Shukla, Sheobhusan 227, 228
Sickert, Walter 206
The Sign of Four 52–3, 55, 61, 62, 77, 82–3, 88, 89, 99, 108
Silent Witness (TV series) 207
Simenon, Georges 5, 6, 7, 117–26; *The Chinese Shadow (L'Ombre chinoise)* 124, 125; *Maigret in Court (Maigret aux assises)* 125; *Maigret in New York (Maigret á New York)* 125; *Maigret's Return (Maigret)* 125; *Pedigree* 125; *Peter the Lett (Petr le Letton)* 118; *The Yellow Dog (Le Chien jaune)* 118–25
Sisters of the Road 165
Sjöwall, Maj 5, 211
The Skull Beneath the Skin 159
Sleeping Murder 99
Slung, Michele 74
Small g: A Summer Idyll 145
Smith, Joan 212
Soitos, Stephen F. 149, 150, 154, 155, 156, 157, 158
Southern Seas (Los mares del Sur) 180–8
Spark, Muriel 190
Spofford, Harriet Prescott 65
Stabenow, Dana 158, 167
Stableford, Brian 64
Starrett, Vincent 95
Stevenson, Robert Louis 87, 191; *The Dyna-*

miter 70, 88; *New Arabian Nights* 88; *The Rajah's Diamond* 88
Stout, Rex 17, 21, 97
Strand Magazine 89, 91, 92, 93
Strangers on a Train (film and script) 134, 137–8
Strip Jack 191
Strong Poison 109–15
A Study in Scarlet 70, 87, 88, 93
Suchet, David 105
Sue, Eugène 4, 49, 62, 221; *The Mysteries of Paris (Les Mystères de Paris)* 55
Sussex, Lucy 72, 73, 74–5, 81, 84
Symons, Julian 13, 22, 53, 54, 104, 106, 113, 116, 129, 136, 137, 139, 145, 146, 154

Taibo, Paco Ignacio II 7, 189
The Talented Mr. Ripley 138–45, 145 (film)
Tales of the Grotesque and Arabesque 34
Tani, Stefano 174, 175, 178
Tattoo (Tatuaje) 180
Taylor, Jenny Bourne 49, 52, 53
Temple, Peter 8
That Affair Next Door 74
Third Girl 105
Tholwe, Dialwe 8
Thomas, Margaret Caldwell 137, 138, 143, 146, 200, 209
Thomas, Ronald R. 35, 43
Thompson, Jim 7, 139, 142
Thompson, Laura 104, 106
Thoms, Peter 48, 50, 53
Todorov, Tzvetan 49, 53, 106
Topin, Marius 63, 64
Total Recall 164
Travels in Hyperreality 176
Treat, Lawrence: *V as in Victim* 191
Trent's Last Case 112
Tuchmann, Barbara: *A Distant Mirror* 176
Turgenev, Ivan 135
Turner, Kathleen 167
Twain, Mark 40

Unnatural Exposure 205
The Unpleasantness at the Bellona Club 107
An Unsuitable Job for a Woman 159

V as in Victim 191
The Valley of Fear 93
"Van Dine, S. S." (Willard Huntington Wright) 4, 7, 21, 73, 97
Vanacker, Sabine 200, 203, 205, 209

Vidal, Gore 145
Vidocq, Eugène François 4, 33, 55
Viewpoint 167
Voltaire (François-Marie Arouet) 40, 173

Waddell, Dan 212
Wahlöö, Per 7, 211
Wallace, Edgar 5, 103
Walsh, John 37, 43
Walton, Priscilla 159, 164, 165, 166, 168
Warren, Samuel 33, 35
Warshawski, V. I. 160–7, 205
Watson, Kate 70, 72, 75
Watson, Nicole 8, 158
Watts, James 100
Watts, Steven 31, 32
Weisz, Pierre 122, 126
Wells, Carolyn 73, 98, 188, 189
Wells, Carragh 181, 189
Wenders, Wim 145
White, Jane G. 174, 178
White, Robert J. 174, 178
The White Company 89
Who Killed Roger Ackroyd? 104, 106
Whose Body? 107, 111
The Widow Lerouge (L'Affaire Lerouge) 56, 88
Wilde, Oscar 88, 89; *The Picture of Dorian Gray* 88
Wilder, Billy 94
Williams, John A. 154, 155, 157, 158
Williams, John B.: *Leaves from the Notebook of a New York Detective* 7, 21, 66, 128
Wilson, Andrew 143, 146
Wilson, Barbara: *The Dog-Collar Murders* 165; *Gaudi Afternoon* 165; *Murder in the Collective* 165; *Sisters of the Road* 165
Wilson, Edmund 97, 106, 113, 114, 116
Wilson, Woodrow 61
Wimsey, Lord Peter 107–15, 162
Wings, Mary: *She Came Too Late* 165
Wittgenstein, Ludwig 175
Wollstonecraft, Mary 24
The Woman in White 44, 45, 47, 48, 53, 72
Worthington, Heather 20, 22, 61, 64
Wright, Richard 154

The Yellow Dog (Le Chien jaune) 118–25

Zamora, Lois Parkinson 174, 178
Zaremba, Eve: *A Reason to Kill* 165
Zola, Émile 62

www.ingramcontent.com/pod-product-compliance
Lightning Source LLC
Chambersburg PA
CBHW051220300426
44116CB00006B/645